Thomas Doubleday

A Financial, Monetary and Statistical History of England

from the Revolution of 1688 to the Present Time

Derived Principally from Official Documents

In Seventeen Letters

Addressed to the Young Men of Great Britain

Elibron Classics
www.elibron.com

Elibron Classics series.

ISBN 1-4021-6946-9 (paperback)
ISBN 1-4212-8308-5 (hardcover)

This Elibron Classics Replica Edition is an unabridged facsimile of the edition published in 1847 by Effingham Wilson, London.

DEDICATION.

TO MY SONS.

Dear Sons,

I dedicate this book to you, because you are, as yet, very young men; and because that which I now address to you is equally applicable to any other young man of a similar age. Do not fancy that I expect that you should now look into this volume, because it is so dedicated. I know well enough, that youth has pursuits and pleasures of its own, which it will not leave to interest itself in subjects like those which are here discussed. This is as it should be;—but this state of youth does not last for ever. It is evanescent; and new thoughts and new motives quickly come in with the march of time.

You are, or in all certainty must in future time be, engaged in some branch of traffic or dealing which will, day after day, bring you in contact with others, engaged in similar objects. From such persons you, even now, begin to hear bitter, though mysterious, complaints of the existing state of affairs: and the sounds of a general and growing dissatisfaction, even now, begin to jar upon your young ears after a manner which, at all events, makes you pause and wonder for a moment, by what strange spell it happens that all the world seems discontented and miserable, in the midst of scenes which appear to afford so many materials for enjoyment.

As time hastens onward, a painful curiosity will at length take its place in your breasts, and urge you to enquire "how" it comes to pass, that men, surrounded with all the natural means of comfort and ease, are eaten up with anxiety and tribulation; and from what secret and evil-working cause, a society which nature seemed to design for happiness, is drawing nearer and nearer to the semblance of a purgatory, or a hell? To these questions, you will, in all human probability, receive replies that cannot be, even in the slightest degree, satisfactory to clear and steady minds—which I take yours to be. In some quarters, you will get answers, which absolutely mean nothing. From others, the response will only mean that which can alone serve to bewilder you the more. You will be told by some, that people complain, because "the times are bad." From others, you will hear, that the country is pining for want of "free trade." Some will inform you, that "over-production" is the root of the mischief. Others will assure you, that it springs from "the want of occasion to produce more!" All your oracles will, however, leave the question in your minds, much as they found it; and when, at last, you are fairly sick, and wearied, to utter nausea, with the sound of the half-blind, half-witted, half-plausible, half-foolish, half-founded, half-empty, half-true, half-false talk, which will meet you at every turn, you will bethink yourselves of looking into this book,—peradventure, as a last, and not very agreeable resource.

You will there, however, at last, find, that which you sought, detailed in their order, as they have been created, or have arisen, the whole of the causes which have really led to the present strange and wretched position of society in this kingdom. You will find them described in such a way, as to enable you, by a moderate effort, made in a diligent and enquiring spirit, to understand them all, and to arrive at a clear and distinct perception of that, which before appeared to you as nothing more nor less than a maze, a conundrum, or a puzzle of the first water.

To do this, however, you must begin at the beginning. You must go steadily on; surely planting one foot, before you put forward the other: and, in particular, you must not, by any means, quit, until you have fully understood and mastered it—the theory of the nature, uses, and phenomena of money, as given in the Second Letter of this Volume.

The mastery of this is as necessary to the Politician, as is the mastery of the Multiplication Table to the learner of Arithmetic. Without it he is nothing. It embodies—to use the phraseology of Shakespeare —"the very heart of his mystery." This, therefore, you must master, or you had better, at once, drop the book: but this being once overcome, all the rest is comparatively easy; and you will not only find instruction, but great amusement in tracing the insidious manner in which the delusions of false money have led the originators and supporters of the Funding System, step by step, into the quagmire where they are now about to sink; how the current of taxation has gradually brought after it that flood of evils, difficulties, distresses, bewilderments, knaveries, and follies, in which the nation is now steeped; and especially, how the ignorance of Ministers of State of that which you will then know, has betrayed them into the disgrace of having actually, by their own deeds, given the *coup-de-grace* to the system which they were hired to support, and plunged themselves and their masters into the gulf which is at hand, and ready finally to receive them all.

This you will trace step by step; and this it is impossible that any good mind should trace, without emotions embracing interests of the deepest description; without feelings, sometimes of wonder, sometimes of indignation, sometimes of pity, sometimes of contempt, at the sight of a nation, once high-spirited, happy, rich, free, and great, brought down to the state of a set of spiritless, half-starved, corrupted, and bewildered slaves, by a body of usurers and villains, as contemptible as any that ever made the sun blush to shine upon them, or the winds of Heaven unable to blow over them, without nausea and loathing.

This, however, is not all that you will acquire; for with this, you will also learn one other truth (which peradventure you may also help to teach), and that is, that the full understanding of these apparently complicated matters is not of such difficult attainment as men have been led to believe; but, that the real difficulty has been to come at the materials for knowledge, which have hitherto lain, for the most part, scattered about, often in obscure corners;—neglected alike by the designing, who might know, and the ignorant, who could not know, their true value. In the getting together of these materials, you will then perceive, lies by far the principal merit of this treatise, provided there be merit of any kind to be found in it.

With a healthy state of society, the compilation, composition, and publication of such a volume ought not, you will see, to excite either surprise or strong feelings of any other description. Under a vicious and corrupt system, however, your own good sense will teach you, that the matter is somewhat different; and hence you may perhaps, at last, be induced to conclude, that a present more valuable could not easily be made by an old man to a young, than this which I now inscribe to you, and that you need not blush, on this account, to own your share in the blood, nor to bear the name which is borne by

Your affectionate father,

THOMAS DOUBLEDAY.

RIDLEY PLACE, *Jan.* 31*st*, 1847.

CONTENTS.

A

FINANCIAL, MONETARY, & STATISTICAL HISTORY OF ENGLAND.

LETTER I.

PREFATORY.

Dear Friends,

Every man who is ambitious to possess the slightest share of that which, in common parlance, is called "Information," ought, in the first instance, to make himself well acquainted with the history of his own country. No one, indeed, who is ignorant of it, can properly, in any extended sense of the term, perform his duties as a citizen, in any country which has made the least approach to a state of freedom and of popular government. A man *may* certainly give a correct vote for a candidate for parliament or for any other popular assembly, judging solely from his knowledge of the honesty and talent of the aspirant, and applying common sense alone as a test of the propriety and policy of the measures to be advocated by his representative. Beyond this, however, persons destitute of correct historical knowledge, are, to a great degree, incapacitated either for forming an opinion or for acting with regard to any national question; and when they do so act, are to be regarded less as "hounds that hunt," than as dogs that merely "fill up the cry;"

—a station not to be envied by any possessing a proper self-esteem, or a proper sense of his responsibility for that which he publicly says and does.

It will soon be discovered, by all who set themselves diligently to acquire an accurate knowledge of the history of this country, that on going back to periods which are anterior to the last century and a half, that is to say, to periods prior to the revolution of A.D. 1688, historical knowledge is comparatively simplified. The causes of events and springs of action are, in fact, more upon the surface; and consequently, the comprehension of the whole is easier to be arrived at, and when arrived at, is more readily grasped and retained by the mind. This somewhat greater simplicity in the history of these earlier times arises from one great pervading cause, and that is, that matters of FINANCE, or, in more homely language, *the money matters of nations*, were then less complicated, less varied, and of far less consequence than they now are, and have been for the last hundred and fifty years.

From the time of the Norman conquest, up to the sitting of that parliament of King Charles I., which is known by the name of "The Long Parliament," the FEUDAL System, first in its original form, and then in a changed and mitigated shape, was suffered to exist, and continued to exist in England. Under this system, the maintenance of the monarch and of the various officers of state, was not derived, as now, from the taxes. Under this system, there was no such thing as a "Civil-List," or sum of money set apart by parliament and raised by taxation, to pay the king or queen, and the different officials who are appointed under the authority of the Crown; but the king lived like any other landed person, from the proceeds of his own estates; the only difference being, that the crown estates were infinitely more valuable than those of any subject, however wealthy; and from these estates, the royal attendants, the ministers of state, the judges, and other public functionaries, were maintained and paid.

Thus, under this system, the kingly dignity was upheld, without the necessity of a constantly recurring application to the people, and without mixing the revenue of the king as an individual, or the revenues of his dependants, real or nominal, with what in modern times is called finance: but the feudal system, which, in its origin, was a system of *national defence*, as well as aristocratic privilege or prerogative, provided for much more than this. Under it, all the lands of the kingdom, whether held directly or indirectly of the king, were held *in chief*, that is to say, by the *first* holders, barons or lords of manors, or by what title soever they might be called, upon a tenure of *military service*. Nor were holders of lands under the church (which, before they were seized by Henry the VIII. and his successors, upon the plea of a reformation in religion, held in possession large portions of the lands of England, as well as tithes) in many cases exempt from military service. Hence, under this system, when wars became politic or unavoidable, there constantly existed a national means for carrying them on, for which all the lands and all the dwellers upon the lands in the kingdom stood charged, by the structure of the feudal tenures. The only ones exempt were the Clergy, who were personally so; and the Burgesses of the few chartered towns, who only stood charged with the defence of their own boroughs, but beyond that were free of the feudal services, and hence styled "Free Burgesses."

Under such a state of things as this, it is evident, that the machinery for raising taxes, as it came to exist in later times, was nearly or altogether uncalled for and unnecessary. In great exigencies, the parliament granted the king occasional "aids," or "benevolences" in the shape of a temporary tax. After a time, this tax was partly imposed by means of an *ad valorem* duty or "poundage" on certain staple articles of commerce. A "Tonnage" and an impost called "Ship-money" were also levied, which at last nearly grew into a prescription; and the levy was attempted to be made part of the royal prerogative. As the various holders of lands grew in power, the feudal services were gradually commuted into payments of money, by the lords "in chief" to the crown, and by the "copyholders," or holders under the inferior tenures of Soccage, Villeinage, Frankalmoigne, etc., to the lords of the manors and lordships, the term "copyhold" alluding to the registration of the payments in the Rolls of the Manorial Courts. These changes took place during the period elapsing between the Norman Conquest, and the sway of the Long Parliament; up to which time there existed nothing that can be called a "financial system" in the present meaning of these words. When wars were made, the chief expense fell upon the *land and its owners*, under the operation of the feudal tenures; and the other aids were temporary in their nature and intent, arising, as they did, in a manner "*per force*," out of the changes made by time in society itself, and the

growth of a mercantile middle class, hitherto unknown.

When, however, that extraordinary body of men who composed the Long Parliament set their arbitrary king at defiance, and assumed the government of this country to themselves, they, at one blow, destroyed all that remained of the feudal system. Whether, as some say, this was done from a pure love of liberty; or whether, as others say, it was done to relieve the land, with which most of them were connected, from these charges, I shall not attempt to decide. The plain fact is, that after the execution of the king, the parliament passed an act to annul all the feudal charges upon landlords, and, to use their own words, enacted "that all sorts of tenures held of the king or others be turned into free and common soccage, save only tenures in frankalmoigne, copyholds and the honorary services, without the slavish part, of grand sergeantry." Up to this time, the English *people* had known little or nothing of taxation, save the name; if they knew that. The plundering of the churches and monasteries, and the seizure of the church lands and tithes by the tyrant Henry VIII. and his degraded and villanous parliaments, had indeed subjected the English people to a perpetual charge of Poor Rates, enacted by the government of Elizabeth, as a compensation for that great refuge and patrimony, of which the robbery of the church lands and tithes deprived the poor of this country. But at this period, these payments were trifling and hardly felt: and therefore we may safely refer to this act of the Long Parliament, as laying the first corner-stone of that system of taxation which has gone on ever

since, until it has at last made questions of finance of paramount national importance, and caused the happiness or misery of a country to depend upon the notion a minister may have of some of the most abstruse points of what is called political economy. The reign of Charles II. being dated from the death of his father, this Act, which was confirmed after the restoration, stands in the statute-book in the twelfth year of that reign. It was, however, the work of the Long Parliament; and was, after no long time, followed by another Act, establishing a system of taxation in its worst form, that of an EXCISE.

It is a curious subject of reflection, but not more curious than true, that the plunder of the church and the confiscation of its property under pretence of "reformation," to which one of the conditions annexed was (as quoted by Sir Edward Coke), that it should bar the king and his successors from asking any more taxes of their subjects, has been a proximate cause of all the taxation that has followed. It caused the Poor Rates, as enacted by the 43rd of Elizabeth. The fears of the holders of the abbey lands, and the lay impropriators of tithes, caused by the Popish leaning of Charles I., joined to the desire of the Presbyterians to clutch what was left, were amongst the grand excitements to the rebellion that overset the monarchy, and, in the end, relieved the landlords of the feudal charges at the expense of the body of the people. And, again, in the year 1688, the same fears, excited by the Popery of James II., caused another rebellion (for this was the real cause of the patriotism of the Cavendishes and Russells), which violently changed the line of succession, and, as we

shall hereafter see, rendered necessary or rather desirable to those in power, that system of borrowing and of paper-money, of the progress and effects of which I am now to give a true and candid view, uncoloured and unobscured by the falsifications and mists which corruption and folly have thrown around it.

Before entering upon the immediate subject-matter of a work like the present, it is a necessary preliminary to endeavour to give the reader a general notion of the state of the country and of the national mind, at the period of the commencement of the narrative: and this I am now to do. At the period, from which we take the first step of our narrative, the Revolution of 1688 was completed, and the new state of affairs and the new government had subsisted for a few years. The position of the new government and of the new king and queen, William III. and Mary, was, however, at best precarious. The nation was torn in pieces, and the national mind subdivided by a variety of sects and factions political and religious, all hating each other, and most of them either in direct opposition to, or else jealous of the existing government. The Roman Catholic portion of the nation were placed by their religion, and for the most part by their political opinions, in bitter hostility to the new order of affairs. The principal cause of the movement of 1688 and its results, was the dread of a resuscitation of the old religion, and the possible resumption of the confiscated property of the Roman Catholic church in England. The whole of the reigns of Charles II., and his brother James II., was, in truth, more or less of a re-action in favour of the old religion: nor is it to be wondered at, that the holders of the plundered property of the church should vehemently dread its results, and foresee in a continuation of the dynasty of the Stuarts, the loss of the enormous wealth got out of the wreck of the Roman Catholic establishment. It could not, even at that period, though one hundred and fifty years had elapsed, be forgotten that the Church of England was established against the will of the majority of the British people; and more decidedly still against the will of the Irish people. Deserted by those whom, up to that time, they had been accustomed to consider their natural leaders, the nobility and great landed aristocracy, and depressed by that power which the remains of the feudal system gave that aristocracy over the smaller holders, who were then the majority of the nation, that majority unwillingly yielded to the first aggressions of the tyrant Henry VIII. and his base parliaments: but it was not until after a series of bloodshed, conflicts, and savage persecutions, extending over nearly four reigns, that the old religion was finally overwhelmed, and the present establishment set up to fill its place; to which last object success was, after all, denied. Hence the Roman Catholics naturally regarded the rule of the Prince of Orange, now William III., as the renewal of a triumph over themselves, and harboured against the government all those feelings of virulent animosity, which this view of the national affairs could not but engender.

Of the virulent animosity which the Roman Catholics of this period cherished against the *régime* of William and his consort, the Tory party, as a body, no doubt availed themselves. Disapproving of that headlong fanaticism or bigotry in James, which induced him to violate the prejudices of a large portion of his subjects on the tender point of religion, and thus jeopardise his crown, without a chance of restoring the supremacy of that form of religion to which he was certainly devoted, they yet could not agree in the policy of that most perilous, to a monarchy, of all alterations, a change in the hereditary succession. They, therefore, beyond a question, looked on with a total distrust of the permanence of the new dynasty; and if it had little of their confidence, it had just as little of their love. In their eyes, it was not only an evil in itself *per se*, but it embodied also in its very existence, as it were, something beyond this, and equally detestable—the victory of a rival faction. How far the leading Tories of that period carried the doctrine of the hereditary divine right of kings, it is not easy to determine. That some of them carried it very far, seems to be evident in the fact, that Atterbury, bishop of Rochester, in the next reign, thought it his duty to peril his life for a family, who, if they had been again restored to the throne, would probably have employed their power in putting down that establishment of which he himself was one of the most distinguished ornaments. Be that as it may, however, it is unquestionable that amongst the Tories of the period, embracing the reigns of William III. and of Queen Anne, were some of the most able and virtuous men of their time. That government could not have little to fear, which had to fear the enmity of such men as Bolingbroke, Swift, Harley, Atterbury, and Pope.

As it often happens in unsettled times, the enemies

of the government were united, and acted as one body, whilst those who called themselves its supporters, did not amalgamate by any means so kindly. Amongst the churchmen of the establishment even, there were great differences. Those who supported it more from a fear of the renewal of the claims of the Roman Catholics, than from any attachment to its peculiar tenets, as a matter of course stood by the Revolution and its consequences. The "High Churchmen," as they were styled, were a different sort of men. Steeped in the doctrines of royal hereditary right; deriding the right of private judgment in matters of religion; followers of the opinions of Laud, Juxon, and the other high church bishops of the time of the first Charles; deeming the Presbyterians and other Dissenters as no better than pestilent schismatics; they secretly meditated a new unity of religion, by a gradual junction of the Reformed Church of England with the Romish Communion; and clung, accordingly, to the Stuart family, as the legitimate and appointed instruments for this healing measure. Of men possessing these opinions, the universities, Oxford especially, were full; and the "Puseyites" of the nineteenth century are only the successors of the Atterburies, Sacheverells, and other high church divines, of the seventeenth and eighteenth.

Next to the "Low-Churchmen," or those who loved the Church "as by law established" principally for the sake of pelf, the Dissenters were the most zealous partisans of the new Government. The king was himself a Calvinist; and this secured him the unanimous favour of the rigid Presbyterians. The other Dissenters were of various shades; Anabaptists, Quakers, Millennarians, Socinians, Fifth-Monarchy-men, Independents, in short, every species of theorist, visionary, or fanatic, that had teemed in the hot-bed of the first Revolution, or sprung into sudden life from the Medea's kettle of the Reformation. Freedom of religious thinking, is not unnaturally apt to be accompanied by a similar freedom of political sentiment. Hence all these sects joined the Whig Churchmen in carrying out the Revolution that had been so successfully achieved, though many of them pushed their political theories much further than was at all palatable, even to the most sincere and best of the leading men of the time. Marlborough, Somers, Locke, Addison, Steele, Halifax, and the other dominant Whigs, were far from being Republicans; and few of them really believed in, or wished to act upon, the dogmas, as to popular government, to which, at the moment, they deemed it politic to yield an assent. On the contrary, they soon formed a pretext for the disuse of triennial parliaments; and to the aggression of the Septennial-Act the great Lord Somers himself was so blinded by prejudice, or insincere in profession, as to accord not only the *fiat* of his legal assent, but the meed of his praise! In fact, the free notions and usages of our Anglo-Saxon forefathers seem to have been upon the decline through many centuries. Some of the ceremony of the coronation even now, goes to prove that the kingship was really in essence elective; yet, in the crisis of 1688, a large portion of the nation was fully imbued with the absurd doctrine of Divine Right. As late as Cromwell's first Parliament, it was proved, that, up to the reign of Henry III., the king called no additional peers to parliament but with the consent of the Commons then and there assembled; yet, since that time, no one has ventured directly and openly to impugn the doctrine, that the Crown, by prerogative, may create peers of Parliament *ad libitum*.

Such was the state of parties, and so distracted was the national mind, at the epoch of the Revolution of A.D. 1688. The system of finance had received little alteration during the period that elapsed from the restoration of the Stuarts until William was seated upon the throne. The truth is, that the arbitrary notions of the Stuarts had, in their composition, to the full as much of folly as of tyranny. They had not the wit to discover, that, though a monarch might dispense with parliaments, and still retain the throne, the real monarchical power was gone, as, without a parliament, it was now impossible to coerce the people into submission to pecuniary exactions. Doting upon the shadow of kingly absolute power, they do not seem to have had metaphysical acumen enough to perceive that the substance had escaped; for the power of a king who has not the power of the purse, is nothing better than a name. Hating the very idea of the existence of a parliament, they seem never to have dreamed, that, under the form of liberty, a king, by means of a subservient and bribed House of Commons, may exercise ten times the power that he ever can dare to attempt through the exercise of a naked despotism. Hence, though arbitrary in the abstract, the restored Stuarts could not extract from the people one moiety of the sums that the Long Parliament and the Usurpation obtained from only a portion of that people; and, like Ferdinand VII. of Spain, Charles II. foolishly imagined himself a mighty prince, and above all control, when he could hardly command the means to get a clean shirt, to such straits was he sometimes reduced by thoughtless habits, joined to a miserable and inadequate revenue. The amount of revenue raised by the Long Parliament is a matter of uncertainty. It seems now impossible to come at any account which can be implicitly relied upon. Sir John Sinclair (History of the Revenue, vol. i. p. 284) quotes a statement which he describes as the best he has seen, that makes the total moneys raised in England from November 3rd, 1640, to November 5th, 1659, to be £83,331,198, or £4,385,850 per annum. A very minute and detailed account, however, published in 1725, though obviously by no partisan of of the Long Parliament, carries the amount as high as £92,391,348, or £4,862,700 a year. The *data* on which the abstract is founded are all given, and though the author's name is kept back, I do not see why the statement is of inferior authority to Sir John Sinclair's. If we contrast the revenue of the second James, as settled by Parliament on his accession, with the expenditure of the Long Parliament, it dwarfs in the comparison.

For the year during which he abdicated, it stood as follows: —

Tonnage and poundage, with wood, coal and salt farm	£600,000
Excise, beer, and ale	666,383
Hearth-money	245,000
Post-Office	65,000
Wine licenses	10,000
Carried forward	1,586,383

Brought forward	1,586,383
New tax on wine and vinegar . . .	172,901
Duties on tobacco and sugar . . .	148,861
Duties on French linen, brandy, silk, etc. .	93,710
Total	£2,001,855

This was more than the average revenue of Charles II., who does not seem to have received more than one million eight hundred thousand pounds a-year on the average; nor was this helped out by the crown estates: the little that then remained ungranted away; that is to say, the fee-farm rents having been sold, with the consent of Parliament (22 Car. II., cap. 6), by the profligate Charles, for a sum uncertain.

Thus, upon the whole, it is evident, that though the government of the Stuarts, during the period betwixt the two rebellions, was often despotic in form, it was not oppressive in reality. The machinery for taxing was not equipped with new wheel or pinion; and though the people were vexed by bickerings and persecutions on account of religion, the mass could not be otherwise than happy, being left in possession of their earnings, and themselves enjoying the fruits of their own industry and skill. Without the form and name of liberty, they had its principal blessings; it being reserved for the next century to hit upon the plan of giving the name and form, whilst the blessings were taken away. Neither must it be supposed that, with a revenue so insignificant to modern ears, the kingdom was left defenceless, or its power as a state dilapidated. This was by no means the case. The wrong-headed James had, when he abdicated, a strong and well-appointed fleet, and an army amounting to nearly twenty thousand men. In estimating money payments, however, at distant periods, the altered value of money must never be forgotten in the calculation; this is a matter into which I shall hereafter more minutely enter: suffice it in this place to say, that the money of King James II. was, beyond a doubt, greatly more valuable than the money of the present day. As a good criterion of the easy state of the people, I would remark, that one year's poor rate, at this period, when rates were distributed with no niggard hand, but liberally, not to say profusely, amounted, it is believed, on the average, only to about *one hundred and sixty thousand pounds*; or, *a twelfth* part of the nett revenue. If distributed in the same manner now, they would amount to *a fourth* part of the present nett revenue. A few years back, that is to say, in 1833, they were equal to *a sixth* of the revenue of that year.

The foregoing considerations afford, I trust, sufficient materials for the formation of a tolerably accurate notion of the state and position of England at the period of the Revolution of 1688. Before addressing ourselves, however, to the actual business of these letters, a further clearance of the ground must take place. It is impossible that any one, however desirous to do so, should understand the details about to be gone into, unless he shall have acquired beforehand; *first*, a clear and complete comprehension of the theory and nature of money; and *secondly*, a full comprehension of the nature of national debts. In letter II., therefore, I shall give as clear and plain an account as I can write, of the nature, uses, and phenomena of money: and in Letter III. as complete an explanation as I can of the invention of national debts and funds. When these are fully understood, we shall then be prepared to go into the history of the steps first taken to create this debt and these funds, called " national", and to add to the quantity of the money in circulation, with a view of enabling those who had it to lend it to the government, and thus become a totally new class of people, under the new and anomalous style and title of "the national creditors." I am, etc. etc. etc.

LETTER II.

THE THEORY, NATURE, USES, AND PHENOMENA OF MONEY.

THE best method, as it appears to me, to come at a clear apprehension of the nature, uses, and value of money, is: *First;* to get a clear idea of the cause of value in general as indicated in all sorts of commodities, necessaries, or luxuries of life. *Secondly;* to apply the knowledge thus gained to the obtaining a notion equally clear of the causes of the value of that particular commodity called money. *Thirdly;* to attain a distinct idea of the use of money, so peculiar to itself, as a measure of the value of all other things; and of the reason why it is peculiarly adapted to be a measure of this kind. *Fourthly;* to come to a distinct knowledge of the phenomena which take place, when the causes, which make money a general measure of value, are disturbed. *Fifthly;* to trace the mode by which money naturally distributes itself amongst nations in proportion to their wants, and thus equalises its value, and keeps that value at this certain level in all its civilised communities having intercourse with each other. *Sixthly*, and lastly; to inquire into and understand the nature of "fictitious money," as contra-distinguished from "real money" and the effects produced by mixing one with the other, or substituting one for the other. All this, to most persons, sounds at first like something very abstruse; and by the mass of mankind, even by those constantly engaged in trading and money transactions, it is very generally held to be so. It is, however, a matter in itself perfectly intelligible: and that which is intelligible in its own nature, that is to say, all pertaining to which a human capacity can grasp, may always be conveyed to others, provided they will set themselves fairly and in earnest to learn and understand; not suffering themselves to be deterred by any temporary puzzle or difficulty at the outset.

First, of the Value of things. In considering this matter, we must make a necessary distinction at the outset; and this is between *value* and *use*, or rather *utility*. Things are not valuable in the proportion in which they are useful. Thus the air, without which no living thing could exist for a single moment, is valueless; because it is supplied by Providence to all, without trouble or pains to obtain it. Thus then, we must not seek for the cause of value in commodities themselves, but in something extrinsic and external; and that external cause *is the quantity of labour* required to obtain them. In this quantity of labour lies the true MEASURE of value; the motives

2

for expending the labour being various and multiform. Sometimes labour is expended upon the acquisition of a thing, because that thing supplies a real want; as, for instance, in mining for coal or for the ordinary and commonly used metals: sometimes, because the desire for that particular thing is ideal, and arising out of a supposed or actual beauty or rarity, quite apart from actual utility, which consists in supplying a real want of our nature. Thus the value of diamonds and other precious stones is great, because to obtain them requires immense labour of research; but the motives for expending that labour are altogether of a fanciful nature, dependent upon arbitrary notions of the great beauty of the gem, and quite apart from any expectations of utility to arise from such possessions. The point here, therefore, to be fixed in the mind is that the amount of labour required for the attaining of anything regulates its value in every case, and that valuable property is merely *hoarded labour* in various shapes and in various amounts.

We now come to the particular commodity called "Money;" and on inquiry we shall find, that its *value* arises, precisely as does the value of all other commodities, out of the proportion of labour requisite to obtain the substances which compose it, and to fashion them into coin. Money is made of what are called "the precious metals" that is to say, of gold and of silver: but whence arises the value of the material? Altogether from these metals being scattered by nature with so sparing a hand, that a vast amount of labour is required to obtain them in quantity; and by that *quantum* of labour is their value measured.

Gold is twenty times as valuable as silver, because, to obtain an ounce of gold takes twenty times the labour that is required for acquiring an ounce of silver. If gold were twice as plentiful, and required only half that labour, it would fall in value accordingly, and be only *ten times* as valuable as silver. Money is only valuable as the material of which it is made is valuable. Money, then, is only like any other commodity, and has nothing peculiar attached to it to give it value, other than that which gives value to the other commodities which it buys.

So much for real value, and its basis, labour. It is, however, here requisite to note that there also exists another sort of value of a secondary and derivative kind. This kind of value shall be more fully adverted to when we come to consider the nature of "fictitious money:" but it is proper, in this place, to explain briefly what it is. As in metaphysics it is an *axiom*, that "things that are indissolubly connected with other things that are necessary are themselves necessary:" so, in political economy, it is also true, that "things that will certainly ensure or command other things that are valuable, are themselves valuable." This is a self-evident truism: but when we consider this sort of value, we must find it liable to this objection, that such "certainty" cannot ever be in truth arrived at. A *high probability* is the utmost that can ever be predicated of any instrument not valuable in its own nature, but only as being held to command other things that are. Let a bond, or note, or debenture, or bill of exchange, be signed as it may, its payment is, after all, still a matter of more or less contingency: this kind of value is, therefore, uncertain, fleeting, and liable to change and destruction, as compared with real and underived value; because it is subject, from its very nature, to greater risk and greater doubt, and exposed to casualties from which the other is free: and this is all that needs be said respecting it in this place. Ample future opportunity will be afforded us to come to a proper estimate of this kind of "representative value," as it is the fashion sometimes to term it; though the phrase be not particularly pregnant of meaning. Its value consists merely in a belief, that an instrument, now valueless in itself, will at some given future time bring its owner something really valuable; and, for this "*paulo-post-futurum*" value, would be as germane an epithet as the unmeaning term "representative;" unless debt be the thing that is meant to be represented.

From the *value*, we come naturally to a consideration of the *use* of money; as to which latter point, precise ideas are as requisite as they are with regard to the former. In order to attain to these precise ideas, the grand object is to fix steadily in the mind the primary truth, that the use of money is to *measure the value of other things*, and that this may be almost said to be its sole use. It certainly facilitates the interchange of commodities between man and man; but it only does this by carrying in itself an unvarying standard or measure of value, in the belief of those who use it, and, for the most part really and in fact. Neither must this term, "measure of value," be imagined to be a metaphorical and not a literal expression. Money is literally, and not metaphorically, "a measure." It measures value as certainly as the surveyor's chain measures acres, or the draper's yard-wand measures cloth. This is the legitimate office of money; and when it is perverted from this, whether intentionally or not, fraud is sure to follow; as will be amply demonstrated in the course of these pages. The next question to be answered is, "*How* does money come to measure value?" To this let us now turn.

Money measures the value of other things by being in itself of one unvarying value. This unvarying value arises from Providence having so distributed the precious metals of which it is made, that their quantity, upon the whole, cannot be suddenly either much increased or much diminished. They are obtained only with difficulty; and as soon as the expense of mining, or gathering them from the bowels of the earth, is equal to the value they bear, the work, of course, stops. Until it does so, more or less is, of course, gradually collected, year after year; but as this only balances the wear, tear, and waste that gradually occurs, the quantity of these metals, available at any given period, is much the same; and as the purposes for which they are wanted throughout the world do not vary materially or suddenly, these metals maintain, as a consequence, a very uniform value; and this value forms *a standard*, by which to measure the various values of more variable commodities. If an article of trade is all at once *increased* in quantity and made plentiful, then more of it is set against the same proportion of money, for which, before such increase, a less quantity of it was usually sold; this is "cheapness": a sudden *decrease* of any article of trade, on the other hand, causes less of it to be set against the same money, for which a larger portion before that decrease took place, was wont to be exchanged; this is "dearness;" and these two circumstances take place, clearly, because, whilst the commodities vary in their quantity and value, the money remains steadily the same in both.

Whilst money continues to be thus invariable, and unchanging in quantity and value, it continues also to be a true and indubitable measure of the value of everything else submitted to it as a standard for comparison: and when prices rise or fall, these risings or fallings are, always and solely, caused by variations in the supply of the various and different commodities, as compared with the demand for them, which become, accordingly, cheaper, or dearer, as the case may be. If, however, by means of natural or artificial causes, a great or sudden increase or decrease of the quantity of money circulating takes place, we then suddenly become aware of a new set of phenomena, unnoticed before, and somewhat puzzling to the persons who are subjected to their effects and influences. If the quantity of money circulating in a country, or in more countries than one, or generally in the world, be suddenly increased, then prices *rise* in the mass. If, on the contrary, a decrease be suddenly brought about, no matter how, in the money circulating in any country or countries, then prices in that case *fall* in the mass; and this without men, in general, being aware either of the manner or cause, or being able to see how such rises or falls are brought about. The cause and manner are as follows. Let us suppose, that by some means or other, for instance, by the discovery of very productive and easily wrought mines, the quantity of the precious metals in a country is suddenly increased. The persons who obtain the metals, getting them at much less cost of labour than before, they become, in fact, depreciated in the owners' hands, and being now much more plentiful than before, are more easily and readily parted with in exchange for anything to which their owners take a fancy. This is the beginning of a general advance in prices; not arising out of any alteration in the quantity and value of commodities, but solely out of an alteration in the quantity and value of money, caused by this sudden windfall of more and more easily obtained gold and silver. The prices of a few articles are only raised at first; but this gradually begets an idea of increasing dearness in all. As the advance goes on, men buy up commodities on speculation, and thus help the advance, which the increased quantity and depreciated value of the precious metals began. And thus, as many lesser streams, flowing towards one point, at last make a great river, so the rise of a few articles, followed by that of others, ends in a general advance of everything. To ordinary beholders, this seems a general dearness of all commodities, and for such they mistake it. It is, however, only a greater cheapness of money, which is the standard of value; and when the *measure is less*, the things measured by it, of course, *seem to cost more:* that is to say, you get fewer commodities for the same weight of gold or silver than you did before; or, for the same quantity of commodity you must give more money than you used to do. Suppose the quantity of money anywhere to be suddenly lessened, no matter how, and the reverse of all this takes place. Money becomes less plentiful and of greater value. Men part with it less easily; prices fall; and gradually a general cheapness of commodities apparently takes place. This *cheapness* is, however, like the *dearness*, only apparent. It is the money that is scarcer and of more value; and not any increase or generally greater supply of commodities. When the *measure is larger*, the things measured by it *seem to cost less;* that is to say, you get more commodity for the same quantity of gold or silver than before; or, in other words, for the same quantity of commodity less gold and silver money is now universally given. As great and sudden alterations in the quantity of circulating money have, however, rarely occurred; and as, when they do occur, they always do so without many persons being aware of what is going on; it has always been exceedingly difficult to make men, in general, see or believe that the alteration, one way or the other, is in the money itself, and not in the commodities which it buys. To dearness and cheapness in articles of sale and commerce they are well accustomed; but of any alteration in the standard of value itself, that is to say, in the money, they have no idea; and hence the consequences of such alterations have always come upon men unawares, and have rarely been understood by them, even when they have actually happened.

The details given above ought probably to be sufficient to give any attentive reader a distinct knowledge of the matters in question. In order, however, to put this last point in a perfectly clear and indubitable light, it may be best to show what *actually* took place on the occasion of a great and sudden alteration in the quantity and value of money, by exhibiting the prices which commodities, especially wheat, bore previously to the great alteration in the quantity of money circulating, and the prices which they brought subsequently. These prices afford full and complete evidence of the truth of the positions which have been laid down; because, although there are constant fluctuations in the prices of particular articles from time to time, without any alteration in the standard of value, money, yet there can be no great permanent change in the prices of commodities in general, nor upon such an article as wheat, *on an average of years*, without such alteration. This is plain, because it is a self-evident axiom, that all the money in a country set against the commodities of that country, is what constitutes price; and where it is impossible to suppose that any vast increase or decrease in the latter has been possible, the alteration must be referred to the former. No combination can affect the price of all commodities together, nor indeed of such an article as wheat; which though it fluctuates, with all other grain, from season to season, must, on an average of years, be much the same both in quantity and value; so great is the bulk, and so universal the use of it, in combination with the inferior sorts of grain.

The grand alteration in the value of the precious metals, and, of course, of money along with them, to which I would refer the reader, is that which took place in about thirty years after the discovery of America, by Columbus, in A.D. 1492. The reign of Henry VIII. commenced in A.D. 1509. Before he had reigned twenty years, the conquest of Mexico and Peru had been completed by the Spaniards; and the Portuguese were busy in the Brazils, which they ultimately overran and subdued. From that time, that is to say, from the early part of the reign of

Henry VIII., gold and silver continued to be poured into Europe, in unprecedented plenty, throughout the period comprised in the sixteenth and seventeenth centuries, causing a continually growing circulation of money, and a rise of prices in all commodities over all Europe, for which men were puzzled how to account, and which began to be sensibly felt in England, about the middle of Henry's reign. This was the first time that men had witnessed the phenomena of a huge accession, all within a few years, to the precious metals then circulating; and to those living at the time the whole was a puzzle and a mystery. The enhanced prices were in England wholly attributed to monopoly; to hoarding; to forestalling; to large farms; to any cause but the true cause; which true cause was *the lowering of the value of gold and silver*, by the discovery of the rich mines of Mexico, Peru, and ultimately of the Brazils. To prove, then, the real effect of this vast and rapid addition to the circulating medium, we have only to take a bird's-eye view of the prices before and after the event. Let us begin with Wheat. The following is extracted from Adam Smith's "Wealth of Nations":—

PRICES OF WHEAT

Before and after the opening of the American Mines.

			£.	s.	d.	
Average A.D.	1423 to 1451	- -	0	10	7	per Quarter.
,,	1453 to 1497	- -	0	8	5	,,
,,	1459 to 1560	- -	0	9	2	,,
,,	1561 to 1601	- -	2	7	5	,,
,,	1595 to 1636	- -	2	10	0	,,
,,	1637 to 1700	- -	2	11	3	,,

Here we see, that, during the period between 1560

and 1601, a space of forty years, the average price of wheat has grown five-fold. Not that grain was scarce during those forty years, but because, throughout the whole of them, the precious metals kept pouring into Europe from Peru and Mexico, with a rapidity almost inconceivable.

To shew that the same effects were produced upon the prices of all sorts of merchandise and commodities, I subjoin a curious document, extracted from Drake's "Eboracum."

TABLE OF PRICES.

Prices proclaimed at York in 1393.				*Prices at York in* 1733.			
	£.	*s.*	*d.*		£.	*s.*	*d.*
Strong Beer per gal.	0	0	1¼	Strong Beer per gal.	0	2	0
A milder sort ,,	0	0	1	Mild Ale - ,,	0	1	0
Finest Claret Wine ,,	0	0	8	Best Claret - ,,	0	17	0
All common White Wines - - ,,	0	0	6	White Port - ,,	0	8	0
				Red Port - ,,	0	6	8
Carcass of finest Beef	1	0	8	Choice carcass of Beef	9	10	0
Next best - -	0	14	0	Next best - -	8	0	0
Scotch Kyloe Ox car.	0	12	0	Scotch Kyloe - -	4	4	0
Ditto Cow -	0	10	0	Cow, ditto - -	3	0	0
Carcass of Mutton, best	0	1	8	Carcass of Mutton, do.	1	10	0
Ditto, worse fed -	0	1	6	Ditto, worse fed -	1	0	0
Carcass of fine Veal -	0	2	6	Carcass of fine Veal -	1	6	0
Another sort, ditto	0	1	6	Another sort, ditto -	0	15	0
A Lamb - - -	0	0	8	A Lamb - - -	0	12	0
A fat Pork Hog -	0	3	4	A fat Pork Hog -	2	10	0
A smaller Pig - -	0	3	0	A smaller Pig - -	2	0	0
A Capon - -	0	0	4	A Capon - - -	0	1	9
A Hen - - -	0	0	1¼	A Hen - - -	0	0	9
A fat Goose - -	0	0	4	A fat Goose - -	0	2	0
A Dozen of Pidgeons	0	0	3	A Dozen Pigeons -	0	1	3
A Woodcock - -	0	0	1¼	A Woodcock - -	0	0	9
A Teal - - -	0	0	1¼	A Teal - - -	0	0	9

Of the latter table, it is to be observed, that different customs duties might render the comparison of some few articles of import unfair; but, upon the whole, there can be no doubt that these returns are substantially correct. The prices of 1393, are *high* for the period, having been assessed by the judges of assize, aided by the bench, when Richard II. and his court were at York. This was done to prevent "combinations" to enhance prices; an operation easy when wealth was generally diffused, and when dealers were few and rich, as well as cunning and avaricious.

From the foregoing topics of discussion, we come naturally to contemplate the manner in which money equalises its value in all countries, having intercourse with each other, and, if brought in extraordinary quantity into one country, quickly spreads itself throughout the rest. The process by which this comes about is very plain. Spain, for instance, was the nation to which came the first great influx of gold and silver, after the conquest of Peru was completed in 1525. This influx of the precious metals, by greatly adding to the money in circulation, at once raised the prices of all Spanish commodities, and all articles of what sort soever used in Spain, far above the level of prices elsewhere. As soon as this took place, a two-fold operation was immediately encouraged. First, foreign nations found an immediate profit arose from sending goods into Spain, and selling them for what they would bring, bringing back the gold and silver received in exchange, in order to repeat the transaction. And secondly, the merchants of Spain found an immediate advantage in sending gold and silver abroad into the neighbouring countries of Europe;

inasmuch as, abroad, gold and silver commanded more goods in exchange than at home, owing to the higher prices. Thus the treasures poured into Spain and Portugal quickly found their way all over Europe; and thus, whenever a country has more than its share of money, it is sure to lose it, in spite of any efforts for retaining it, by the excessive import of goods, which the enhancement of prices is sure to occasion, until the value of the circulation, and prices along with it, are equalised, and *at par* with the money and prices of surrounding nations. And this principle of money, to equalise its own level everywhere, it is which renders reciprocity of trade between nations absolutely necessary to trade being carried on at all without the greatest inconvenience. Because if one nation shall take goods from another nation, without the other also taking an amount nearly equal, so much money is necessary to be sent away by the first in payment of the balance, as to derange and throw into confusion every thing at home, by the loss of circulation and the gap thus caused in it. Hence, to render trade between countries profitable and easy, each must take from the other the same amount in commodities. In that case, those who have money to pay abroad have only to buy the bills of those who have money to receive abroad; and by this *exchange* of bills the payments in each country are met and settled without the necessity of remitting cash in payment from either side. To render this operation complete, however, the amounts in goods exported and imported on each side respectively must be nearly equal. When this is not the case, "the course of exchange" is said to be "against" the country which has *imported most;* because from that country *a balance* is due to the other, for payment of which no bills can be had; and which must, therefore, be liquidated in gold or silver money, transmitted it to the amount of the balance, whatsoever that may be. In a future page, the great effects, sometimes consequent upon this state of things, will be detailed and explained. At present, all that is requisite is a clear apprehension of the really simple principles which regulate the amounts of money in various countries, respectively; and which govern the exchanges between such as carry on any considerable inter-trading and commercial dealings with each other.

We have now arrived at the sixth and concluding point necessary to be touched upon in this letter,—the nature and effects of *fictitious money.* By the phrase "fictitious money," I mean a money made of paper or anything else, of no intrinsic value, or valueless in itself, but which has yet a secondary or derivative value, arising from an opinion, founded upon the good credit of those who issue this sort of money, that it will, at some future given time, command a given amount of real money or real-money's-worth, though in itself it be worth nothing. Strictly speaking, all sorts of bills of exchange may be included under this sort of money; though to style them "money" at all is rather an abuse of the term. They, in fact, do not pass through many hands, nor from hand to hand at all, excepting under strict limitations; whilst each man who passes them adds his own security to that which the bill originally had from its drawer and acceptor. An instrument of this kind for a considerable sum cannot properly be held to be money. From perceiving certain conveniences in bills of exchange, however, men were, past doubt, gradually led to sanction the issue of promissory notes for small sums, payable to bearer on demand, and transferable from hand to hand, without either limitation or increase of security by the transfers. It is a circulation of this sort that is properly to be called a circulation of "fictitious money"; and of the phenomena that arise from the employment of this description of money, we are now to treat.

Promissory-note money may be divided into two species; that is to say: notes of this sort may pass as money, upon the understanding that they will be paid in gold and silver money, on demand of the holder, by those who issue them; which is a "convertible" paper money: or, such notes may pass as money merely on the general credit of the issuers, under a law making them a legal tender as money, and upon an understanding that no ultimate loss shall be suffered by those who hold them; and this is "inconvertible" paper money. That any nation of men should be brought to accept instruments of this kind, and most especially of the latter kind, in lieu of real and valuable coin, seems, at first sight, almost to include an imputation against their sanity. Men, however, always act, and often unconsciously, from mixed motives. It appears to me certain, that neither of the kinds of paper money are taken so much on the credit of those who issue them, be they who they may, as upon a confidence of their certainly passing, without demur, from the hands of the taker into other hands, whether in satisfaction of a debt or in purchase of merchandise; and without this sort of mutual confidence, however arising, amongst men, it seems sufficiently evident that no fictitious money could hold its ground, whether the makers of it were private individuals or a government. Men, in short, never take paper money to hoard it, nor even to keep it by them for any great length of time, to any amount; and it is only its constant transition that preserves its credit or men's confidence in it. That such a basis of credit as this is false and fallacious in the highest degree, is evident enough; and that it should succeed so often and last so long, only proves the short-sightedness of the views upon which men are prone to act, and how easily they will sacrifice a dictate of reason for a petty and temporary advantage or convenience.

In inquiring into the appearances which present themselves when an issue of fictitious or paper money is added to a circulation of gold and silver money, the first point to be observed (and it is one of great importance), is, that whilst such fictitious money *preserves its credit*, it produces the same effect that an equal addition of gold and silver money would do, and no other. Whilst its credit is preserved, whether it be "convertible paper money," or "inconvertible paper money," the effect is the same; that effect being a depreciation of the whole of the money circulating, gold and silver, and paper, and all together, and a rise of prices consequent upon such depreciation. After this general advance of prices has, however, gone on for a certain time, a great importation of goods necessarily takes place; and the ultimate effect of this over importation upon the paper is highly perilous in any case, but much more perilous when the paper is convertible into gold and silver on demand, than when the paper is actually inconvertible. This happens as follows:—when paper money is issued, those who issue it cannot, in doing so, get gold and silver in exchange for the paper they issue. If they did so, there could be neither profit nor convenience to any body. To take gold and silver to a bank counter, and get notes in lieu of them, could be of no immediate benefit either to the banker or his customer, and certainly of none to the latter in any case, or at any time. To get his paper out, the issuer must discount Bills of Exchange for merchants, or lend them to government upon security of Exchequer Bills, or Government Securities of some sort or other. Having done this in the usual manner, the banker cannot, of course, be in possession of any such stock of gold and silver coin as to be able to pay, or nearly pay, *all* his notes on demand, if they were presented to him for payment; because to obtain it safely, and without discrediting the paper, he must not only issue more notes, but must also put himself to an expense which would either destroy or diminish his profits. If, then, the paper issued be put out upon the understanding that it is to be paid, on demand, in gold and silver, or, in other words, if it be "convertible" paper; then, in that case, the issuer is always liable to the danger of having more of his notes brought in than he can find coin to answer. This danger—an *over*-importation of goods to a great extent, and for a length of time, is sure to bring about; because, when the course of exchange turns against a country, gold and silver must be sent to liquidate the balance, and the only certain way of getting this gold and silver is to go to the bank and demand it in exchange for notes, an operation which, if continued, must end in the stoppage of the bank. From this cause, if there were no other, an issue of paper money, "convertible into gold and silver," if not managed with the utmost caution, and by means of notes of the larger denominations, is certain, by overcharging the amount of the circulation altogether, to destroy itself; and after having caused most of the metallic money to be exported, to leave the country without a currency at all.

With an issue of "inconvertible" paper, this sort of danger is avoided. If, by an addition of this sort of money, the circulation of a country is so swelled as to produce high prices, over-importation, and adverse exchanges, what happens is, that gold and silver are quietly sent out of the country, and the inconvertible paper supplies their place. This, however, brings on another kind of danger, equally fatal to the paper portion of the money. It is this—when gold becomes very scarce, a high *premium* is necessitated to be secretly given for it by those who must have it to transmit abroad. This state of affairs of course puts the paper at a heavy *discount* as compared with the coin. When this becomes excessive at last, and notorious, the public at length get alarmed; and the chances are, that the paper sinks into total discredit and is no longer negociable. Under a circulation of inconvertible paper, however, there is another cause for the disappearance of coin which it is proper to explain. This disappearance happens thus:—the circulation being principally paper, and gold and silver not being demandable for it at the bank at a certain standard price, this not only causes a rise in the price of gold and silver bullion, but it also causes a rise in the price of bills drawn upon foreign countries, with a corresponding fall in the price of bills abroad, drawn upon the country with an inconvertible paper circulation. The reasons for these things are as follows:—gold and silver bullion rise because persons who want gold and silver must buy them as they can, gold and silver, in the shape of coin, not being demandable anywhere. The price of foreign bills, or bills drawn upon foreign countries, rises, because, being mostly paid for in paper money, the owner of the bill, which commands silver and gold abroad, asks for it as much of the circulating money as would buy on the spot that quantity for which the bill of exchange is drawn. The price of bills abroad falls, because foreigners who pay in silver and gold will only give as much gold for it as the paper money in which it will be paid will purchase in the country upon which it is drawn. Under all these circumstances the holders of coin are irresistibly tempted, either to melt it quietly into bullion and sell it as bullion, or else to send it abroad in some shape or other, and invest it in foreign goods or in a bill of exchange drawn abroad. To use it as money on the spot is to use it at a loss, as, *in the shape of money*, its power of purchasing on the spot is only the same as the paper. This is of course seen, and hence the coin disappears in the melting-pot, or goes abroad. Under such circumstances, it is sufficiently clear, that the dangers of an entire stop to trade, or of a total discredit of the paper, are immense. In the course of these letters, I shall, indeed, have to show, that, for a period of twenty-two years, an inconvertible fictitious money was maintained in this country; but I shall, at the same time, fully explain the peculiar and extraordinary circumstances which could alone cause so desperate an experiment to succeed.

In the meantime, we have possessed ourselves of all at present necessary to be known on the subject. We have seen what is the cause of "value" in general, or rather in the abstract; and of money in particular. We have seen what constitutes the peculiar use of money, as a measure of value. We have looked at the consequences which follow, when this quality of money as a measure, so useful to society, is disturbed. At the same time we did this, we learned also how money distributes itself over the world, and finds one level of value in all countries, that have any intercourse with each other. And, lastly, we have noted down what may be expected to happen, when fictitious money is made to rival, or supplant, money made of the precious metals and having an intrinsic value of its own. Having done this, we have seen all that is requisite of "money" in the abstract. Of the various strange fallacies as to fictitious, or paper money, we shall see more in the course of this narrative. Before entering upon that narrative, it will, however, be requisite to devote another letter to inquire what is the nature of the things called "National Debts," and "Funds;" and to that inquiry let us now apply ourselves.

There is one important point, however, which, before proceeding to our next letter, I must earnestly impress upon my reader's mind, and that is, never to forget the distinction between money in actual circulation from hand to hand, which is denoted by the word "Currency"; and money not circulating, but locked up in the hands of individuals, in various shapes of valuable securities, or in the shape of deposits of actual coin, which may be called "Capital". It must never be forgotten, that it is only *money in circulation* that affects prices. Locked-up money, as long as it remains so, has no such effects. Hence it may happen, and sometimes does happen, that there may be a superabundance of "Capital" or "hoarded money" in a country, whilst the "circulating money" is too little for the wants of the community of that country. This must always be the case, more or less, where any cause or causes shall be present, to scare or deter men from investing their capital in trades, and other adventurous channels;—as for instance, when a country is so over-taxed, that the residue of currency left, after paying such taxes, has become insufficient to enable the people in general to pay such prices for necessaries and articles of consumption, as will afford a profit to those who deal in them. When this is the case, capitalists become more and more indisposed to invest their money in commerce, or agriculture, and more and more resolute in hoarding it; and thus we come to behold the, at first sight, contradictory spectacle, of a nation getting poorer and poorer, and more and more straitened, at the very time that the surplus-capital in the hands of hoarders and usurers, is daily upon the increase. This is the case with England at present; and this is seen to be the case with any country, where the interest of its debt and its current revenue absorb so large a portion of the people's labour, that the remainder will not enable them to command a sufficiency of money, to empower them to pay proper and remunerating prices for the things which they themselves consume.

Having fixed this distinction firmly in our minds, let us now turn to the subject of Government debts, contracted in the name of a nation; their nature and phenomena.

LETTER III.

ON THE NATURE OF NATIONAL DEBTS AND FUNDS.

FROM the time when I first knew how to think for myself on subjects of this kind, I have never once wavered in my opinion as to the mingled absurdity and wickedness of the things called "National Debts" and "Funds." This is thirty years ago; yet, during the whole of that not very short period, I have met with few persons of that class who style themselves *par excellence* "the educated and thinking," who would openly say they agreed with me in this opinion. I do not, however, adhere and have not adhered to it the less firmly on that account. When I commenced to teach myself the art of thinking, I began luckily at the right end of the science; and, when reflecting on the many complicated topics connected with national economy and national morality, I early schooled myself to the constant recurrence to FIRST PRINCIPLES. In short, I saw that in such cases, and on such topics, the way was to begin at the beginning; and, therefore, I trust, no one need be surprised if, upon a subject, the name of which would lead an uninformed person to believe it to be a mere matter of money-account, I take you back with me to the origin of society, and of its rights, and of the duties of the individuals who compose it.

If there is to be such a thing as society at all—and it is impossible to conceive mankind to exist except in such a state—then it follows, as a matter of course, that such society must be upheld by human means. This is the foundation upon which all civilians build the superstructure of natural civil law. What says Puffendorf, the clearest of all the writers on natural law? He says this: "In jure naturali, aliquid faciendum asseritur, quia per rectam rationem idem ad socialitatum inter homines necessarium colligitur" (Puffendorf, *Præfatio*, p. 99). "Natural law is only the determination, by reason, of that which must be done to preserve the social state of mankind." Again, "Adparet *fundamentalem legem naturalem* esse hanc; cuilibet homini, quantum in se, colendam et servandam socialitatem" (Puffendorf, lib. i., cap. 3, p. ix.). "It follows that the *first law of nature* is this; that the social state is to be guarded and preserved to the uttermost, by and for every man." He then proceeds, "Ex quo consequitur, quia qui vult finem, vult media etiam, sine quibus finis obtineri nequit; omnia, quæ ad istam socialitatem necessario et in universum faciunt, jure naturali præcepta." "Hence it also follows, as all who determine upon an end determine upon the means which are necessary to that end, that whatsoever is necessarily and fully requisite for the preservation of society, is also decreed by the first law of nature."

Thus says Puffendorf; and so says Grotius; so says Vattel; so says Montesquieu; so says Locke; so says Paley, and every writer upon the origin of society and upon natural law. The preservation of the social state being the *first* natural law, it is, as a matter of course, laid down by all civilians, that a man's *first* duties are to the state. This position, indeed, flows necessarily from the other; because, society being of more consequence than the individual, the rights of society must, of course, take precedence of the rights of individuals. It is thus succinctly laid down by Puffendorf (lib. ii. cap. 18., § iv.): "*Erga totam civitatem officium boni civis* est, ut ejus salute nihil habeat carius; ut vitam, opes, fortunasque suas, ad eandem servandam *libenter* offerat." "*This comprehends the duty of a good citizen towards the state*, that nothing shall be preferred by him before the safety and integrity of that state; and that he shall, *freely and at all times*, offer his life, his means, and his fortune, to preserve that State's safety and integrity." As the general always includes the particular, it follows, as a matter of ordinary reasoning, from the foregoing, that "all citizens shall, as they possess means, contribute to the necessary *expenses* of the state in peace or war." And thus says Puffendorf (lib. ii. cap. 7, § vii.): "Quia, porro, nec belli nec pacis tempore, civitati negotia sine *sumptibus* geri possunt: summi imperii est adigere cives ut eosdem suppeditent." This, in ordinary times, "prudent rulers," says Puffendorf, will obtain by an "equal system" of taxation, "æqualitatem observando." But in a passage immediately following, he lays down expressly this all-important law, which also flows necessarily from the premises, and the justice and common sense of which cannot be too strongly insisted upon. — "Urgente reipublicæ necessitate, bona subditi cujuspiam, quibus præsens tempus maxime opus habet, ad usus publicos arripi et adplicari queant; licet ista longe superent ratam partem quam iste ad sumptus reipublicæ conferre tenebatur." "In a pressing necessity of the common weal, the goods of any subject which are absolutely required at the time, may be taken and applied to the public service; though the value should far exceed that of the ordinary *quota* which he is accustomed to be called upon to contribute" (Puffendorf, lib ii. cap. 15, § iv.). He indeed adds, that the excess "should be" made up by the state or by a contribution from the other citizens; but he puts all upon the necessity of the case, and upon that supreme law of nature which, in case of real urgency, calls upon a citizen to *give*, not only all his fortune, but his life to his country. In this maxim of natural law, Puffendorf is supported by all other eminent civilians, and especially by the high authority of Grotius, who lays down in "De Jure Belli et Pacis" (lib. ii. cap. 2, § vi.): "In gravissima necessitate reviviscere jus illud pristinum rebus utendi *tanquam si communes fuissent.*" "In cases of great urgency, the law of nature revives *to use all things as if they were common property.*" Such are the maxims of natural civil law as to the duties of citizens, and especially as to *pecuniary* contributions for public purposes. They flow directly from the necessities of our common nature, and have been ratified, at all times, by the common sense of mankind.

These being the acknowledged dictates of Civil Law, and of the sense of mankind upon these subjects, they were, as might be expected, adhered to and acted upon by governments, through all ages of the world that we know anything of. We, indeed, read in history of occasional "borrowings," and of occasional "debts"; but though public in name, they were private in fact. For instance, it has been no uncommon thing for monarchs to borrow money of private wealthy individuals, and apply such money to the furtherance of their schemes of ambition or aggrandisement. But then, this was as private individuals borrow, and upon security of estates belonging to the crown, and mortgaged to the lender. In this way the famous Flemish family of Fugger, who made enormous riches, during the great rise of prices in Europe, by linen-weaving at Antwerp, lent large sums, both to the Emperor Charles V., and Maximilian, his predecessor. In this way, also, the crown estates, and even the crown jewels of England have been frequently pledged and put in pawn by needy and extravagant Princes. In this fashion, the corporation and citizens of London, more than once, lent large sums to the Long Parliament, upon security of the forfeited estates, and in anticipation of taxes already voted. Still, all these were private transactions, in which the people were not implicated. It has also frequently happened, both in England and elsewhere, that particular services have been "in arrear;" that is to say, that the funds, applicable to these services have fallen short of the real expenditure needed or permitted; and hence individuals have become creditors of the Government, for such arrears owing on account of services performed, and have been compelled to take treasury notes and bonds for balances due to them. Still, however, this was altogether an affair betwixt these individuals and the government for the time being; neither parliament nor people being held to be legally implicated in the matter; and parliament has frequently refused to entertain any question as to these arrears, some of which remain unpaid to this hour, and perhaps properly so.* Up to times of comparatively modern and recent date, therefore, the idea of any persons, in a real national exigence, when perhaps national existence was at stake, offering to *lend* money TO THEIR COUNTRY "at interest," was deemed just as absurd as would be *a child* offering to *lend* its pocket-money to its *father* "at interest," when both were in danger of wanting a dinner! It was reserved for what is strangely termed "an enlightened era," to hatch this monstrous absurdity, which, until it was put into practice, would not have been deemed wicked, but silly. Strange turn for matters to take at an "enlightened era"; and stranger still, that such a notion should first strike root in the skull of a countryman of "Grotius": but so it was. It was in the muddy and huckstering brain of a Dutchman, somewhere about the middle of the seventeenth century, that this pestilent scheme was engendered; and in the huckstering country of Holland was first presented to the eyes of the world, the spectacle of a

* The Old French debt was of this sort; and was contracted mainly by Louis XIV., to carry on his endless wars. Louis was (to use his own words) "himself the state;" and all that the people had to do with it, was to pay such taxes as the *Grand Monarque* thought fit to impose.

"National Debt." The "Lernæan Fens" engendered the "Hydra"; and amidst the swamps of the "Zuyder Zee" was generated this far worse than the fabled monster of the poets! After all, however, the soil is sufficiently worthy of the tree. The Dutch, though they have produced one or two great men, are a nation remarkable for low, peddling, greedy, and huckstering notions: but they have this excuse, that, being a small and weak state, they have been continually, by their position, compelled to make efforts beyond their strength; and this it was, no doubt, which first tempted them to plunge into that most preposterous and wicked system, of which I am now to give the detail.

With a country almost naturally defenceless, engaged by position and religion in conflicts far beyond their real national strength, surrounded by strong and often hostile powers, the Dutch at length became so exhausted by the pressure of the taxes they paid, as to sacrifice before the shrine of mammon those liberties which they had preserved from ambition.

After throwing off the yoke of Spain and the Duke of Alva, they destroyed the Inquisition to set up the Bourse; and having risked all, to battle with those who would have taken from them their religion, they were at last reduced to sacrifice all to those who would lend them money. "Republicans" in name, to get money, they made more than a king of wealth. They invited the wealthiest citizens to throw off the rights of citizens, so that they would open their money bags. They in effect said, "*Lend*, and to your country; and its citizens shall be the lenders' slaves!" To get this money, they covenanted to guarantee it against all the casualties to which all other property is subject. They covenanted that it should feel the effects neither of misfortune nor mutation; that it should not be lessened, and that it should not be lost; that it should be intact even in the hour of national pressure, and unquestioned when everything else was questionable: they swore, for themselves and their children, that, until it was paid again, themselves and those children should work for the interest, were that repaying delayed till the day of judgment. Nay, they gave assurance, that rather than that interest should not be made up in full, those children should starve; and that, for the "principal," not only the soil and those who lived upon it should be mortgaged to all eternity, but that the necessity of borrowing should, in their eyes, be the last necessity, and their being, as a nation, should be endangered rather than *it* should be endangered, and "national honour" yield the place to "national faith." To ears which hear it for the first time, this sounds either like preposterous extravagance or sheer banter; but, unhappily, it is neither romance nor irony, for these are literally the conditions on which "national debts" are contracted! The monstrous mixture of wickedness and absurdity did, to be sure, originate amongst a people whose very existence as a people depended on "huckstering." It certainly was concocted (probably by the brain of a Dutch Jew) amid the cheeses and the salt-fish, the pickled herrings and the butter, the spicery and the crockery, the cockets, the clearances, the manifests, and the tallies of the Bourse of Rotterdam. But the example was too catching wherever there existed a profligate prince, an unprincipled minister, or a time-serving senate;

and in the course of not many years, this moral pestilence reached, not only England, but every state that had credit worth pawning, or subjects worth hood-winking. It is not, however, with the history, but with the theory, of "national debts" that we at present have to do. Let us examine this theory.

If we examine this system, without reference to the barefaced violation of the dictates of natural civil law, and of the principal duties of citizens which it involves, we shall still find it entangled amidst absurdities and evils, legal and moral, of almost every conceivable sort, meeting us at every step.

In the first place, we have the enormous absurdity of borrowing money, which is sunk without idea of a profit at simple interest. In ordinary concerns, if men are compelled by circumstances to borrow money which is to be sunk rather than profitably employed, as corporate bodies sometimes are, the mode preferred is ever that of terminable annuities upon lives. The reason and good policy of this are obvious. The interest, as it is called erroneously, payable to annuitants is, no doubt, at rates much above that of simple or legal interest; but the term "interest," as applied to it, is a misnomer. The truth is, the greater part of it is a repayment of capital by the borrower to the lender, who, by this device, contrives to spend his whole principal probably as well as interest, and if he be a long liver somewhat more. Still, however, the whole transaction has limits and a termination; and if the borrower gains nothing, neither can he lose much, whilst, by the other mode, unless the principal sum can be quickly repaid, which in national borrowings cannot possibly be the case, war being the cause of borrowing, an endless annuity is entailed, by means of which a nation may be paying the entire sum obtained over and over and over again, without gaining one single step towards ultimate relief. All the money borrowed a century ago by the English government has been repaid five times over in the shape of interest, without one jot of progress towards ultimate relief. Monstrous absurdity! When we reflect that had *one per cent.* of this interest been held to be *repayment of principal* (which might at a slight sacrifice have been bargained for), the whole would by this time have been redeemed.

Another absurdity is, that this mode of borrowing bars that effect of *time* which the law allows, and most rationally allows, to affect all other sorts of property. Thus, if Queen Boadicea had borrowed money to enable her to fight the Roman armies, we should, according to this, have been legally compelled now to pay the interest of it, impossible as it would be to prove, whether the documents and claims of the creditors might not be *in toto* forgeries and falsehoods; and though it is impossible to suppose that these sums of money (if not so *immortalised* by a fiction) could have been kept and preserved through all the mutations that have happened in the seventeen hundred years that have elapsed since that time. Strange notion, when twenty years' possession of an estate undisputed will bar a recovery, and a simple contract debt, six years unclaimed, is no debt at all!

A third absurdity is, that the effects of each loan in making "a national debt" renders, in the *ratio* of its extent, another loan more certain to be wanted; so that, being once forward a few steps in this course, it is impossible ever to get back. This is quite evident, if we reflect that the interest of each preceding loan, being paid in taxes on commodities, must to that extent enhance the prices of the articles in which the succeeding loans are to be spent. Hence every succeeding year of a war carried on by loans must, of necessity, cost more than the year that preceded it, to the close; because, as the interest, as it accumulates, is laid upon articles nearly all of which are used by the troops and by the people connected with their management, provisioning, transport, etc., in that degree the pay of the men, and the cost of all supplied to them, must be enhanced. Thus, in the war which was begun in A.D. 1793, and ended A.D. 1815, and which was carried on principally by loans, the expenses grew almost regularly with the years. A glance at the total expense of the army for the last seven years of that war is sufficient proof of this. It must be observed, that the expenditure of each year appears under the date of the year that follows, as the accounts for the *financial year* end on January 5th.

A.D.	1810	Expenditure of the Army	£18,463,094
	1811	ditto	18,536,300
	1812	ditto	23,869,359
	1813	ditto	24,987,362
	1814	ditto	29,469,520
	1815	ditto	33,795,536
	1816	ditto	34,207,384

This was the progress of expenditure through the last seven years of the last war with France; and thus borrowing and loans go on making themselves, at every step, not only more and more inevitable, but more and more burdensome.

That after a short continuation of such a process as this, *redemption* is impossible, must be evident enough to any man capable of reflection. If, at the times and periods when national exigences and emergencies occur, men cannot be made to advance the means requisite for the salvation of a country, how are such advances to be expected, or asked for, or obtained, when the exigency is past? The thing is plainly impossible, as long as human nature shall continue to be what it is Another absurdity of a very striking sort arises also out of this state of affairs: it is this. If a country clear of debt and unencumbered cannot defend itself out of its own immediate means, how is that same country, when loaded with debt, to sustain itself when another similar state of peril shall arise? "By contracting more debt," is the only conceivable answer. This may go on for a while; but then we come at last to this *reductio ad absurdum*, that as the incurring of debt, even by the richest nation, has a limit, it follows, that the doom of an indebted nation is thus far fixed, that it is easy to foresee a time when it must either be subdued or turn upon its creditors, or both! Such are the contradictions that arise out of schemes and systems like these. They are, however, of minor importance, when compared with others, to which we shall now address ourselves.

If a nation contract debt to a considerable extent, it follows, as a matter of necessity, that both the soil and the people must be virtually and actually *mortgaged* to the lenders; inasmuch as the interest of such debt can only be paid to the "national creditors," as they are styled, out of the produce of the labour of

4

the people, principally as exerted upon that soil. Now it is not difficult to see, nor does it need much reflection to convince any man of ordinary comprehension, that such a mortgage as this, is totally inadmissible upon any grounds of reason, and at open discord with every dictate of natural law as well as of common-sense. To convince ourselves of this, we have only to reflect, that he who has the power to *mortgage* has the power also to *sell;* for it is a maxim of law that one includes the other;—but what power can a people have to sell their country? The very idea includes absurdity of every description. If they were to sell, how could they give possession; for to give possession includes quittance, and having quitted whither could they go? If it be said, that the *rents* only are mortgaged; then we have the difficulty:—if the debt is small, who is to apportion out the estates? If the interest of it be equal to the whole rents; then follows the absurdity:—that if the owners of soil alone are to suffer in a national exigence, land would be nearly valueless! And after that, follows the question:—If the soil alone be mortgaged, why is the interest not paid out of rent, rather than out of the general taxes?

A short reflection must, however, suffice to convince most minds, that a nation can neither sell nor mortgage; because a nation, on the whole, can only have a *life-interest* in the soil which they inhabit. An abstract *right* without any *power* to enforce it, is a mere nonentity or chimera of the fancy. It is like the abstract idea of a right to life without the means of living; a mere absurdity or rather contradiction. A nation can have *no right* to alienate, because they can have *no power* to alienate, their soil; for how can they *control their successors?* A whole nation cannot possibly be bound to a bargain of their ancestors, making them serfs or aliens for ever! A *life-interest* then, is all that a people living at any given period can have in their soil; but persons having a mere life interest such as this, cannot have any imaginable power either to mortgage or sell nationally, because every day must bring into being parties not included in the bargain. Hence the whole idea of a nation mortgaging its soil falls to the ground, and is totally untenable; notwithstanding some great authorities have seemed to admit the contrary, though in a very limited way. The principal of these authorities is the illustrious Thomas Jefferson, President of the United States. In a letter addressed to Mr. John William Eppes, and written in the year 1813, about four years after the close of his presidency, this admirable man enters upon the following course of acute, but in one point (in my humble opinion) erroneous reasoning. With this exception, the whole passage is instructive in the highest degree, and ought to be impressed upon the mind of every man who is in a situation to influence to the slightest extent the political measures of any government or of any country.—The passage is as follows:—

"It is a wise rule, and should be fundamental in a government disposed to cherish its credit, and at the same time to restrain the use of it within the limits of its faculties, never to borrow a dollar without laying a tax, in the same instant, for paying the interest annually, *and the principal within a given term:* and to consider *that tax* as pledged to the creditors on the public faith. On such a pledge as this, sacredly observed, a government may always command, on a reasonable interest, all the lendable money of its citizens; whilst the necessity of an equivalent tax is a salutary warning to them and to their constituents against oppression, bankruptcy, and its inevitable consequence—revolution! But the term of redemption must be moderate; and, at any rate, *within the limit of their rightful powers*. But what limits, it will be asked, does this prescribe to their powers? What is to hinder them from creating a perpetual debt? I answer *the laws of nature*. The earth belongs to the living, not to the dead. The will and power of man expire with his life by nature's law. Some societies give it an artificial continuance, for the encouragement of industry. Some refuse it: as our aboriginal neighbours whom we call Barbarians. The generations of men may be considered as bodies or corporations. Each generation has the *usufruct* of the earth during the period of its continuance. When it ceases to exist, that usufruct passes on to the succeeding generation, free and unincumbered; and so on, to and from one generation to another, for ever. We may consider each generation as a distinct nation, with *a right* by the will of a majority, *to bind themselves;* but *none to bind the succeeding generation*, more than the inhabitants of another country. Or the case may be likened to the ordinary one of *a tenant for life*, who may hypothecate the land for his debts, during the continuance of his usufruct; but at his death the reversioner (who is for life only) receives it *exonerated from all burthens*. The period of a generation, or its term of life, is determined by the laws of mortality, which, varying a little only in different climates, offer a general average to be found by observation. I turn, for instance, to Buffon's Tables of 23,994 deaths, and the ages at which they happened; and I find that, of the numbers of all ages living at one moment, *half* will be dead in *twenty-four years and eight months.* But, leaving out *the minors* who have not the power of self-government, of *the adults* [of age] living at one moment, a majority of whom act for society, *one half* will be dead in *eighteen years and eight months.* At NINETEEN YEARS then, from the date of a contract, the majority of the contractors are dead, and their contract with them. Let this general theory be applied to a particular case. Suppose the annual [*male?*] births of the State of New York to be 23,994, the number of its [*male?*] inhabitants, according to Buffon, will be 617,703 of all ages. Of these, there would constantly be 269,286 *minors*, and 348,417 *adults;* of which last 174,209 will be *a majority.* Suppose that majority, on the first day of June, 1794, had borrowed a sum of money equal to the Fee-simple of the State, and to have consumed it in eating and drinking and making merry in their day; or, if you please, in quarrelling and fighting with their unoffending neighbours. Within *eighteen years and eight months*, one half of the *adult citizens* are dead. Till then, *being the majority*, they might rightfully levy the interest of their debt annually on themselves and their fellow-revellers, or fellow-champions. But, at that period, say at this moment, a *new* majority have come into place, in their *own* right, and *not* under the rights, the conditions, or the laws of their predecessors. Are they bound to consider the debt; to consider the preceding generation as having had *a right* to eat up the whole of the soil of their country in the course of a life; to alienate it from them (for it would be an alienation to the creditors); and would they think themselves either *legally* or *morally bound* to give up their country and to emigrate to another for subsistence? Every one will say 'No!' The soil is the gift of God to the *living* as much as it had been to the *deceased* generation; and the *law of nature* imposes no obligation on them to pay this debt. And, although, like some other natural rights, this has not yet entered into any 'Declaration of Rights,' it is no less a law, and ought to be acted upon by all *honest* governments. It is, at the same time, a salutary curb on the spirit of war and indebtment; which, since the modern theory of the perpetration of debt, has drenched the earth with blood and crushed its inhabitants under burthens ever accumulating. Had this principle been declared in the British 'Bill of Rights,' England would have been placed under the happy disability of waging *eternal war*, and of contracting her thousand millions of public debt!" (Jefferson's Correspondence, vol. iv. p. 202. *Letter to John W. Eppes, June, 24th*, 1813.)

To the reasoning of this striking passage, there is, as it seems to me, one objection to be taken, and that is with regard to the *minors*. By this scheme, minors wanting a few days only of legal age might be bound for nineteen years *nearly*, in a system of which they disapproved, which they detested, and to which they ought not to be subjected *per force*, when of age to assert their other political rights. Mr. Jefferson forgets, that probably in every day of his *nineteen years*, one or more minors must come of age, and thus add to the minority who never consented to, and could not be bound by the contract in question, when *the minority*, in lapse of years, became *a majority*. But this would happen in much less than nineteen years. In *eleven* years, *one-half of the majority*, or a fourth of the entire adults, will be dead. This reduces the majority to 37,105 persons, at the end of *eleven* years. But during those *eleven years*, half of the minors must have come of age. If they all lived, this would add to the other side 134,642 persons; which would then be a *great majority*, not bound by the contract. Making all reasonable deduction for deaths, however, there would still be an ample majority unbound by the contract, which would thus be at an end. To borrow money to be repaid within *eleven years*, would hardly answer the purpose of any government; yet this ought, as it seems to me, upon the president's own reasoning, to be the extreme term, if to lend money at all, by citizens to their country be an admissible transaction, which I contend it is not, involving, as it does, a breach of the duties upon which society is really based.

The grand and most fatal objection to all the extended systems of national borrowing, is, however, that they, in reality, create a mortgage upon the *labour* of universal posterity; for it is out of the fruits of the national labour alone, that the annual interest can be paid, and such small portions of national debts as have ever been repaid, have been so from the same source. This is a violation not only of all natural law, but of all laws whatsoever. There never was a code on earth, which made the children liable for the debts of the parents, unless those parents left those children something wherewith to pay. To mortgage the future labour of a child to pay the interest of a debt, contracted before it was born, is in fact, to enslave that child. An infant, so mortgaged, is born a helot and a serf. His body is no more his own than is that of the bondsman; and under whatever pretence or name, the fruits of his exertions are taken from him and made the property of another, a slave he is to all practical intents and purposes, and a slave he ought to be called. The definition of "a slave" is that he is "a man whose bodily toil and the fruits of it are the property of another;" and under this category comes every man whose labour is mortgaged, to pay the interest of a National Debt.

That such a monstrosity as this is totally at variance with all the usages and maxims of any state pretending to the slightest freedom of government, it needs little penetration to discover. One of the primal maxims of a "free government" is, that under it "no one can be taxed without his own consent, as expressed by a majority of freely elected national representatives." Next to the deprivation of life, deprivation of goods at the arbitrary will of a ruler or rulers, stands second in the list of the different species of tyranny. Taxes imposed without national consent are a public robbery; yet this is what must be perpetually done, if posterity are to be bound to pay the interest of a debt, and "consent" is forestalled and mortgaged as well as labour. That men, with the word "freedom" in their mouths, should ever have assented to the theory of a national debt, is just as surprising, as that men should have submitted to the practical consequences. It affords one proof more of the soundness of Chancellor Oxenstiern's aphorism, "Go, my son, and see with how little wisdom mankind are governed"!

The closing *item* of this black catalogue, is the spirit of gambling, of which such systems are the prolific parents, and which in fact forms an essential part of their nature. It must not be supposed, that men who lend money to governments in huge masses, either do or can engage in such transactions upon the footing of ordinary lenders in the ordinary business of life. Suppose the interest offered for each hundred pounds be at the highest rate allowed by law, or current at the time, the government borrowing cannot get the full hundred for that interest. The reason is, that the lenders must, of necessity, sell a large part of the "scrip," as the government receipt is called, to others, in order to obtain the necessary amount; and to do this, a large margin, in order to allow of profits upon successive sales of this kind, is requisite. Hence a perpetual school of speculation and gambling, attended with all conceivable sorts of trickery, in order to enhance the value of the "scrip" or "stock," is fostered; and out of the fortunes thus made by lending money to their country, in a real or pretended exigence, the gamblers who do it find added means to negociate other and larger loans, which are rendered more and more necessary by those which preceded them. Thus, not only are the laws of society violated by the system of "national debts," but society is plundered and swindled in the very act of borrowing, and a state gambling-house is erected, compared with the mischiefs of which, lesser "hells" as they are termed, dwindle into insignificance, and seem scarcely worthy to be struck by the sword of justice.

Such is the theory, and such the consequence of the things called "national debts." That they are based upon the violation of all national law and all national morality, seems to be a conclusion inevitable, by those who examine them with an unprejudiced eye. It is perhaps difficult to determine whether the folly or the wickedness of those who have abetted such transactions predominates. Different minds will decide this question in different ways: be the decisions, however, what they may, it is certain, that here honesty can only be defended at the expense of common sense and common foresight.

We have now arrived at the conclusion of such abstract matter as forms a necessary preliminary to the following pages. Of such importance, however, do I deem a clear understanding of these points, as a preparation for the narrative that is to ensue, that I cannot end better than with a sentence of that earnest pleading for freedom of teaching attributed to Spinoza, in which he expresses himself as follows. "Denique, quoniam hæc, quæ hic ostendimus, præcipua sunt, quæ in hoc tractatu intendo, volo, antequam ulterius pergam, lectorem enixissime rogare ut *hæc duo capita* attentius legere, et *iterum atque iterum perpendere* dignetur; et sibi persuasum habeat, nos non eo scripsisse animo, ut *nova* introduceremus, sed ut *depravata* corrigeremus, quæ tandem aliquando correcta evidere speramus". —*Tractatus Theologico-Politicus*, cap. xiv. p. 166. "Lastly, since the topics, upon which we have here enlarged, are the foundations, as it were, of this work, I would, before, proceeding further, earnestly entreat my readers to peruse *these two chapters* most attentively, and, if necessary, *to give them more than one perusal;* and I must beg of them to be assured, that I have not written with any view to introduce pernicious *novelties*, but to lay bare *modern errors*, which we may, at length perhaps, hope to see beginning to yield to common-sense."

LETTER IV.

THE REVOLUTION OF 1688.—THE ESTABLISHMENT OF THE BANK OF ENGLAND.—THE BEGINNING OF THE NATIONAL DEBT.—ITS EXTENT AT THE END OF THE REIGN OF WILLIAM THE THIRD; THE VALUE OF MONEY WHEN IT WAS BEGUN TO BE CONTRACTED.—EXCHEQUER BILLS INVENTED.—DEATH OF WILLIAM.

We are now in readiness, almost, to commence the active business of this narrative; but, before doing so, it will be expedient to cast back a retrospective glance at the summary of the state of parties, which formed the closing portion of the first letter of this series. We shall there find, that, on the success of the revolution in 1688, which seated the Dutch stadtholder upon the throne of Great Britain and Ireland, under the title of *King William the Third*, the nation was split into numerous and violently contending parties. First, there were the strong party of the Roman Catholics, excessively numerous in Ireland, and in England embracing in their body many persons of all ranks of society and retaining great wealth and influence, enraged, and naturally so, at this second crushing of their hopes of a gradual and complete re-establishment of their religion. Secondly, there were the high churchmen, calling themselves partisans of the Church of England as by law established, but hardly concealing their desire for a re-union, in some shape or other, with the ancient religion of their forefathers. Thirdly, there were the adherents of the church, who were hostile to the Roman Catholics, and who were determined to preserve the ascendancy of the Reformed Church as it then stood. Fourthly, there were the Presbyterians, who held episcopacy only second in degree, after the church of Rome, in its deserving of all detestation. And, lastly, there were the Independent Dissenters, of all grades, and containing amongst them divers colours of religious persuasion or fanaticism, down to absolute deism, but all preaching toleration and the injustice of establishments of any sort: these were the religionists. In politics, there were: first, the Tories, disapprovers of the revolution, though by no means abetting the exiled king in his popish or arbitrary notions: secondly, the Whigs, who had made the revolution, principally for the sake of the church property which they held and feared to lose. And, lastly, there was the Democratic and Republican Party, who supported the revolution from principle; and who, in religion, sincerely held the propriety of full toleration, and the right of private judgement in matters of faith, as in politics they did the right of the people to choose their own government; doctrines very grudgingly admitted by the Whigs, and held by them as abstract notions, rather than as doctrines to be acted upon. Such were the perilous divisions of the time; and from them the new king and all his friends and advisers deduced, without a dissentient, one conclusion; and that was, that every and all conceivable means of attaching a strong party to the government, and of rendering that government in itself as strong as possible, were to be resorted to. The necessity for this was, indeed, palpable and evident enough. That the revolution of this period was not brought about by any effort on the part of the English people in the mass, seems to be certain. James they unquestionably disliked; and some of his tools, such as Kirk and Jeffries, they naturally detested. The Reformation, unpopular at first, had made some progress, through the many sectaries to which it gave rise. Still, however, the people, well off and little oppressed as they were, proved by no means ripe for a violent change in the succession: and of their want of sympathy when the new dynasty was many years afterwards in danger, we have the strong testimony of Horace Walpole, an unwilling witness; for though he cared nothing for the reformed religion, and as little for popular freedom, he was unquestionably a zealous Whig and partisan of the House of Hanover, and was deeply vexed by the popular apathy, which in 1745 he was compelled to admit and describe.

Under these circumstances, with the people indifferent, and the weight of the aristocracy adverse, there was only one course for the revolutionary government to take; to enlist the multitude as far as it seemed safe, by the concession, in words at least, of popular rights, and to attach the middle or commercial classes, by measures which might give it a pecuniary if not a patriotic hold, upon their feelings and expectations. The "Bill of Rights" was the first fruit of this policy; the establishment of "the Bank of England," and the simultaneous commencement of a "national debt" the second. The first is a matter for general history. It is with the second, only, that, as author of these letters, I am to deal.

The year 1694, when this last event took place, was the sixth of the reign of the new dynasty of William and Mary. The revolution had added fresh virulence to those wars which the designs of the French monarch, Louis XIV., against the Protestant religionists, and the general independence of Europe, were exciting. Ireland had been the scene of a long conflict, which the victory of the Boyne terminated; and the theatre of war was now transferred to Flanders. In that tract of country, at present known by the name of "Belgium," numerous battles were fought, with various success, between the French armies and the allied English and Dutch, and other troops, commanded by King William in person, until 1697, when the contest terminated, for the time, in the peace of Rhyswick. The expenses of these wars bore heavily upon the treasury of the new government. James, on his abdication, certainly left his Dutch successor an army, considered large in those times, and an efficient and well-equipped navy; but he also bequeathed to him, a revenue of *barely two millions of pounds per annum*, and a people whom the ease of two inglorious and disgraceful, but not expensive reigns, and the recollection of the exactions of the Long Parliament, rendered naturally abhorrent of taxation, even though the tax-gatherer came dressed up with the cap of liberty on his head. Hence it was found, after no long time had elapsed in warfare, absolutely necessary to discover, if possible, some means of rendering an increased expenditure more palatable to the middle or commercial classes, who were the principal supporters of the government; and at the same time to raise the supplies necessary for these foreign wars, without adding to the discontent of any large portion of the people. In Holland, the country of his birth, the Dutch king and his advisers found both a precedent to quote, and an example to follow. By its position and circumstances, this country, inconsiderable in size and population, and not naturally defensible, had been compelled to act the part, for a series of years, of a leading power in Europe; and, this it had only been enabled to do, by that novel arm which a very extensive foreign trade is sure to create, and by the money drawn together by successful trading. Venice had at an earlier period played a similar part; but a series of struggles at last led the huckstering genius of the Dutch into a system, at which the Venetian republic had not arrived; and this was the fabrication of paper money, the erection of a bank to issue it, and the systematic borrowing of that money, and the creation of debt on the part of the government, for only the interest of which taxes were demanded of the people. Here was machinery set up and at work; and, in the opinion of interested or superficial observers, working successfully. It was, accordingly, soon proposed to set up a copy of this machinery in England, and in A.D. 1694, the blow was struck, which has been destined to have effects so monstrous, so long continued, and so marvellous on the fortunes of England and her people; and the establishment since known as "the Bank of England," was erected under the sanction of the government.

The first proposal or scheme of a bank has been attributed to a Doctor Hugh Chamberlayne. That which was adopted, however, was supposed to be the concoction of Gilbert Burnet, the bishop of Salisbury, a Scotchman, a native of Dunfermline, and a favorite of the king, assisted by William Paterson, another Scotchman, who had the principal active management of the entire scheme. Burnet had himself seen the system in full operation in Holland; and he seems to have thought of nothing but the facilities which it would afford, to clear off the incumbrances, and replenish the means of the revolutionary government, and to create an appearance of prosperity in the midst of fast-increasing debt, and more gradually and stealthily growing taxation. That the new government was in urgent need of such assistance is very certain. The amount of taxes, appropriated to the various services, had fallen far short of the expenditure; and so low was the credit of the government, that its securities, such as exchequer tallies or debentures, etc., were at an enormous and ominous discount, and such as threatened to end in a stoppage and total disruption of its means and resources. In the scheme of "the bank," were to be found the means to remedy this precarious, not to say desperate position of affairs. It was eagerly grasped at by the cabinet and the king. The houses of parliament were, after a severe struggle, prevailed upon to sanction it; and on the 27th day of July, A.D. 1694, the first charter was issued, a day fifty times more really important and memorable, than epochs of dynasties, or eras of victories and conquests.

Before entering upon such details as must, of necessity, follow the announcement of this event, so all important in its consequences, it is requisite that we should come to some precise judgment of the actual value of money at the period when this event, destined in its after effects so often to alter that value, took place. We must know the value of money then in England, in order to know the extent of the mutations and fluctuations in that value afterwards brought about, under the agency of the system now commenced. Into this inquiry let us now enter. The reduction of Peru and Mexico having been completed by Spain, in A.D. 1525 ; and that of the Brazils by Portugal subsequently; the influx of metallic wealth upon Europe which followed these grand events, had continued through the greater part of two centuries, and had now nearly exhausted itself. The diamonds of Brazil were discovered late: but the Brazilian gold was now in full circulation; so that at the period of 1694, the supply of the precious metals was rapidly finding a level, the additions year after year from the mines being now greatly absorbed by the wear and tear of the quantities of coin now in use all over Europe; and in the domestic purposes to which both gold and silver were now more commonly applied. In order to come to a judgment of the value down to which money had depreciated, by the enormous influx of the metals, we can only use such *data* as we possess. They are scanty in the extreme. One of the surest tests is a comparison of the average price of wheat at this period with the average prices of the present time; and for doing this there are materials in existence. The tables of the market-prices of wheat at

Oxford, the averages being constructed from the highest and lowest prices, calculated at Lady-day and Michaelmas, give the following results, upon the eleven years which preceded the year 1694, when the bank-scheme was begun.

years.		*prices of wheat.*			*years.*		*prices of wheat.*	
		s.	*d.*				*s.*	*d.*
1683	. .	35	3	per qr.	1689	. .	28	2
1684	. .	36	8		1690	. .	27	6
1685	. .	43	8		1691	. .	29	11
1686	. .	26	8		1692	. .	39	7
1687	. .	27	7		1693	. .	56	3
1688	. .	23	2					
							181	5
		193	0				193	0
						11)	374	5
					per quarter average.		34	$0\frac{5}{11}$

By the above calculation, the average price of wheat at Oxford, for these years, is as high as *thirty-four shillings* and a fraction per quarter. It must, however, be observed that the last two of these years were the commencement of a series, which not only concluded the century, but spread into the next, and which has been recorded as being most disastrous to the crops, not only in England, but over the larger part of Europe. It must also be borne in mind, that the *Oxford returns* are always fouud to be above those of *Mark Lane*. Now, as the returns at Mark Lane are undeniably higher than an average which includes the whole country, we must deduct considerably from this price to arrive at any safe conclusion.

Taking all the circumstances together, I am inclined to think that *five shillings per quarter* is *the least* that can be deducted on these accounts; which brings the price to *twenty-nine shillings per quarter.* If with this we compare the average price of wheat for the *seven years* which preceded the war with France in 1793, as given by the Oxford tables, we come to the following result.

years.	*prices of wheat.* s.	d.	
1786 . . .	41	10	per qr.
1787 . . .	49	9	
1788 . . .	49	5	
1789 . . .	53	7	
1790 . . .	57	10	
1791 . . .	51	6	
1792 . . .	53	4	
	7)357	3	
	51	$0\frac{4}{7}$	per quarter average.

If we deduct *five shillings per quarter*, from this price of *fifty-one*, we make the average for the country *forty-six shillings per quarter;* and this we may justly do, as these years were, upon the whole, rather years of scarcity than of plenty; the conclusion of the eighteenth century being similar to that of the seventeenth. This comparison, then, gives the value of money in the years 1694, and in 1792, as *twenty-nine* is to *forty-six;* or, in round numbers, money in 1694 must have been nearly as *two-thirds* are to a *unit*, when compared with money in 1792, *inversely.* The plain way of stating this is, however, to consider that *twenty-nine* shillings, of 1694, would buy as much wheat as *forty-six shillings* would in 1792, on an average of seasons;—and, therefore, the money of 1792, must have *depreciated* a *full third;* or, in other words, must have been *a full third less valuable* than the money of 1694.

It is more difficult still to come to a certain conclusion as to what the value of money at this present time is, compared with the value of money in 1792. This difficulty arises out of the Corn Laws, which tend, in a great majority of years, to keep both the prices of grain and the rents of land above their natural level. The only way, then, is to take any years in which great plenty made these laws for the time imperative, and compelled wheat to sink to *its natural price*, according to the value of the money of the the time. The following were three years of great plenty; and these are the results,—the prices here being *average prices*, and not for one market.

year.	*prices of wheat.*	
1834 . .	51	11
1835 . .	44	2
1836 . .	39	5
	3) 135	6
	45	2 per quarter average.

This agrees with the result of 1792, very nearly; and, upon the whole, I should deem these comparisons as affording a fair approximation to the truth. The money then, of 1792, was a full third of less value than that of 1694; and the money of to-day is about the same.

The comparison, between 1694 and 1792, is also borne out by the "provision tables" of Greenwich Hospital, which go up nearly to the former period.

If the rental of the land of the kingdom at this time, which was estimated by *Mr. Locke* and others, at about *twelve millions sterling per annum*, be compared with the rental of the present day, it would seem, on a first view, to point to a different result. The best consideration I can give the matter, however, convinces me that this is only in appearance. We must recollect, in the first place, that the rent of land at that time was based upon considerations, and circumstances very different from those which prevail at this day. The interest of money was *six*, or even *eight per cent*, in ordinary cases. The profits of trade were commensurate with this high interest for money. No one, therefore, who saw tradesmen making the great returns which all traffic then afforded, would give a heavy rental for land. Lands, consequently, were let low, and on long leases, the competition for farms being moderate. Again, we must take into consideration the effects which the vast increase of population, since that time, has had upon the rental of England. It has caused, in the first place, nearly *seven millions of acres* of "common lands," which paid no rent at all, to be inclosed. This land is probably worth *twenty shillings* an acre, on the average. In the second place, it has, by augmenting the towns, raised the rent, enormously, of all the lands in their neighbourhood; that is to say, tripled and quadrupled it. If to all these causes of augmentation, be added the low interest which money now bears, and the unnatural competition for land, which our now redundant population has caused, we shall conclude, that Locke's low estimate is not to be, by any means, attributed totally to the different value of money. Upon all the considerations, we may safely, I think, estimate the money of this day as a *full third* of less value than the money of 1694, but hardly more than that; and, having fixed this in our mind, we shall be able better to appreciate the extraordinary fluctuations in that value which, during the intervening period, the establishment of a paper-currency has caused, as well as the terrible effects of these fluctuations upon the welfare and morals of society.

Having fixed in our mind the general fact, that the money of 1694 was more valuable by a *full third*, than money is now; or in other words, that *two* pounds then, would buy rather more of any thing than *three* pounds will now; we now proceed to the details of the scheme of "the bank," and the proximate reasons for that scheme. Had the Revolutionary Whig Government intended to govern soberly, and without mixing the country, against the advice of its wisest citizens, in foreign wars and broils, in which it had no concern, they would not have needed any scheme which was sure to involve an alteration in the value of that money, sooner or later. It was not, however, their intention so to govern. The sudden change of the dynasty, and the mere fact of the successful adventurer being the Dutch stadtholder, and prince of Orange, rendered a series of continental wars inevitable. These wars and the debt which they created were, however, beyond a doubt, considered as a sort of "god-send" by the friends of the new government; who were taught to consider them as a means of binding the moneyed classes to the government, and of consolidating and perpetuating the new order of things. To enable the ministers, however, to impose upon the people additional burthens, sufficient even to discharge the interest of any debt that might be contracted, a resort to fictitious or paper money was necessary. To have forced an addition of coin into the kingdom, to meet these new expenses, would have involved a pressure which, under the critical circumstances of the Whig *régime*, could not be risked. This peril, their opponents, the French, either could not see or else despised; and in due time they paid the penalty. The pressure for money caused by the expenditure and debts of Louis XIV., at this period, laid the foundation of that growing discontent, which, deepening and increasing as that expenditure and that debt swelled and deepened, at length, after the expiration of just a century, levelled the throne, the church, and the aristocracy, in the dust; and, as by a moral earthquake, changed the whole face of society in France. The entire circulation there was, and continued to be, metallic. The amount was calculated by the minister, M. Neckar, in 1789, to be about ninety millions of English pounds sterling. The *annual taxes* (exclusive of course, of the rents of the royal domains, etc.), wrung from the French people, never much exceeded a *fourth part* of that sum; and yet the pressure caused by this, under the French system, at last stopped the wheels of the government, and brought on the revolution. The new king of England and his advisers were, therefore, "wise in their generation," when they originated the scheme of a bank and paper money; for this not only enabled them to run into interminable debt, but, to avoid the pressure which must have been resorted to, in order to force a larger supply of the metals into circulation, by supplying the money wanted for interest, year after year, in the shape of bank-notes.

We are now arrived at the period for looking at the general detail of the scheme for a national bank. It was as follows: but before recapitulating it, we may observe the curious fact, that the scheme, instead of being brought prominently forward, was smuggled under the long tail of an act of parliament for raising moneys generally, and is described as a means merely "for securing certain recompenses and advantages to such persons as shall voluntarily raise fifteen hundred thousand pounds towards carrying on the war with France"! In the act itself, certain clauses enact, that if subscribers under the act shall raise £1,200,000, they shall be formed into a corporation under the style and title of "the Governor and Company of the Bank of England." The remaining 300,000*l.* was also to be subscribed; but for this the lenders were to receive annuities from the government, for one, two, and three lives. The New Bank Company were, in return for their charter, to lend the whole of the subscribed capital (1,200,000*l.*) to Government, at an interest of *eight* per cent. per annum. They were also to have four thousand a year for management; in all, one hundred thousand a year for lending twelve hundred thousand. Such being the terms offered, the subscription-list was filled up in ten days, and on the 27th July, 1694, their charter was sealed: and this, it may be truly said, was "the opening of the first seal"—for England. The name of the first governor was John Houlbon, Knt.; and amongst the directors stands the ill-omened name of William Paterson, the contriver and concoctor of the whole scheme.

Thus the beginning of "paper money," and a "bank," was the beginning of "national debt," properly so called. There were, before this time, *arrears* owing by Government, and also some sums taken up on *terminable* annuities *for lives*; but this is the first sum standing on the debit side of the national account, *for the redemption of which no provision was made, or attempted to be made*, and of which the *interest* only was provided for. Thus did "the debt" first strike root; and thus was the first seed sown. It will soon be seen how rapidly and how surely it spread itself. There are some plants which seem useful enough in their way, but which no wise gardener will ever suffer to enter his confines; because, when once in, it is impossible to extirpate them, and even to prevent their spreading almost over the whole ground. Of the same nature are national debts. Let them once strike root in a country, and they never stop, nor can be stopped, until they have impoverished the whole land. It must not be supposed, that even when first proposed, this scheme did not meet with great opposition. Quite the contrary. It was from the beginning predicted, that this institution must, from its very nature, be either the tool of Government, or its master; that it must create a swarm of jobbers and usurers, and in various ways corrupt the morals of the nation. The whole danger was not, however, seen, even by sagacious politicians, until many years afterwards, when it had become more palpable in its effects; and such objections as were advanced were treated as the effusions of faction. The example once set, was soon followed. In four years after this, the East India traders, who had before existed as a company, lent the government *two millions sterling*, at the same interest as that paid upon the original bank loan, as the price of a charter and extended privileges. Other schemes followed; but of them I shall treat in their proper place, it being better now to give a brief detail of the proceedings of the Bank up to the end of the reign, and then ascertain the progress which the debt had made during the life of King William, which ended in A.D. 1702.

On its commencing business, the Bank seems to have charged the highest legal rate of interest, six per cent., upon all bills discounted, whether foreign, or inland, or home bills. In a few days, however, it appears to have been found politic to reduce the rate of discount upon foreign bills to four and a half per cent. In 1695, in January, in order to increase the business of the concern, another course was adopted. Foreign bills, excepting at short dates, were again discounted at the rate of six per cent., and inland or home bills at four and a half per cent.; but to persons who would *keep an account with the Bank*, an inducement was held out for doing so, in the shape of a reduction to *such persons* of half the discount on foreign bills, the rate of which was thus, in these cases, reduced as low as *three per cent.*,—a novel rate in these days! In the following May, despite of these relaxations, the "Governor and Company" seem to have been driven to further expedients; and for a time, all short-dated running bills, or notes, were taken for discount at the novel rate of *three per cent.*: and not content with this, the Court of Directors at last gave notice of their readiness "to lend money"; that is to say their notes, "upon plate, lead, tin, copper, steel, and iron," at *four per cent. per annum!*

From these manœuvres, it is sufficiently evident, that the Paper Money system flagged at first, and was received with distrust. Two years after this, however, both their own credit and that of the new Government were subjected to another severe ordeal, which had well nigh ruined both. In the year 1697, whilst war was yet going on, so disgracefully bad had become the state of the coinage, from the clipping and sweating which the Jews had made it undergo during the confusion of the change of 1688, that a fresh coinage became absolutely inevitable, and not to be postponed. The difficulties attending this transaction put both Bank and Government "to their trumps." So great was the run for the new coin, that to avoid paying change, the Directors prevailed upon persons keeping accounts with them, to transfer even sums as low as five pounds, from one credit to another. To diminish the number of their notes in circulation, they prevailed upon rich merchants to hold bills in lieu for a time, at an interest of *six per cent.*; and it has been asserted that, to gain time, they sometimes paid in *new sixpences*, when the pressure of the demand became excessive! The Government was placed in a predicament not very dissimilar. Their credit ebbed so low, as to be, to all appearance, upon the very eve of dissolution; and with their credit would have perished that of the Bank, which was, from the very first, regarded as a mere instrument and tool of the revolutionary Government. To such a pass did the general alarm reduce them, that at last Exchequer tallies, and orders upon the Exchequer, were at *sixty per cent. discount;* whilst the notes of the Bank itself were at a discount of *twenty per cent.!* In certain emergencies, the greatest rashness is said to be the greatest prudence: and so it proved in this dilemma. The credit of the Bank being much better than that of the Exchequer, a device was adopted, which certainly does honour to the *nerve* of "the Governor and Company." They advertised for an additional subscription of a million to their capital, and, as a bonus to adventurers in this way, actually offered to receive *four-fifths* in the *discredited Exchequer tallies and orders*, and the remaining fifth in their *own notes*. This was a master-stroke! In *this* way, the million was eagerly subscribed; and thus, at one cast of the dice, they relieved the tottering Exchequer of eight hundred thousand pounds of "promises to pay," and implicated the subscribers of the whole million in the absolute necessity of carrying the Bank through, if possible, which, in spite of the gibes and jeers of the Tories and the Jacobites, as well as of the opinions of the more disinterested opponents of the new system, was at last done, though after a severe struggle. Precarious as all artificial money-systems are, they sometimes have such runs of luck in their favour, as to appear to spectators to have, in vulgar phrase, "nine cats' lives." This was the first mortal struggle which the system had to front and get through. It succeeded to a miracle, and almost *by* a miracle: and of the reaction, caused by this unlooked-for success, the Chancellor of the Exchequer,

Montague, afterwards created Lord Halifax, very cunningly and adroitly availed himself. He obtained a renewal of the Bank charter for five years, with an exemption from all *rate*, *tax*, *assessment*, or *imposition*, of their capital stock or real fund, with all profits thereon: and it was also enacted, that forgery of their notes, or their seal, should be a "capital felony." These proceedings had the effect of raising the credit of the Bank to a height far beyond anything it had reached before: and it also put upon the minister the invention of a new instrument, known, from that day to this, by the name of "Exchequer bills." These bills were and are nothing more than promissory notes, *due at certain dates* and bearing interest, issued by Government when in want of money. These bills the Bank undertook to help to circulate, and also to help (if needful) *to pay* when due; and these bills, accordingly, took the place of the old "tallies" and "orders," which had so shortly before been in the very gulf of discredit and bankruptcy, along with the Government which was party to them.

Thus were now fairly established in England, paper-credit and paper-money in the shape of "Exchequer bills" and "Bank notes," formally for the first time. This novelty, destined to be so disastrous in its after effects, was only brought about by an open and avowed union between the Government and the Bank, and a combination of the credit of both; which continued as time elapsed, though with more of secresy; and which, despite of all assertion to the contrary, continues at this hour. Sometimes, indeed, the Bank has appeared to rule the Government, and sometimes to be ruled by it; but their interests no set of governors, in either place, have ever been able to dissever; nor will their fates now, in all probability, ever be disunited, be those fates what they may.

In conclusion, I must observe, that it is not meant to be asserted, that up to this period, no kind of paper security connected with banking had ever passed from hand to hand. The fact is, that "Goldsmiths' receipts" for *coin*, lodged with them in their capacity of bankers, had, for convenience, been sometimes transferred from hand to hand; and this was the nearest approach to paper-money that had been accomplished. The transaction, in all cases, was, however, limited to a few merchants, and is unworthy of notice, except as a point in financial history.

I shall conclude this letter with a statement of the debt, fixed and floating, contracted during the reign of the third William, whose memory unthinking and ignorant zealots have chosen to designate "glorious and immortal." If "the tree is to be known by its fruits," it may be justly styled the most unfortunate reign that England ever saw; inasmuch as, during its pernicious progress, were sown the seeds of a system which has poisoned the happiness of Englishmen, and reduced their country from a state of exuberant and equally diffused wealth and universal comfort and ease, to a land of toiling slaves and spirit-broken paupers, lorded over by a moneyed and landed aristocracy who have divided the government between them, and, by a mixture of crime and error spread over a century and a half, have induced a state of suffering and consequent insecurity, that bids fair to involve their own safety, as well as that of such remaining fragments of the ancient institutions of the land as they have left undestroyed or unchanged. It is not, of course, any part of the plan of this work to give a minute or detailed history of the steps by which, with the aid of the paper-money, the monster of the debt progressed and grew. Records there are of this progress, not only in the statute-book itself, but in various annals compiled from it. These minute details are, however, neither very useful nor very interesting. It is sufficient to note, from period to period, the increase of its weight; and in the varied and plentiful crop of miseries which have attended it, we shall find ample evidence of the intensity and dreadful virulence of the evil.

The following statement is extracted from Sir John Sinclair's "History of the Revenue," a work of which there is no doubt of the accuracy and general value, whatever may be thought of the soundness of the views of its author.

NATIONAL DEBTS ON THE 31ST DAY OF DECEMBER, A.D. 1701.

Perpetual Funded Debts bearing interest:—

	Principal.			Interest.		
1. The original stock of the Bank of England	£1,200,000	0	0	£96,000	0	0
2. The original stock of East India Company	2,000,000	0	0	160,000	0	0
3. The Bankers' debt made by Charles II.	664,263	0	0	39,855	15	7
	£3,864,263	0	0	£295,855	15	7
Annuities and debts charged on certain taxes with a view to redemption	9,861,047	2	2	853,122	18	8¼
Unfunded debts unprovided for -	2,669,391	19	5	161,963	10	5
Total of debt -	£16,394,702	1	7	£1,310,942	4	8¼

Thus, in seven years, with the exception of the debt of the Exchequer of Charles II. to the goldsmiths and merchants, sixteen millions of debt had been contracted—a trifle in modern eyes, but the *fomes* or original germ of a plague which has ravaged England from that day to this. The debt of Charles II. was a sum of money lodged *for security* in the Exchequer by various traders, but upon which the unprincipled Charles, in a strait for money, laid his hands! It was now made part of the "National Debt"; and for this unprincipled robbery, the toiling people of England have been made to pay interest for nearly two centuries—a worse robbery than the other!

LETTER V.

QUEEN ANNE.—PROGRESS OF THE BANK.—LORD BOLINGBROKE'S ACCOUNT OF THE SYSTEM AND ITS EFFECTS.—SUCCESSION WAR.—DEBT AT THE QUEEN'S DEATH.—GEORGE THE FIRST.—SOUTH-SEA BUBBLE.—DEBT AT HIS DEATH.—GEORGE THE SECOND.—WALPOLE MINISTER.—"CATSKIN WAR."—ITS COST.—FRENCH WAR.—THE SINKING FUND FIRST TRIED.—HUME'S PROTEST AGAINST FUNDING.—DEATH OF GEORGE THE SECOND.

IN our last letter we left "the system" fairly launched, and at length brought over the shoals, reefs, and broken water which greeted the commencement of her voyage. Unopposed by the people at large, who knew not what was preparing for them; acquiesced in, perforce, by those whose opposition could alone have been effectual, and fostered by the new Government which, without such assistance, would itself have been in a precarious position, the "Paper money and Funding System" may now be considered, at the commencement of the reign of Queen Anne, as established in England. Had it been possible that the people could have been possessed of such knowledge as might have led them to oppose the completion of this pernicious and insidious scheme, it is pretty evident that, even at this period, they would have lacked the power to do so. The truth was, the people of England had little or nothing to do with the Revolution of 1688. Putting apart a few religious zealots and theoretical Republicans, who aided the Whig party, it was altogether the work of an aristocracy alarmed for the safety of their ill-gotten possessions. If the people had little to do in it, their services were not necessary, were neither wished for, nor acceptable; and the few privileges that were formally conceded to them by the Bill of Rights, were, at the very first opportunity, and upon the earliest shadow of pretext, withdrawn from them. The Septennial Act was passed; and under the tutelage of the new system, a practice of corruption, both within and without the walls of Parliament, commenced, which quickly rose to a height, astounding even to modern ears; and the evidence of which has been in vain attempted to be discredited by those who deem it inconvenient to have such practices attributed to a party upon whose lips "purity of election and representation" has ever hung as a watchword!

In the mean time, the Bank went on increasing in credit and in capital; and as these grew, so did its advances to the Government, some of which were repaid by extensions and renewals of its privileges and charter. In 1707, the subscription of a million, which had been, at a former crisis, taken, for the most part, in the shape of discredited Exchequer orders and tallies, was repaid to the subscribers. This raised the credit of the establishment higher than ever; an additional strength was gained by a renewed charter, which gave the Governor and Company a monopoly of their new trade, by preventing all other banks from having more than *six partners*; which at that time was almost a prohibition. In order to obtain these new privileges, the Bank lent the Government four hundred thousand pounds without interest; and *cancelled* "Exchequer bills" in their possession, amounting, with interest, to 1,775,027*l.* 17*s.* 10½*d.* To enable the Company to fulfil these expensive bargains, a large further dose of *bona fide* capital became necessary: and by means of three several subscriptions, their capital was raised to the nominal amount of *five millions and a half*: a huge sum; the greater part of which was to be employed in assisting the Government, as usual. For another extension of charter, they agreed to circulate a sum equal to their whole original capital in Exchequer bills; and shortly after agreed to cancel similar bills in their hands for *two millions more!* In return for this, they obtained the lucrative office of managing future loans to Government; and, in fact, effected a transfer of the whole business of the Exchequer to their own shop, where it has ever since remained. In the midst of these rapidly growing involvements of debt on the part of the Government, Queen Anne died; and with her again died the hopes of the Tory party, who had grasped a short-lived power, of which they made no good use, and which, it is possible, that they had not time to use as they intended. Certain it is, that the best and most illustrious men of the Tory and High-church party bore, from first to last, strong testimony against the system that was now erected with such fatal success. The chief of these was the famous Henry St. John, Lord Bolingbroke; who, in his "Letters on the Use of History," delivers himself as follows:—

"Few men, at the time (1688), looked forward enough to foresee the necessary consequences of *the new constitution of the revenue* that was soon afterwards formed, nor of the method of funding that immediately took place; which, *absurd as they are*, have continued ever since, till it is become scarce possible to alter them. Few people, I say, saw how the creation of funds, and the multiplication of taxes would increase yearly the power of the Crown, and bring our liberties, by a natural and necessary progression, into more *real*, though less *apparent danger*, than they were in *before the Revolution!* The excessive ill husbandry practised from the very beginning of King William's reign, and which laid the foundation of *all that we feel and fear*, was not the effect of ignorance, mistake, or what we call chance; but of design and scheme in those who had the sway at that time. I am not so uncharitable, however, as to believe that they intended to bring upon their country *all* the mischiefs that we who came after them, experience and apprehend. No: they saw the measures they took singly and unrelatively, or relatively alone to some immediate object. The notion of attaching men to the new Government, by tempting them to embark their fortunes on the same bottom was a reason of State to some; the notion of creating a new, that is a moneyed interest, in opposition to the landed interest, or as a balance to it, and of acquiring a superior influence in the City of London, at least, by the establishment of great corporations, was a reason of party to others: and I make no doubt, that the opportunity of *amassing immense estates*, by the *management of funds*, by *trafficking in paper*, and by *all the arts of jobbing*, was a reason of private interest to those who supported and improved this SCHEME OF INIQUITY, if not to those who devised it. They looked no further. Nay, we who came after them, and have long tasted the bitter fruits of the corruption they planted, were far from taking such alarm at our distress, and our dangers as they deserved. . . . Your lordship, I am sure, sees how much a due reflection on the passages of former times, as they stand recorded in the history of our own and of other countries, would have deterred a *free people* from trusting the sole management of so great a revenue, and the sole nomination of those legions of officers employed in it to their chief magistrate. . . . Nay, your lordship sees not only how much a due reflection upon the experience of other ages and countries would have pointed out national corruption, as the natural and necessary consequence of investing the Crown with the management of so great a revenue, but also, *the loss of liberty*, as the natural and necessary consequence of national corruption."—Bolingbroke's *Study of History*, Letter II, p. 45.

This was written about the year 1735, not half a century after the revolution; and we shall see, in due time, from the testimony of the same writer, as well as of others, how deeply, even at that era, corruption and the basest spirit of lucre had sapped and ruined the boasted, or rather pretended, safeguard of the nation's liberties, the House of Commons.

The great cause of the profusion of Queen Anne's reign was, however, another fatal gift from the "Pandora's box," of the revolution,—the notion of our being compelled to preserve "a balance of power in Europe." This scheme of a *balance of power* was the invention of the Dutch king, who, no doubt, looked with a paternal eye to his hereditary power in Holland, where his family were perpetual "stadtholders," or governors. It was a specious pretext for involving England in the fortunes of Holland; and, before Queen Anne had been well seated on the throne, it gave rise to the long war, called "The War of Succession." The first offence taken, was the proclamation of the Pretender by Louis XIV. as king of England, on the death, in A.D. 1701, of his father, James II. This was a violation of the peace of Ryswick. The real cause of the coalition which was formed against France was, however, the attempt to place the crown of Spain upon the head of Philip, a grandson of the French king, and thus to consolidate the power of the two monarchies. At this scheme, the ruling powers in England affected great alarm; though it seems to have been the opinion of many, that the junction thus to be effected, would have been apparent, rather than real; such having always been the antipathy of Spaniards to a French connection, that no amalgamation of feeling between them seems possible. The result was, however, a coalition between England, Holland, and some of the German states against France and Spain; which, after a series of victories, under the generalship of Marlborough and Prince Eugene, was at last finished in 1713, by the treaty of Utrecht. Though the greatest share of the expense of this very questionable war, was managed (as has been the case in every future coalition) to be thrust upon England, yet this peace was not palatable to the nation at large. The new mode of raising supplies, by mortgaging posterity, and paying the interest in paper money, had not then begun to be felt seriously by the people at large; and the national vanity had been roused, so far as to make even wise men aspire to raise these islands into an arbiter of all other nations; and a supreme court to which were to be referred all the disputes of all the wrong-headed and arbitrary rulers of Europe. These foolish notions, the treaty of Utrecht, effected by the Tory Government in the latter years of the Queen, barred for the time; much to the dissatisfaction of even such men as Lord Somers, who ought to have known better; but who seems to have been thoroughly infected with every folly and every wickedness of his party, during these eventful periods.

Queen Anne died soon after the peace of Utrecht; that is to say in 1714. It seems to be a dubious matter to state the exact amount to which the debts of the Government had risen during her reign, as writers disagree upon the subject. One thing is certain, that the Tories, who had, from the first, opposed the system, made these debts no less. There can be no doubt that during their short term of power, during the last years of Anne, they must have felt the ease of borrowing, rather than raising taxes directly from the people; and whatever Swift or Bolingbroke might think, there is reason to suspect that Harley, Lord Oxford, a man of more supple character, was imbued with the folly of this system of financial anticipation, nearly as much as his opponents. The following is the outline of Sir John Sinclair's statement of the Government debts, on the demise of the Queen in 1714; making the account up to the 31st of December, of that year. In this account, amongst other speculative and gambling modes of getting supplies, "*lottery funds*," occur for the first time.

General View of Debts up to 31st December, 1714.

	Principal.	s.	d.	Interest.	s.	d.
Perpetual Funds, Bank Loans, cancelled Exchequer bills, East India Loan, etc.	£21,094,071	3	2	£1,288,603	18	8
Temporary Annuities, Lottery Funds, etc.	26,017,042	13	4	1,861,384	4	10
Unfunded Debts, Navy and Army, balances, and other deficiences.	7,034,249	14	10	201,369	19	9
Total debt - -	£54,145,363	11	4	£3,351,358	3	3

Here, so rapid was the increase, we see the interest of 1714 is nearly equal to the perpetual debt of 1701; and the whole amount of incumbrance is quadrupled in the short space of thirteen years!

To Queen Anne succeeded the elector of Hanover, under the style and title of George I. Before going into the financial deeds of his reign, we must advert to the spirit of gambling, and fraudulent speculation, which the invention of the funding and paper system soon began to evoke. The first grand break-out of this depraved love of lucre, and total decay of public spirit amongst the higher classes, occurred in the plunder and pillage of "the Reformation," so called by those, principally, who profited by it. The same leaven worked in the Long Parliament, and amidst the licentious profligacy which became fashionable after the Restoration. On the establishment of the Bank, and the commencement of borrowing, in the name of the nation, this degraded spirit, the disgrace and ultimate bane and ruin of every people, amongst whom it gets head, was not long in showing itself; and it soon went lower, and became more widely spread than it had been, even when the enormities of the tyrant, Henry the Eighth, and his infamous parliaments and tools were in their full blow of iniquity. The reader will have already remarked, that with the admirers of funds and fictitious money, *lotteries* became also a favourite means of raising cash for a craving government. In a few years after, this method of public gambling was put quite into the shade by the publication and establishment of a scheme, known then and since by the name of the "South-Sea Scheme;" a scheme which, for extent of fraudulent and insane speculation, has eclipsed all others, before or since. The date generally assigned to the "South-Sea Bubble," is that of 1720. The South-Sea trading company scheme, out of which it gradually arose, was patronised, however, by Harley, Lord Oxford, about 1712, though the spring-tide of the grand fraud did not arrive until some years after. This ruinous and infamous scheme arose out of the wants and necessities of a weak and reckless Government; and its history is, briefly, this:—

As the growing operation of the increasing taxes began to act upon private expenditure, and silently to decrease and cut down the large and ample profits, then always derivable from ordinary trades and professions, men began, not unnaturally, to hanker after schemes of short and compendious methods for realising fortunes. This baleful spirit, the encouragement given by the revolutionary Government to public gambling in various shapes, fostered and nourished; until, at last, those classes who might have been thought to have possessed the greatest prudential guards against this sort of fascination, seemed smitten with a sudden madness of absurd speculation, and became the prey of a set of villains, who exhibited a scene of folly and fraud, unmatched either at the period when it happened, or, even, in future time—prolific as that future has been of such exhibitions. This vein of gambling, into which the nation had been gradually led by the schemes of the Government, and the various speculations which were the natural and assured fruit of those schemes, was at last taken advantage of by a set of men who were connected with the "South-Sea Company," a trading company established for the ostensible purpose of gaining a commerce with the Spanish American possessions, and for whaling in the South Seas; at that time almost unknown. This company was set on foot in the last years of the queen's reign; but their transactions, up to 1719, consisted merely in sending a vessel or two, under a license from the king of Spain, to some of the Spanish settlements. In the year 1719, however, the Directors conceived a plan of obtaining a charter of exclusive privileges, by offering to relieve the Government of large irredeemable annuities granted in their distress for money at ruinous rates, and other incumbrances of a similar nature. Having sent in proposals to the Government containing the most tempting offers, these proposals were, at last, after much rivalry from the Bank, which naturally feared this new aspirant to Government influence, of which they boasted of a monopoly, agreed to by the ministry, and an act was passed to give them the necessary powers, and as a basis for a charter of privileges. The act met with violent opposition from the Tories, and also from Archibald Hutcheson, Esq., member for Hastings, one of the few men of the time who combined sterling sense with sterling honesty, and undaunted courage; but it was at last carried in favour of the South-Sea Company. Its outline was as follows:—It enabled them "to increase their capital stock, by redeeming certain public incumbrances and debts therein mentioned." It further enabled them "to raise money, to be applied to such lessening or redeeming of several debts and incumbrances before specified." It further enabled them "to call in certain uncancelled Exchequer bills, and to make new bills in lieu of the same"; which bills were "to be circulated and exchanged on demand, in or near the Exchequer." This affair was completed about the Christmas of the year 1719; and for their services, exclusive privileges of trading within certain latitudes were assured to them, and the favour of the Government guaranteed, in various modes, not now worth recounting. As soon as the act had fairly passed the Houses, the stock of the company at once rose to *three hundred and nineteen per cent.;* and a mad epidemic of speculative gambling seemed, at once, to seize the whole nation, with the exception of Mr. Hutcheson, and a few others, who not only preserved their sanity, but energetically warned the public of the ultimate fate of the scheme and its dupes. The public, however, was deaf. The first sales of stock by the "Court of Directors" was made at *three hundred per cent.!* Two millions and a quarter were taken, and the market price at once reached *three hundred and forty:* double the first instalment according to the terms of payment. To set out handsomely, the Court voted a dividend of *ten per cent.* upon South-Sea stock, being only a *half-yearly dividend*, payable at Midsummer, 1720! To enable persons to hold, they also offered to lend *half a million on security of their own stock;* and afterwards increased the amount to a million, or nearly so. These bold steps gained the whole affair such an increase of credit, that, upon a bare notice that certain irredeemable annuities would be received for stock, upon terms hereafter to be settled, numbers of annuitants deposited their securities at the South-Sea House, without knowing the terms! About June, when the first half-yearly dividend was becoming due, the frenzy rose to such a pitch, that the stock was sold at *eight hundred and ninety per cent.* This extravagance, however, made so many sellers, that the price suddenly fell, and uneasiness began to be manifested; when the Directors had the inconceivable audacity to propose to create new stock at *one thousand per cent.*, to be paid in ten instalments of one hundred pounds each: strange to relate, this desperate villany turned the tide again; and, to use the words of Anderson, "in a few days the hundred pound instalment was worth *four hundred!*"

This last act was the zenith of the bubble-mania, and the tide flowed in upon all the other schemes of the day. The price of Bank stock advanced to *two hundred and sixty;* and of East India stock to *four hundred and forty-five* per cent.; whilst the prices of a host of minor bubbles were dragged up by the success of the greater. The pretended value of all the sorts of stock in the scheme-market was, at this time, computed to be equal to *five hundred millions sterling;* and, as at this time the rental of all the lands, houses, etc. of the kingdom was not calculated to exceed *fourteen millions per annum*, this, at sixteen years' purchase, gives only *two hundred and twenty-four millions*, being only half the sum pretended to be employed in these outrageously swindling chimeras! After midsummer, the madness began to decline, and doubt to take the place of frenzy. The minor bubbles burst first; when the South-Sea schemers were foolish enough to apply for a "*scire facias*" against their projectors, on the ground that *their* schemes injured the credit of the grand scheme. This turned *quondam* allies into furious enemies. The "*scire facias*" was issued on the 13th of August, 1720, when the downfall began; and Mr. Hutcheson saw his predictions completely fulfilled. The South-Sea villains, in sheer desperation, declared a *half yearly dividend of thirty per cent.* due at Christmas, and offered to guarantee fifty per cent. per annum for twelve years! They might as well have declared it for "the thirtieth of February!" Everything was done to prop the reputation of the directors, but all was in vain; and when the stock fell at last to *one hundred and seventy-five*, a panic ensued, and all went to the ground together, totally ruining thousands, and nearly dragging the Bank and East India Company along with it. The end of the catastrophe was a parliamentary interference; the expulsion of, and infliction of heavy fines on some of the guilty (amongst whom was the Chancellor of the Exchequer, Aislabie), and a *re-absorption* of some of the stock into the "National Debt," where it stands, at this hour, as "South-Sea Annuities' Stock!" This terrible lesson had a temporary good effect upon the nation; and extravagance, it will be seen, was checked for a time—though only for a time.

George I. succeeded to the throne in 1714, and died in 1727. During this period, there is little to record financially. The War of the Succession had exhausted all Europe; and, with the exception of a short rupture with Sweden and three years of languid hostilities with Spain, the reign of the first of the Hanover family was peaceable. The outstanding debt was not diminished certainly under this monarch, but it was *not increased;* the administration of affairs was upon the whole sober; for though Walpole was in office, he was not in full power, and his wholesale briberies were reserved for a later period. At the death of George I., the debt appears to be a trifle less than it stood at his accession; the pressure of the taxes, however, and perhaps the ruinous effects of some of the trading schemes, had now begun to affect the amount of *poor's rate*, which, it will be seen, increased, after a few years more, year after year. This, with the amount of *convictions for felo-*

nies, affords the true " test" of the real prosperity or adversity of a country; and to these two conjoined tests we shall, henceforward, amid all the mutations caused by the paper-money, have frequently to look. In doing so, it must, however, always be borne in mind, that when money is depreciating in a country, from whatever cause, these *rates* must rise somewhat without additional poor, because more must be paid for the commodities which the poor receive as relief. When the poor's rates, however, rise in a *ratio beyond* that of any possible depreciation of money, there can be no doubt as to the cause, and as to the really diminishing means of the people amongst whom such appearances occur.

George II. succeeded to the throne in 1727, and the twelve years of his reign, from his accession until 1739, were a period of national tranquillity. During these years, the minister, Sir Robert Walpole, although he held his power in the House of Commons by means of the most barefaced and wholesale bribery and corruption, carefully preserved a good understanding between his country and other nations; and when his own power, and that of his party (the Whigs) were not at stake, appeared inclined to husband the national resources. Under his administration, however, was amply displayed that destructive effect upon the characters of public men, and thence, by necessary sequence, upon the liberties of their country, which a system of funding is sure to produce, and always has produced, wherever it is encouraged or tolerated. For the rapid growth of these vices through the reign of Queen Anne and of the first George, we have the strong attestation of

Lord Bolingbroke, who paints them thus:—"Since the Revolution, our kings have been reduced, indeed, to a seeming annual dependence on Parliament; but the business of Parliament, which was esteemed, in general, *a duty* before, has been exercised, in general, as *a trade* since. *The trade of Parliament and the trade of funds have grown universal.* Men, who stood forward in the world, have attended to little else. The frequency of Parliaments that increased their importance, and should have increased the respect for them, has taken off from their dignity: and the spirit that prevailed whilst the service in them was a duty, has been debased since it became a trade. Few know, and scarce any respect, the British constitution: that of the Church has been long since derided; that of the State as long neglected; and both have been left at the mercy of the men in power, whoever these men were. Thus, the Church—at least the hierarchy—however sacred in its origin, or wise in its institution, is become a useless burden on the State: and the State is become, *under ancient and known forms, a new and undefinable monster;* composed of a king, without monarchical splendour; a senate of nobles, without aristocratical independency; and a senate of commons, without democratical freedom! In the mean time, my lord, the very idea of wit, and all that can be called taste, has been lost among the great: arts and sciences are scarce alive: luxury has been increased, but not refined: corruption has been *established,* and *is avowed.* When Governments are worn out, thus it is: the decay appears in every instance. Public and private virtue—public and private spirit—science and wit, decline altogether." This noble passage was written by a Tory; and more such passages, from the same quarter, might have done much to rescue the name from the obloquy into which it has, too justly, fallen. The evidence of Sir Nathaniel Wraxall is more directly to the point. This gentleman, in his "Memoirs of his own Time," a gossiping book, but with no marks of intentional falsehood on its face, asserts, that he himself was actually assured by a person, formerly in the employment of the minister, that a part of that employment was to stand in the lobby of the House of Commons, on certain questions coming on, and to deliver sums of money to certain members, secretly, as they passed. This assertion, some of the writers of the Edinburgh Review, some years ago, took a great deal of very suspicious pains to laugh down and discredit. There is nothing in the complexion of the times to weaken the statement; and I, for one, see no reason to doubt that Sir Nathaniel and his informant both told the truth. Lord Bolingbroke's description refers to a period when taxation had created great corruption, without having gone far enough to create great national pressure and difficulty. Necessity is the mother of invention; and when "science" became imperiously needed, we shall see the history and effects of its return.

It was in the midst of all this corruption, openly avowed and practised, that in spite of the pacific minister, a war with Spain at last broke out. It has been asserted, that this war, which was commonly called the "Cat-skin War," was fomented by the enemies of Walpole, who calculated upon its depriving him of the means of securing his bought majorities. This was said to be the secret of his aversion to hostilities; and he was held up as one ready to sacrifice the honour of his country for the continuance of his power. Such assertions are easily made; and they were made; and thus, the war had the appearance, at all events, of a vindication of national character. The Spaniards, emboldened, it was believed, by the pusillanimity of the minister, had barbarously tortured and maimed some English mariners who attempted to trade at Nootka-Sound for furs. Sailors, whose ears had been cut off, were actually exhibited at the bar of the Commons; and the warlike spirit of the nation was so effectually roused, that, despite the pacific minister, a declaration of war against Spain ensued. When this event took place, the minister had, notwithstanding his lavish House of Commons' expenditure, considerably reduced the public debt, and thus far his conduct is entitled to praise. On the breaking out of the Cat-skin War, in 1739, the amount of public incumbrance was 46,954,623*l.* 3*s.* 4½*d.* (as stated by Sir John Sinclair), which shows a reduction of *five millions* from the time of the demise of George the First. Sinclair, in his History of the Revenue, strangely enough, treats this good example as a trifle. It was *ten per cent.* upon the whole debt; and, considering the money Sir Robert Walpole was compelled to lavish in order to keep the Hanover dynasty in any tolerable security, his conduct here, certainly deserves more praise than it seems ever to have obtained. The war which began with Spain, was extended into a war with France, owing to a disputed succession to the empire of Germany, in the consequences of which this country was involved. In the midst of it, the Rebellion of 1745 broke out, and was at last quelled, after the people of England had evinced, according to the published confession of Horace Walpole, the most perfect apathy as to the result. In short, had the French possessed the means of affording the Pretender, Charles Edward, any reasonable degree of aid for such an expedition, it seems probable, that the Stuart family would have been a second time restored, and the whole affairs of this kingdom changed, not, in all likelihood, for the worse. Troops, however, were recalled from Germany, and the adventurer, whom *nobody opposed*, though few joined, was at last beaten by mere mercenaries, at Culloden, and the succession of the Revolution preserved. This rebellion, however, gave a shock to the funding system, which it felt for some time. Owing to pouring out of paper, the interest of money had been so reduced, that when the rebels took the field, the *three per cents.* were actually as high as *eighty-nine!* When, however, it was perceived how easily the whole might have been swept away had forces enough joined Charles Edward to enable his army to march from Derby upon London, those who had begun to look at these things as a sort of "Property," stood aghast at the narrowness of their escape; nor did this feeling of insecurity subside for some years. In 1748, the Peace of Aix-la-Chapelle was effected, and something like security again established. This war of nine years, however, was more expensive than its predecessors; the cause of which has been already explained, by showing, that as the interest of former debts must enhance the prices of every thing used in war, each succeeding war must of necessity be more of a drain in the *ratio* of the incumbrances contracted prior to its being begun. Of this we now have a small proof in the war of 1739, which nearly doubled the public debt as it stood at its commencement, and quickly undid the retrenchments of Sir Robert Walpole.

The account stands thus:—

	Principal.				Interest.		
	£	s.	d.		£	s.	d.
Debt on Dec. 31, 1748 .	78,293,313	1	10¾	.	3,061,004	11	1¾
Debt on Dec. 31, 1739 .	46,954,623	3	4	.	1,964,025	10	1¼
Increase . .	31,338,689	18	6¾		1,096,979	1	0½

The peace concluded at Aix-la-Chapelle lasted seven years; and during that interval, the minister, Mr. Pelham, contrived, by taking advantage of another fall in the interest of money, to reduce the capital of the funded debt by a sum of 3,721,472*l.* 1*s.* 8¼*d.*, besides reducing at the same time the rate of interest upon much of the remainder. In this way, issues of paper-money sometimes act against those who generally profit by them; the same paper which enabled debt to be made, working afterwards a reduction of its interest. But this is only another proof, that no evil is so unmixed as to be unattended by *some* good —not even the evil of funds and paper-money.

In the year 1755, broke out that war with France which was destined to out-last the life and reign of George II. It is curious that its principal object was the defence of those splendid American colonies, which now formed one of the brightest gems of the British Crown; and which, within a few years afterwards, were doomed to be lost through the insane obstinacy of a mad king and a besotted ministry, who were all equally incapable of appreciating their value, or their quality. The French nation, vain of their military character, and hating the English as formidable rivals, had neither forgotten nor forgiven the victories of Marlborough. Resolved upon revenge, they secretly, by means of agents sent from their settlements in lower Canada, formed an immense confederacy of the Indian tribes inhabiting the South-Eastern Bank of the great river St. Lawrence, and occupying those regions which are now the state of Maine. This being done, they suddenly marched against the British Colonies, committing cruelties unexampled, and spreading ravage and terror far and wide. The Colonists, taken by surprise, had little means of resistance; and when the news reached England, the French and their savage allies were within one hundred miles of Philadelphia, which was, even then, a splendid and flourishing city. Under such circumstances war was inevitable; and war accordingly was begun, which carried on, as it was, at immense cost, lasted until the year 1762, almost doubling the debt of the country, during its progress. Its effects will make a part of the detail of the evils which marked the long, insane, tyrannous, and disastrous reign of the third George. With the death of his predecessor, this letter must conclude. It took place in 1760. It was financially remarkable for two things. First; the establishment of the first "sinking fund" by Sir Robert Walpole, which was abandoned after it had paid off five millions of debt: and next the famous declaration of the sagacious and celebrated David Hume, against the funding system. In an Essay, "on Public Credit," written before the war of 1755, he depicted, in colours the most vivid, and in language most unequivocal, the enormous wickedness and folly of this mortgaging of posterity; and predicted, with all the confidence, and more than the coolness of a prophet, the various consequences which were sure, in the ripeness of time, to flow from it. In these opinions he was supported by his friend, Dr. Adam Smith, author of "The Wealth of Nations." Some of their predictions are now fulfilled; and few who shall read these letters, can, I trust, doubt as to the inevitable fulfilment of the remainder.

In our next, we shall enter upon the long, gloomy, mad, and wicked reign of George III. We shall there trace the workings of the paper money and the funds, tearing up, as it were, all that is valuable in society by the roots! We shall behold the whole community changed and distorted in face, body, and limbs, and the very character of Englishmen altered or effaced. We shall see the industrious classes crushed into pauperism, crime, and destitution, whilst the wealth of the country is drawn into huge masses, and placed in the grasp of Jews, loan-mongers, contractors, gamblers in stock, commissaries, and every conceivable species of swindler and peculator. We shall see the very name of "yeoman" forgotten in England, and the noble class so designated trodden down in the dust. We shall contemplate a country of equally diffused wealth and happiness metamorphosed into a land of teeming, discontented, rebellious paupers, kept quiet with difficulty by a standing army, and lorded over by a knot of capitalists, and gigantic landed aristocrats. In short we shall see this system work national changes, far beyond the reach of the worst tyrannies of former times: and, under the forms of liberty and law, the whole integrity and happiness of a county sapped and mined, until public virtue, public morality, and national ease, are become chimeras of the past, and empty and unintelligible names.

LETTER VI.

ACCESSION OF GEORGE III.—WAR ENDS IN 1763.—AMOUNT OF DEBT AT THE PEACE.—NOTES FOR FIFTEEN AND TEN POUNDS, COINED BY THE BANK.—RAPID INCREASE OF THE PEACE ESTABISHMENT.—GROWTH OF THE POOR'S-RATE.—FIRST ATTEMPT TO TAMPER WITH THE POOR-LAW.—DISTRESS OF TRADE.—LORD BUTE BECOMES MINISTER.—PARTITION OF POLAND PERMITTED.—LORD BUTE DETERMINES TO TAX THE AMERICAN COLONIES AGAINST THEIR CONSENT.—OPPOSITION OF LORD CHATHAM.—THE COLONISTS RESIST.—AMERICAN WAR.—MR. PITT MINISTER.—HIS FINANCIAL MEASURES.—PROGRESS OF THE COUNTRY BANKS.—DEBT IN 1793.—COTTON TRADE FIRST ESTABLISHED.—REFORM OF PARLIAMENT FIRST ADVOCATED.

GEORGE the Second was succeeded by his grandson of the same name; a youth of ungainly manners, and hurried and awkward address; of a frame somewhat athletic, with bold, strong features, and that marked and peculiar depression of forehead, which is found to denote an utter absence of all the higher mental and intellectual qualifications, whilst the animal passions and lower propensities of our nature are allowed a full and complete development. He found his kingdom engaged in that war which the aggressions of France, in America, had provoked; but which had been brought, in these regions, to a triumphant close, chiefly by the successes of General Wolfe, a brave young officer, who died, in the midst of victory, during that last battle before Quebec, which really secured the conquest of Canada. This event took place in 1759: but hostilities lingered, between the two countries, until the year 1763, when peace was at last concluded, and Canada ceded to the British; an acquisition unfortunate in the consequences it helped to cause. This war again all but doubled the national debt, although it lasted little more than seven years. We have already seen how *great borrowings*, in their effects, augment the necessity for *still greater;* but this war was, in itself, naturally costly, being carried on in another hemisphere. On the breaking out of the conflict in 1755, the debt, after the reductions effected by Mr. Pelham, stood thus:—

	Principal.	Interest.
Total of funded and unfunded debt in 1755 . .	£74,571,840	£2,416,717
Add funded and unfunded debt contracted up to 1763 .	72,111,004	2,424,104
Total debt up to 1763 . . .	146,682,844	4,840,821

Thus seven years of just and unavoidable hostilities plunged the country, or rather the government, doubly deep in the bottomless quagmire of public incumbrance; but in addition to this, the unfortunate people now began to find out another secret; and this was that Government debts not only enhance the cost of carrying on war, but, also, of carrying on peace! The indirect taxes on commodities, of necessity, cause an increase in the pay of every functionary of Government, from the throne down to Jack Ketch; and hence, under such a system, peace-establishments grow with war-establishments,—the loans contracted for during each war, rendering the next peace establishment more onerous. To give the reader a bird's-eye view of this part of the question, all that is wanted, is to put together the different peace-establishments from the period of the revolution, when the borrowing and funding commenced. In looking at the different amounts, we must here, as in the case of poor's-rates, make some allowance for the rise in prices caused by the putting out of more and more paper, and the gradual depreciation of the value of money, of which these enhanced prices are, in part, the effect. Up to this date, the grand cause of the rapid growth of the peace expenditure was, however, beyond a doubt, the additional taxes on commodities caused by the interest of the growing debt; for as yet the Bank had been unfurnished with the power rapidly and greatly to depreciate the currency of the kingdom. During the war, notes for *fifteen pounds*, and then for *ten pounds*, had been permitted to be issued; twenty pounds having, before 1759, been the lowest sum for which notes were made; but this sort of issue, coming only from one Bank (for, up to this time, the transactions of the few country bankers were too insignificant to be noticed) cannot have much effect upon the value of a national currency, consisting mostly of gold and silver. We must, therefore, ascribe to the workings of the Government debts and taxes, that rapid augmentation which we shall see in the different peace establishments, from the Dutch king, down to George the Third. In a peace establishment, are included the ordinary expenses of government, and such of the king's expenses, as come out of the taxes, excluding, of course, the interest of debts, which is separately provided for. When both are put together, they form the "ordinary revenue," unless, as is seldom the case, there happens to be some *surplus*.

		Peace establishments.	Revenue.
1688	William III.	£1,907,455	£3,895,205
1706	Queen Anne	1,965,605	5,691,803
1714	George I.	2,583,000	6,762,643
1727	George II.	2,766,000	8,522,540
1770	George III.	4,322,972	9,163,793

As to the above, it is only requisite further to remark, that, in the peace establishment of William III., was not included the large item, known by the odd name of the "Civil List." The expenses of the monarch, up to Queen Anne's reign, were, in a great measure, if not wholly, paid out of such of the Crown lands as had been recovered from the grasp of the rapacious grantees, or buyers, of the long Parliament. On the accession of Anne, however, an arrangement was come to, by which the Sovereign surrendered the control of these lands (save and except the Duchy of Cornwall, which is the property of the Prince of Wales), to the Houses of Parliament, upon condition of an annual allowance, in lieu of the rents of these lands, to be paid out of the taxes. This allowance was, to Queen Anne, made £600,000, per annum: but as debt and taxation waxed heavier, the Civil List, of course, grew with them, as we shall have occasion to see, afterwards. They who invented this arrangement, were no true friends to the monarchy. It must ever be kept in mind, that this List embraces not only the king's or queen's actual personal expenses, but also the pay of the judges and various other functionaries, some sinecurists, and some not, besides a class of pensioners, constantly varying in number, who are quartered upon this fund. Thus, instead of living, as used to be the case, upon his own estates, the monarch is placed in the invidious position of *pensioner-in-chief;* and is made to appear to dissipate sums enormous, over which, in fact, he has not a shadow of control!

Such were the effects of the Funding System and Paper Money, as evinced in the ordinary expenditure of the kingdom. Upon the poor-rates they soon began to act, in a way not to be misunderstood. There do not exist, unhappily, any accurate records of the amount of the poor-rates raised in England, at a date so distant. It has been estimated, however, that,

in 1698, the poor-rates reached	.	£ 819,000
in 1700	ditto	1,000,000
in 1714	ditto	1,000,000
in 1776	ditto	1,720,316

These are the lowest estimates which I have seen; and I leave out others, which I deem excessive, to avoid the chance of overstatement. It is also to be borne in mind, that all *general* statements of poor-rates, include various sums paid for parish litigations, vexatious removals, and numerous other charges, with which the poor have little or nothing to do. Under all the circumstances, however, it is certain enough, that the growth of these rates, joined to the distress, which now began to be visible in various staple trades, had already produced alarming effects upon the public mind. It is amongst the aphorisms of that quaint and wordy, but once admired, author, Harrington, the writer of "Oceana", that "a people cannot see; but it can *feel*"! This feeling had, prior to the accession of George III., been shown in no equivocal manifestations. As far back as 1740, the press teemed with complaints of the distress of the woollen, and other staple manufactures, which, oppressed by the effects of the growing taxes, could no longer sustain the competition of more lightly taxed foreigners. This state of affairs in trade, circumstances, not to be foreseen, after a few years relieved. The growth of the poor-rates was, however, not to be stopped; and even in the reign of the first George, this growing rate produced one of those cruel attempts to tread, as it were, poverty out of existence, which have occurred at intervals ever since the Reformation, when the poor, as well as the church, were plundered of a patrimony, which they had enjoyed for ages.

The poor-laws had, from first to last, been disliked by the aristocracy. Rapacity of wealth in some has no bounds; and, as with water in a dropsy, unhappily possession only increases the thirst. Hence even the original poor-law—the justly famous "Forty-third of Elizabeth"—was not passed until misery had, again and again, been attempted to be silenced by cruelty enormous, and until a rebellion became imminent, if some substitute for the share of the poor in the church-lands and tithes were not provided. From the same feeling of cruel greediness, a hard-hearted merchant, named Sir Josiah Child, had absolutely the astounding audacity to propose, in Charles the Second's reign, to vest a power in commissioners to transport the poor to the plantations in America! In the ninth year of George I., however, the increasing poor-rate gave birth to an act of Parliament, which may be termed the first attempt to strip the poor of that restitution of their rights which the law of Elizabeth had made. This act enabled the overseers of any parish, with the consent of a majority of the parishioners, to purchase or hire houses to be used as work-houses, and to contract with persons for lodging and maintaining the poor therein: and it further enabled the overseers to *deny relief* to any poor person who should refuse, if ordered, to inhabit these work-houses. This atrocious act was founded, *first*, upon a notion that this method was cheaper than affording out-door relief; and, *next*, upon an expectation (better founded), that the idea of imprisonment might *deter* poor persons from application to their parishes! This was the case at first; and in numerous places where work-houses were tried the rates fell, for a year or two, below their usual average. The treatment of inmates, however, being on the whole good, the diet substantial, and the restraints moderate, the dislike soon wore off. The consequence was, that ultimately the rates rose higher than before; the maintenance of a large body of poor in this way being (unless starvation be resorted to) much more expensive than is out-door assistance. This blew up the whole scheme, which quickly fell into desuetude; and the act, after becoming obsolete, was repealed. Such was the end of the *first attack*, after the passing of the famous compensation act of the forty-third of Elizabeth, upon the rights of the poor.

I have already stated, that the war with France and Spain, which gave us Canada, ended in a definitive treaty of peace, which was ratified early in 1763. This famous war might be said to have put the whole of the vast continent of North America virtually in our power as far as the Gulf of Florida; and if England had, at this period, possessed an ordinarily wise or decent government, the wonderful colonial field thus obtained might have been made the finest acquisition that ever nation won. We were now doomed, however, to taste, and by whole mouthfuls, the bitter fruits of the pernicious and suicidal system into which we had been plunged by the Whig Revolution in 1688. The death of King George II., soon after Wolfe's victory, ruined all these fair prospects. The imbecile young king was ruled by a profligate mother; and by her influence the conduct of affairs was, in spite of the most commanding talents and virtue of the highest order arrayed to prevent it, committed to the hands of a needy, villanous, and dissolute gang of courtiers, headed by an unprincipled Scotch paramour of the vicious old dowager, the Earl of Bute. They found the nation gratified, indeed, by the noble conquest which its arms had achieved; but oppressed and murmuring under the weight of enormous debts, laid upon it by former causeless wars, begun upon views the most chimerical, and rushed into with all the rashness engendered by the preposterous swindle of mortgaging posterity to pay for the folly and wickedness of their ancestors. In this state of affairs, the profligate and greedy administration of Legge and Bute, not daring to touch the already dilapidated resources of the country at such a time, cast their rapacious eyes upon the American colonies, now consolidated by the addition of Canada, and forming a noble and rich tract, with boundless resources, and already numbering three millions of inhabitants of European origin. These splendid colonies they determined to tax, and to apply the moneys so to be obtained to their own purposes; and not content with this, and as if determined to shew the world that the ministers of a half-idiotic king could be more wickedly infatuated than their miserable master, they determined not only to tax these colonists, but actually to tax them without and against their own consent, whether expressed through representatives, or in any other manner.

Against this atrociously villanous proceeding, all the sound-hearted and all the unbribed sound-headed portions of the nation were loud in their expostulations, from the very beginning. The pompous and overpraised bully, Johnson, wrote, to be sure, a dull pamphlet in its defence, to which he gave the characteristic title of "Taxation no Tyranny," and for which he, in due time, got a pension; but when to the name of this very slavish, and very impudent pedant, we oppose that of the immortal Chatham, his clumsy sophistries are at once despised and forgotten. I regret that it is foreign to the purpose of these Letters to go into any detailed account of the character of this last named illustrious man. Suffice it to say, that by means of his transcendant accomplishments, his moral courage, and unflinching patriotism, he rose from the station of a cornet of horse, and the rank of a Cornish squire, to the highest offices of the state; that to the last he deserved and retained the love and admiration of the people of England; and that he was one of the very few statesmen on record who have united to undoubted honesty, wisdom the most profound, and eloquence the most astonishing and unapproachable. Be it permitted to my pen, however, also to record, that this great man was the bitter enemy of those wretches whom he aptly designated "the Cannibals of Change Alley"; and that on being told that some of his measures had caused "a panic in the funds," he nobly replied, "when the funds are falling, we may be sure the country is rising"!

In spite, however, of the energetic remonstrances of the great and virtuous Chatham, backed by those of every wise and honest man in the kingdom,—the boorish semi-idiot, who nominally governed, and the profligate Scotchman and regal demirep, who really ruled the destinies of the state, were infatuated enough to persevere. Notwithstanding the loud and powerful protests of the American Colonists against their tyrannical proceedings, they caused a bribed and subservient parliament to pass a stamp act, and to lay a duty upon tea, in direct opposition to the votes of the Colonial assemblies; and, not content with this insane aggression upon the liberties of three millions of people, they added to injury, insult to the deputies sent by the Colonists to carry their complaints to the English legislature. The assured and just result, was armed resistance on the part of the outraged

Colonists, which broke out in 1774; and in the midst of which the illustrious Chatham died, struck down by the hand of death, in the midst of that House of Lords which he had so often astounded by his indignant eloquence; and where he expended his last accents in protesting against these unnatural hostilities. The event was for some time dubious; until the French, burning to revenge the loss of Canada, aided the insufficient means of the excellent Washington, the American general-in-chief, by subsidies both of men and money. After that, the result was not long doubtful; and after having lost three entire armies, the half insane king, and his equally infatuated satellites of ministers, were compelled, in 1783, to acknowledge the independence of those states which they had hoped to plunder with impunity. This disgraceful conflict, amongst other consequences, of course, added enormously to the existing debt, in which preceding governments had plunged the country, and which at the conclusion of this war stood thus. In the interval between 1762, when the French and Spanish war ended, and 1775, when the American war was actually commenced, about *ten millions* of debt had, by the expiration of annuities and other means, been got rid of. If to this reduced debt we add the debt incurred during the American conflict, the amount stands thus.

	Principal.	Interest.
Debt as it stood in 1775 - - - -	£135,943,051	4,476,821
Added by the American war - -	121,269,992	5,192,614
Total Debt in 1783 - - - - - -	£257,213,043	9,669,435

Thus, by this pre-eminently wicked war, was the debt again all but doubled, and the interest made equal to the amount of the whole revenue, when the at once weak and obstinate tyrant who helped to cause it mounted, in an evil hour, the British throne. Many of the other consequences of this war, which shall be adverted to in the proper place, we are also feeling at this hour; for the fruits of the crimes of rulers of nations are commonly tasted "even unto the third and fourth generation."

The event of the American conflict nearly drove the royal idiot upon the throne, and the much-abused people, whom this half-witted incubus seemed to be fated to lead to destruction, actually frantic. The first was astounded by the exhibition of Mr. Adams, the late rebel, presented to him as "ambassador" from "the Republic of the United States of America," and its "President Washington;" the second by a Flemish account of accumulated debts, ruined armies and fleets, and decayed trade, which one would have supposed might have been a lesson, not merely to the people, but to their aristocratical rulers for ever. Men whose power, however, seems absolute for the time, invariably despise the most solemn warnings of experience. History is to such an obsolete record; and this lesson like the rest was, accordingly, speedily to be forgotten. But the immediate effects of the catastrophe in America were very striking. The bank, despite a reduction of its issues, from nine millions, in March, 1782, to five millions and three quarters, in October, 1783, was reduced to great straits; its cash being only 473,000*l.* The profligate administration was broken up, and the nation, now thoroughly roused, seemed resolved, if possible, to obtain for themselves a government, which, by means of a wise economy and the preservation, if possible, of peace, might rescue them from the gulf, into which they now plainly saw themselves to be on the point of plunging.

The financial position of the country, bad as it was, was not, as it now seems to be, too bad even to be talked about. The country was, therefore, agitated from end to end, with schemes, proposals, and plans, not only of economical, but of political reform. The predictions of Lord Bolingbroke, Swift, and others, were now clearly seen to be fulfilled. It was felt by all keen-sighted and honest men, that the means of direct and indirect corruption, which the enormous expansion of the revenue, and the workings of the funding system, had put into the hands of those engaged in it, made them, in fact, the masters of the country. The constitutional power and influence of the monarch and his privy council were gone. The minister summoned to that council those only whom he wished to meet there. By means of the decayed boroughs, and the enormous county patronage, and materials for bribery, possessed by the existing administrations, the independence of the House of Commons was totally subverted, and the little influence possessed by the people at large over their self-called "representatives," reduced to nothing. In point of fact, an oligarchy, composed by the junction of a moneyed with a landed aristocracy, had become absolute; and, with the name and forms of freedom, the English people had now, without well knowing how, become slaves, as complete, as if they had been vassals of the Dey of Tunis, or the Czar of Muscovy.

In addition to all this, it was felt by competent observers, that all this debt, and all this enormous taxation; and all this dislocation of the moneyed and commercial affairs of the country, had not, in fact, added one jot or tittle to the national power and influence. All it had done was to afford encouragement and aid for repeated exhaustions through foreign wars, mostly unjust and unnecessary, which at their close left the national energies and moral power less efficient than before. During the interval of repose which took place between the conquest of Canada, and the unhappy breach with the American colonists, the three powers of Austria, Russia, and Prussia encouraged by the exhausted state of France and England, had been permitted to consummate an act of political perfidy and robbery, more monstrous than anything that modern times had yet seen. This act was the partition of Poland, a deed of enormous and unblushing robbery upon a grand scale (the perpetrators being three crowned heads), which took place in 1772-3; just before the commencement of the American war. It was planned by that wonderfully intellectual but most vicious woman, the empress Catharine II. It was the first grand step in that series of aggression and appropriation, which has ever since been pursued by Russia, and which, at this moment, we see without daring effectually to resist. This act of spoliation was the corner-stone of that "empire at Constantinople," which is the ultimate aim of Russia. In vain did the great Lord Chatham see it and denounce it. England and France were too jealous of each other, and too exhausted by mutual aggressions to save Poland. The American struggle commenced; and the three crowned robbers were left to lacerate unhappy Poland at their will.

That the grief and dismay consequent upon a retrospect so lamentable as this, should cause a ferment of no common kind in the nation, was only just. Financial and Parliamentary reform came, therefore, to be agitated for the first time; and the feelings, speeches, and views of men in general, of all the higher grades (for the lowest, as yet, were totally ignorant of all that was transacting), thenceforward assumed a tone and a colour new and changed, and indicative of the novel circumstances in which the country, at last, saw itself to be placed. The press teemed with publications of all sizes, in which the difficulties, distresses, and multiform evils of the body politic were set forth, commented on, palliated, or exaggerated, in every conceivable way. The titles of these books, if not their substance, have at all events been preserved, and the list affords curious food for reflection, even at the present day. The authors are of all ranks; and of their lucubrations the titles of some are amusing, of others ominous. Amongst the writers, we find the Earl of Stair, Earl Stanhope, Lord Newhaven, Lord Dundonald, Pulteney Lord Bath, the Bishop of Cloyne, Baron Gilbert, Sir Matthew Decker, Sir John Dalrymple, Sir John Barnard, Edmund Burke, Samuel Johnson, Daniel Defoe, Mr. Eden, Sir John Sinclair, Dr. Price, Henry Hartley, Arthur Young, Dr. Shebbeare, &c. &c. Amongst the works named, we find the following, which speak for themselves with an eloquence quite their own. " The National Debt no National Grievance, 1768." " A Scheme to pay off the National Debt, by *a Repeal of the Marriage Act* [!] 1767." " An Appeal *to the Public* on the Debt, by

Richd. Price, D.D., F.R.S., 1772." "A Candid Enquiry into the *present Ruined State of the French Monarchy*, 1770." "A Scheme to pay the Nation's Debt *in thirty years* without an additional tax, 1778." "The Debt compared with the Revenue, and impossibility of War without Economy, 1781." "*Old Funds* sufficient for a *New Loan*; a Proposal to lower the Interest of Money and *tax the Funds* [!] 1781." "Means to raise the Supplies *within the Year*, 1780." "Plans for redeeming Public Debts, by R. Price, D.D., 1783." "Thoughts on paying off the Debt by a *Lottery*, the *Prizes* to arise out of a *Diminution of the Annual Interest* [!] 1784." "A Plan for *consolidating into one Rate*, the Land and all other Taxes, 1784." "Plans for *future national Defence*, by the Duke of Richmond, 1785." "Dangerous Situation of England; and Address to the Landed, Trading, and *Funded Interests*, 1786." "*National Debt* productive of *National Prosperity* [!] 1787." "Efficacy of a *Sinking Fund* considered, 1786." "National Debt discussed, towards a *Radical* and *Speedy Payment*, 1786." "Renovation, or *New Modes* of Representation, and raising Supplies" [no date, probably 1787]. "Machiavel's *Infallible* Means to pay off our Debts, 1788." To these, and to all other similar "redeeming" schemes, it is a sufficient answer to observe, that, if nations will not raise supplies *when they are wanted*, they never will *afterwards*, *when the exigence has passed*: and that, if they would submit to any really efficient process of redemption, the mutations of the world come too frequently ever to permit such plans to be carried out. These works, however, amply prove the agitation and alarm which now pervaded the country, and which continued until rapidly recurring events of an unexpected nature, forced the public mind after a few years to take a new direction.

Of the party struggles which followed the catastrophe of the American war, it would be foreign to the plan of these Letters to give any detailed account. It is proper to remark, however, that the pressure upon the country, caused by the mortgaging system, had now, in addition to the two old factions of Tory and Whig, produced a third party, who were advocates of a reform in the House of Commons and for a return to the constitution, as it existed before the two Acts of Henry VI., which vested the right of voting in counties in the forty-shilling and other freeholders. To this party, the second son of the illustrious Chatham, the too celebrated William Pitt belonged, before he was made minister; and he only condensed its sentiments when he uttered his famous assertion, that "under the existing system no minister could be an honest man." A principal supporter of this party was the Duke of Richmond, who actually drew up and printed a bill to be brought into the House of Commons, enacting Universal Suffrage, and Sessional, or Annual Parliaments; a proposal which was, of course, scouted. When, however, the struggles of party, in 1783, ended by fixing Pitt in the post of Prime Minister, he abandoned his parliamentary reform notions, though the earlier days of his power, like those of Nero, gave no symptoms of the extravagances of his later years.

That Mr. Pitt took sway with excellent intentions, upon the whole, must be still admitted by all candid minds. Of fair abilities and a fluent speaker, it is probable, that he admired and intended to form himself upon the character of his great and good father; and this idea all his earlier acts confirm. As soon as he felt the reins of power firmly in his grasp, Mr. Pitt set about the great task of arranging the financial affairs of the country, which were in no little disorder. He arranged and simplified the whole tariff. He newly moulded the regulations of the Excise; and having put the system of taxation upon the best footing, he, with certain exceptions of the malt and some other annual duties, formed the whole into "the Consolidated Fund," upon which the interest of the debt, and the Civil List had a priority of charge. He also established a "Sinking Fund," which was to arise out of a *real surplus* of revenue; unlike the delusion which he afterwards patronised when introduced by his mouth-piece, Addington, many years afterwards. Neither is there any reason for supposing that, prior to the French Revolution, and the coalition against the new republic, in 1793, Mr. Pitt was not favourable to such ameliorations in the constitutional law as the times would permit. The bill of Mr. Fox, in 1790, for the regulation of the law of libel, which declared the jury judges of the law as well as of the fact (before which, any one accused of libel was, under the then construction of the common law, completely at the mercy of the judge), was no doubt passed with the tacit approbation of Pitt. His "Indian Bill" insidious as it was called, and hollow as it certainly proved to be, was also an improvement upon that of his great Whig rival. In short, could Mr. Pitt's life and administration, have been preserved for a length of years, throughout a period of peace, he might have possibly turned out a benefactor, instead of a curse to his country, and emulated the fame and the name of his illustrious parent. He was, however, surrounded by men, whose hopes, whose fears, whose passions, and whose prejudices, were constantly liable to be excited to violence amidst the mutations of political events; and whose impetuous wills, whether directed towards good or evil, he had not the means to resist. To the selfish terrors and burning jealousies of these men, he was fated, in a few years, to become the victim; and after a short administration of affairs, in which honesty, frugality, moderation with statesman-like talent of no mean order, were exhibited, he was violently pushed over the precipice into a raging ocean of war, difficulty, and consequent desperate extravagance, from which he never emerged, and in the midst of which he perished, with a broken heart and shattered constitution, the consequences of the remorse, anxiety, and dismal forebodings, arising from the false step which he had taken, and the dissipation, contrary to his natural character, to which it drove him.

Before the rash plunge of 1793 was made, however, the condition of the country had become much ameliorated, and the effects of the disasters in America were fast wearing away. The weight of debt and taxes, undoubtedly, was still enormous; but science and ingenuity had stepped in, and by the substitution of machinery for human labour, averted for a time the evils of foreign competition, by the creation of a manufacturing system, which has, however, produced some fruits almost as bitter. I allude, of course, only generally to the improvement of the steam-engine, by Watt, about 1770, and, in particular, to the commencement of the cotton manufacture, and the invention of spinning cotton, wool, flax, or silk, by machinery. In 1767, the spinning-jenny was invented by Mr. Hargreaves; and, in 1769, Arkwright took out his first patent for spinning with rollers. The invention of the power-loom, by the Rev. Dr. Cartwright, followed in 1774; and in two years more, the mule of Samuel Crompton was added to the list of inventions for rendering the human hand almost a superfluity! The whole was crowned by Watts' perfected steam-engine, of which the patent was dated in 1782. These inventions, in their first effects, gave England a mastery in manufactures that seemed to defy fate and fortune; and, through the dreadful conflict that was soon to ensue, enacted wonders, that, at an early period, might have well passed for some stupendous triumphs of sorcery. Whether the first light, in which they were naturally viewed, was the true light, we may afterwards see occasion to doubt. At all events, like paper-money, they were "strength in the beginning", and, I am willing to hope, may yet be made to produce happiness in the end. I can see no reason for asserting, that the employment of machinery is *necessarily* connected with human degradation, if properly regulated. It cannot be shown *why* the men, women, and children, employed in a cotton mill, should not be as happy, and as moral, as any other set of persons so congregated. In point of fact, under proper regulations, and with adequate wages, they might be just as happy as any other operatives. All that is proved by the squalor and vice now to be seen in our great seats of manufactures, is the truth, that even the advantages of machinery have not availed to counteract the evils of taxation; which has compelled their employers to abridge their wages, and lengthen their hours of work beyond the proper medium. To attribute these evils to the machinery itself, is perfectly absurd. A steam-engine is no more connected with poverty or immorality than a plough; and the vices of Glasgow and Manchester are common to all large cities.

Whilst these wonders of ingenuity were starting into strange life, the great weight of the taxes, and the consequent necessity for constant additions to the money in circulation, had also called into existence another set of traders, little noticed until now, who took upon them to coin and put forth a paper-money of their own, under the name of "Country Bankers". For a considerable period downwards, after the changes of 1688, they were so obscure, that no records as to their numbers, or even existence, remain. They were little noticed by the Governments that succeeded the revolution; and one of the first traces of their trade is in an Act of George III., in the year 1775, to prevent their issuing notes for sums under *twenty shillings!* Two years after that, *five pounds* was made the *minimum* for the note of a country banker. By a clause in the monopoly of the Bank of England, all other banks of issue were restricted to six partners; and under this regulation, in the year 1793, the country bankers had grown up into a very opulent and considerable body of traders, their numbers being supposed to be comprised in about two hundred different banks, though as to the exact number the *data* are uncertain. In a future stage of this narrative, we shall see the great effects which they were destined to assist in producing.

Before concluding this letter, it is proper to state the position of the Government Funded Debt, up to the important era of 1793. It shows a decrease of more than four millions of pounds. This is, indeed, inferior to the saving effected many years before by Mr. Pelham: but then it consisted wholly in diminished expenditure, and the proper application of the revenue so set at liberty; whilst Mr. Pelham's diminution was the fruit of the falling in, or falling out, of various fortunate contingencies, as well as of saved revenue. It was effected, likewise, in a time of greater difficulties. The figures stand thus:—

	Principal.	Interest.
Debt at the end of American war .	£257,213,043 .	£9,669,435
Paid off during the peace . . .	4,751,261 .	143,569
Amount in 1793 . . .	252,461,782 .	9 525,866

Such was the debt at the ever-memorable era of 1793. With such pressure upon the means of the people, the *poor's-rate*, however, went on, with a steadiness of growth, which nothing but repeated hardenings of the laws could arrest for a day. From 1783 to 1793 it averaged *two and a quarter millions, nearly.* To this growth of *pauperism*, we shall shortly see added a crop of *crime*, which all the schemes for "education" that followed, and all the increase of "churches," and spread of religious sectaries of the austerer tenets, seemed powerless to decrease or cure. In the meantime, having thus cleared the stage for the grand tragic drama that is to follow, we not inappropriately close this letter.

LETTER VII.

THE FRENCH REVOLUTION BEGINS.—ITS CAUSES.—TERROR OF THE ENGLISH ARISTOCRACY AND CLERGY.—THEIR APPEALS TO THE PASSIONS OF THE PEOPLE.—JUNCTION OF THE WHIGS AND TORIES.—MR. PITT COMPELLED TO DECLARE WAR AGAINST FRANCE IN 1793.—PANIC IN THE FUNDS, AND TERRIBLE BANKRUPTCIES FOLLOW.—MR. PITT FORGES AND DESTROYS THE FRENCH ASSIGNATS.—FIVE-POUND NOTES.—SUCCESS OF THE FRENCH REPUBLICANS.—PAINE'S RIGHTS OF MAN.—PAINE A MEMBER OF THE FRENCH CONVENTION.—MR. PITT LENDS TWO MILLIONS TO THE MERCHANTS.—PAINE PREDICTS THE STOPPAGE OF THE BANK OF ENGLAND.—INCREASING ALARM OF INVASION.—PANIC AND RUN UPON THE BANK.—BANK STOPS 27TH FEBRUARY, 1797.—RESTRICTION ACTS.—SECRET COMMITTEE.—PAPER-MONEY ESTABLISHED.—DEBT UP TO A.D. 1797.

We have seen, that when the American colonists entered upon their just and successful resistance to that conspiracy against their liberties, hatched by the infamous Lord Bute, and carried on by the scarcely more respectable Lord North, the government of France, burning with revenge for the loss of Canada, made common cause with Washington, Adams, Jefferson, Paine, Franklin, and their associates, and by sending out a strong army under Rochambeau and La Fayette, turned the scale in favour of freedom revolting against aristocratic and regal tyranny. By this blow France, no doubt, stung her English rivals to the quick; but, as the bee is said to do, she left her life in the wound. Her victorious troops returned from their triumphant campaign in North America, flushed with conquest indeed, and covered with laurels, but also deeply imbued with republican feelings, and with republican principles. In France, they found a field ready tilled and manured for the reception and successful nurture of such seeds. The despotic government, which was wholly in the hands of the court and noblesse, was now, in consequence of the extravagance of Louis XIV. and Louis XV., so beset with debt and difficulty, as to be nearly crippled and powerless. Paralysis, the consequence of an overwhelming weight of debt, had seized upon every limb and energy of rule. The monarch, Louis XVI., was an amiable, but very weak person, totally governed by an unprincipled, spendthrift, and profligate Austrian wife, who, in her turn, was ruled by the minions who basked about her on all sides. In the midst of all this, the press, though nominally chained, teemed with writings of the most speculative and republican character, which being put forth in the name and guise of "philosophy," the government either wanted the instinct, or else the power to suppress; and amidst a people daring and rash by nature, fickle in disposition, and goaded on to the desire of sweeping change by crushing oppression and hopeless want, were these insidious writings suffered to circulate. From such a seed-time there could be only one harvest. The "wind" was "sown," and "the whirlwind" was "reaped." The return of the troops from New York to France, with the amiable enthusiast, La Fayette at their head, applied the match to the train. France became from top to toe enamoured of republican institutions. The old worn-out monster of despotism, like a boa constrictor after too full a meal, had become torpid under the weight of what it had swallowed. The French people became alive to its helpless condition; and every man was ready, with lance or spear, to fix it to the earth on which it lay. It expired amidst the shouts of the people, headed by the National Assembly. The laconic "*ça ira*" of Franklin became the watchword and motto of change. The Bastile was levelled with the ground; the tricolor streamed, like some new and ominous meteor of the storm; and, at last, amid the lightnings and corruscations of national convulsion, THE REVOLUTION broke forth, in all its lurid splendour, like a volcano in the night, throwing its flashes far and wide, alarming the nations, and rousing men from their sleep.

At this terrible outburst of a long-oppressed people, the English aristocracy soon, as was natural, became dreadfully alarmed. A portion of the Whig party, at first, hailed the dawn of popular freedom in France with gratulations which seemed to be real. This, however, did not last long. As the revolutionary fire in France went on increasing in volume and power, the aristocracy on this side of the Channel shrank and quaked. "*Proximus Ucalegon*" seemed now to be written in handwriting of flame upon the wall; and at last the strength of the Whig party, headed by Burke in the Commons and Fitzwilliam in the Lords, went over to the Tories to urge on a mad crusade against republican France. The cruel death of the unfortunate Louis XVI., the savage barbarities of the French democrats, their atheistic monstrosities and anarchical schemes, at last drove the frenzy to its climax; and the dread of violent and immediate revolution seized on all the higher orders of the state. The Lords denounced, the Commons echoed the Lords, and the clergy re-echoed both. What seems strangest of all is, that it was actually attempted to give the conflict the shape of a religious crusade! That the English aristocracy should feel alarmed at the course of events in France is not to be wondered at. They were conscious, that in England there were liberties to be vindicated and wrongs to be redressed; and that though, at this time, neither discontent nor disaffection had reached the millions whose comforts had not yet been seriously dilapidated, there existed, in the breasts of a certain portion of the middle classes, aspirations after a better order of things, which the events across the Channel could not but encourage. The clergy, however, were in a different position. From the period of the plunder of the Roman Catholic Church by the detestable monster Henry VIII., it had been their policy to paint the old religion in colours the most unfavorable. The Pope was called " Antichrist," as if the religion of which he was the head was actually opposed to Christianity. The Roman Catholic hierarchy was styled " the scarlet whore of Babylon drunk with the blood of saints." In short, " Popery" was described as a something worse and more dangerous than open infidelity, and as the parent of atrocities the most repulsive and abhorrent to all good men. From this, most people would have supposed, that when the French republicans seized the revenues of the Gallican church, and drove her priesthood into exile, the English clergy, if they could not applaud, could hardly have blamed the deed. Strange to say, this very clergy became the most bitter denouncers of the French revolutionists. To take the tithes and lands of "Antichrist" was held up from every pulpit as sacrilege; to ridicule the orgies of "the scarlet whore" was loudly proclaimed from the same places to be blasphemy; and, to crown all, when numbers of the "drinkers of the blood of saints" sought in England a refuge from their enemies, they were actually received as martyrs! Upon sensible men, all these proceedings could have only one effect; but upon the unthinking part of the nation the effects were very different. They were soon taught to consider the French nation as a sort of demons broke loose; and to be a "Jacobin," or to question the "divine right" of kings to their thrones, became, singular to say, as dangerous, as it would have been a few years before to assert the claims of the Stuarts, or question the justice of the Revolution made by the Whigs for their own purposes in 1688!

To do Mr. Pitt justice, there is every reason to believe, that he resisted, as long as he was able, this torrent of violence and folly, and would have taken the wise course of a guarded neutrality, allowing the French people to work out their own salvation after their own fashion. With the exception, however, of a small part of the House of Commons, headed by Charles James Fox, and a fraction, and not an influential one, of the middle classes, there was no one to aid him in maintaining this prudent position.

The lessons of the past were thrown to the winds. The overburdened state of the finances was disregarded or forgotten. In an evil hour, Mr. Pitt was persuaded that a single campaign would settle all; and under the influence of this notion, he yielded at last to the frenzy that had seized on the rest of the nation, and war was at last, in spite of the remonstrances of the few thinking men that dared to remonstrate, declared in the spring of the memorable year of 1793.

In spite of all these confident prognostications, the revulsion in the public mind, when the "Rubicon" was thus passed, and the overloaded nation actually plunged into new and desperate hostilities, was tremendous. Many who had not dared to speak in remonstrance, were now impelled by their fears to act in self-defence. A commercial panic ensued; and before the year was out, hundreds of bankruptcies, to an extent unknown before, had taken place, and nearly a third of the country banks then in existence had stopped payment! From the commencement of the paper money and the debt, bankruptcy, a thing almost *unknown* before in England, had grown and increased; but on this occasion, the "Gazette" exhibited a list that out-did all former precedent. The number of banks that suspended payment are stated by Chalmers to be *seventy-one.* This estimate, however, I believe, treats branches of the same bank as separate establishments. Of the exact numbers of bankruptcies in any one year, at these remote periods, it is not easy to come at an accurate account. The comparative lists that I have examined vary, though not materially. The following, which is principally taken from Sir John Sinclair's book on the revenue, is probably near the truth, and it sufficiently bears out the important fact to which I have already adverted, that bankruptcy, funding, and paper money, all grow and thrive together.

Years.	Bankrupts.	Years.	Bankrupts
1700	38	1768	351
1701	38	1769	344
1702	39	1770	397
1713	200	1771	433
1714	173	1772	523
1726	416	1773	507
1727	446	1774	337
1744	197	1775	350
1745	200	1776	435
1746	159	1777	535
1748	130	1778	636
1749	91	1779	522
1750	169	1780	458
1751	172	1781	458
1752	153	1782	558
1753	242	1783	532
1754	238	1784	521
1755	213	1785	502
1756	279	1786	510
1757	274	1787	509
1758	315	1788	707
1759	254	1789	502
1760	221	1790	585
1761	182	1791	583
1762	230	1792	636
1763	243	1793	1802
1764	322	1794	816
1765	239	1795	708
1766	342	1796	760
1767	360	1797	869

Here we see, such was the consternation excited by the infatuated crusade of 1793, that the number of bankrupts all but tripled those of the preceding year. Of the *seventy-one* banks, and branches of banks, which closed their doors, *twenty-six* are recorded to have been made bankrupts. The others were either wound up, or enabled to resume their business. The rapid fall in the price of consols, also, strongly marked the misgivings felt when the country was found to be nearing the precipice over which it was eventually hurried. In the summer of 1792, three per-cent consols were as high as ninety-two. In the December of the same year, when war became all but certain, they had tumbled down to seventy-four; and in February, 1793, they were at seventy-two, having fallen twenty per cent. in a few months: affording, thus, full proof, if any were wanted, that the opinions of those who gamble in them, so far from resting on them as a species of unchangeable property, perpetually point to a time when they shall cease to exist.

When the heretofore cautious, moderate, and economical British minister was, at length compelled, much against his better judgment, to join the coalition of vindictive and alarmed despots, against the French republicans, it was the opinion of both the friends and enemies of liberty, that the revolution would be now stunned and smothered by the weight of forces that threw themselves upon unprepared France. The clergy and aristocracy doomed to a certain destruction enemies who heeded little either throne or altar; and the distempered king, who had been actually and ravingly mad, from about September, 1788, to the spring of 1789, did every thing, personally, in his power to drive the two countries into mortal hostility; amongst other modes, even stooping so low, as actually to recommend an Anti-gallican tirade of the accomplished but hollow Burke, who had now deserted the tattered colours of Fox and the few who stood firm, for the gilded pennons of Pitt, and a pension of five thousand a year! The grand reliance of the minister himself, however, was upon the notoriously desperate state of the French finances, and the consequent destitute condition of their armies, if armies they could be called, which consisted of hasty levies of undisciplined volunteers, unprovided with the commonest necessaries for a campaign, and marching in the snow destitute of shoes and stockings. The truth certainly was, that, in the judgment of all men, the money affairs of the French convention were, at that period, quite desperate. Finding it impossible amidst the viccisitudes of the times, to collect any efficient amount of taxes in metallic or real money, the revolutionary government, after the seizure of the property of the church and of the emigrant noblesse, issued a paper money secured upon these now "national domains," and styled "assignats," because to the holders of this paper was assigned a certain lien upon these immense estates. This abstractedly considered, forms a better security for a paper currency than the world had ever before, or has ever since seen, without any exception whatsoever; but when the Austrian and Prussian veterans prepared to cross the French frontiers, even this security began to lose its credit rapidly; and when England at length joined the ill-omened confederation, that decline was vastly accelerated. In the mean time the necessity of increased preparation, and the rise in prices which the increased issue and growing depreciation of the paper caused, hurried on the whole towards the final catastrophe of panic and total discredit, which Pitt at last contrived to render complete. In vain did Robespierre and the convention threaten with the guillotine those who made any difference between the paper assignats and actual coin. The threat had only the effect of causing all the coin *to be hoarded*. In vain did they decree a *maximum* of price for bread and other necessaries, it only caused *the markets to be deserted*. Those who would not sell were denounced as traitors; they then *hid their goods*. In short, the fear of death upon the scaffold could not conquer public opinion; and when he joined in the war, Pitt had predetermined to complete the discredit of the assignats, by forging and distributing the forgeries over France; which he did. The consequence was, that the assignats became "waste paper," and they may to this hour be seen pasted against the walls of cottages in France, as memorials of the time when they fell. This act of Pitt has been confidently denied; and it has been asserted that if done, it was not with the knowledge of the heads of the government.

Both denial and assertion are, however, false. In consequence of the fraudulent dishonour of a bill of exchange, the whole was divulged in a court of law; and the paper of which the forgeries were made, is now known to have been manufactured, by direct order of government, at Langley paper mill, situated near the city of Durham, a site chosen, probably, for this purpose, on account of its remoteness from the seat of government: and, indeed, the whole transaction was worthy of the genius of the minister, who was singularly destitute of military notions, excepting in so far as they were intertwined with the grand question of "ways and means."

The blowing up of the French currency of "assignats," was the first and last of Mr. Pitt's triumphs. When the campaign of 1793 was commencing, everybody regarded the conquest, and dismemberment of France, as certain. Burke had declared she should be "blotted from the map of Europe." Pitt had described her as "in the very gulf of bankruptcy." The pious king, with the whole clergy and aristocracy, had pronounced her "regicide government" to be utterly "abandoned of God." Alas! events falsified all. Those who thus talked, knew little what a nation of thirty millions of people can do, when they have set their hearts upon doing it. The inkstand of the "blotters" was quickly twisted from their hands, and sent with a vengeance at their own heads. The curses of the parsons went the wrong way, and operated as blessings. The raw levies of enthusiastic republican lads of sixteen years of age, routed the Austrian and Prussian veterans contrary to all tactics, and completely "hors de les regles." The war was quickly carried into the enemies' country, and made to pay its own expenses. As confidence was restored, the hoarded coin quickly re-appeared, and took the place of the discredited assignats. In fine, the dukes of Brunswick and York, who by English influence had been chosen as the heroes of the intended "March to Paris," were beaten with every circumstance of disgrace and disaster that can possibly be conceived. Holland, Belgium, and Switzerland, were over-run; Italy was threatened; the French troops swarmed across the Rhine; the French marine was rapidly augmented;

all Europe trembled before the French Republic; and the invasion and conquest of England was now loudly threatened, and, as afterwards appeared, most potently believed by those most concerned!

After the disastrous step of the war of 1793, the character of the minister, Pitt, became totally changed. Desperation seemed to have seized upon him. Loan after loan was borrowed and squandered, with a reckless extravagance, upon ill-planned expeditions, which almost invariably failed, and upon coalitions which, as invariably, were dissolved by defeat. Whilst this was going on, he had the mortification of finding his financial prophecies turned against himself, and the bankruptcy, with which he twitted the convention, predicted just as confidently and as truly of the system he was then carrying on. At this time, in consequence of the continual loans, the issue of paper by the Bank necessarily became excessive; and in order to facilitate the circulation of these additions constantly thrown into the amount of the paper currency, the Bank was empowered, for the first time, to fabricate notes for sums as low as *five pounds*. These proceedings did not go on unobserved by the keen eye of one, more capable of estimating their ultimate consequences than were either the men who issued, or the minister who urged on the issue of these delusive instruments. This observer was the celebrated Thomas Paine. Originally a staymaker, and then an exciseman, he emigrated to America about the time of the commencement of the disputes with the colonists. Paine took the side of independence; and, by his talents, raised himself to the important post of Secretary to the Congress, whilst by his writings he helped to secure the success of the great cause which that Congress was elected to maintain. After the peace of 1783, he returned to England, and on the appearance of the book of the apostate Irishman, Burke, against the proceedings which were occurring in France, Paine answered it in a treatise called "The Rights of Man," in which he boldly and most ably advocated the right of a people to choose their own form of government. It was one of the hardest blows ever dealt to despotism and tyranny. Paine was prosecuted for writing "a seditious libel"; and having retired to France to escape the fangs of the enraged Government, he was elected a member of the French Convention. Whilst in the United States, he had witnessed the workings of paper money, and state borrowing; and, understanding the symptoms, he was easily able to predict the catastrophe. Paine saw very well that the fabrication of the smaller notes would speedily enable the reckless minister to depreciate, by his over-issues, the whole body of the currency. He was well aware that this, joined to the necessity of sending subsidies and pay for the troops abroad and to the alarm now augmenting at home, would and must, and in no long time, drain the Bank of England of her last guinea. In a short pamphlet, accordingly, entitled "The Decline and Fall of the British System of Finance," he not only foretold the certain ruin which England would eventually bring upon herself by the Funding System, but also the impending difficulties of the Bank, and the extreme probability that her notes might, in no long time, share the fate of the French assignats. This prophecy was put forth in the year 1796. In England it was despised, and its author burned in effigy. In France, it gave additional confidence to the revolutionists; and it is more than probable, that a design of Clavière to stop the Bank of England by an alarm of forged notes, and a run, to be fomented by secret agents, which is known to have been entertained about this period, might give additional confidence to the predictions of Paine. Be that as it may, within two years, the prediction as to the Bank was fulfilled, as far as it pointed to stoppage, and the inability to pay in gold.

In the meantime, from the very commencement of hostilities, difficulties, numerous and novel, beset the unfortunate minister. The pressure of commercial distress, caused by the panic and want of confidence, arising out of the ill-omened rupture of 1793, was perfectly unprecedented in the commercial annals of the country; and this soon forced upon Pitt, *for the first time*, one of those measures, the policy of which is always questionable; and which, at all events, set an example ever impolitic, and generally dangerous to be followed. This measure was *the lending of money by the Government to merchants*, in order to prop mercantile credit for the time. The minister, scared by the mischiefs which his first plunge into war immediately occasioned, having signified, through the Bank. his readiness to do this, it appears by the report of the commissioners for the issue of Exchequer bills in that year, that the number who applied for loans were *three hundred and thirty-two*. The amount which these modest applicants proposed to take, was no less than 3,855,624*l.* sterling! Of the number who applied, *two hundred and thirty-eight*, were successful in obtaining loans. The amount lent stood thus:—

Obtained on personal security .	£2,015,000
On security of goods	187,200
Total lent	2,202,200

and to the honour of the borrowers, and of the general solidity of trade at that period, the whole was faithfully repaid; much before it was due. The precedent, however, was most mischievous.

The effects of the first alarm in 1793, were got over in the manner described; but it unfortunately happened that alarm became one of the necessary engines of the administration. In order to reconcile the people to the stoppages in the channels of trade, the raising of more and more troops, the continual impressment of seamen, the growing and extraordinary annual loans, the hardships of the militia conscription, the arming acts, the rapidly augmented taxation, and the prospects of a struggle becoming every hour more desperate, it became absolutely requisite, to persuade them that they were fighting, not for the defence of aristocracy and corruption, but for actual existence; that the national independence was in imminent danger; and that liberty, religion, and even the name of Englishman, were in danger of being ingulfed in one grand chaos of Jacobinism, Atheism, and universal anarchy. For a time, these perpetual horrors, dinned by a host of venal and foolish prints, day after day, into the ears of the people, answered the purposes of those who so dinned them; but after the successes of the French began to be overwhelming, and their actual means of invading either England, or Ireland, or both, imposing and apparent, the matter with all men, got beyond a joke, and the alarm spread over society, became deep and feverish.

Now began to exhibit themselves, those symptoms which Paine, in his "Decline and Fall of the English System of Finance," published some little time before, had described as being the assured consequence of an issue of five-pound-notes, in the midst of increasing taxes, and increasing national alarm. Towards the close of the year 1796, the Bank of England began to experience *a scarcity of cash*, which first became chronic, and as time went on, increased in virulence. This was the natural fruit only of the measures that had been taken during the three preceding years. The usual way, in which the metals reach the vaults of the Bank, is not by purchase, in the ordinary sense of the term, but by *cash* being paid in on account of taxes, which taxes are paid out again in *bank notes* in the shape of dividends, government warrants, etc.; and also by merchants, who have sums in *bullion* remitted to them, lodging the same in the Bank on their own account, but receiving payment, in ordinary times, for their draughts upon the Bank, *in notes*. In 1796, as Mr. Paine had foretold, these two sources began totally to fail. After the circulation of bank paper for sums as low as *five pounds*, the whole of *the taxes* were paid in these notes, and gold in any quantity was hardly to be had. The rise in prices, also, caused by the quantities of paper issued, stimulated the importation of all sorts of goods so strongly as to render the exchanges unfavourable, and to stop any large remittances of *bullion* from coming into the country. As the alarm increased, the people began also to *hoard the gold coin;* so that when the year 1796, at last come to a close, it was evident to the few persons who, at that time, understood these matters, that *a crisis* was approaching and one of no common description.

During the last months of the year just concluded, some negociations for a cessation of hostilities had been attempted, but early in 1797, it was seen that they must certainly fail. Here was a source of more irritation upon the public mind; and the venal newspapers, ignorant all the time of the position of the Bank (which was kept secret, almost to the last, even from Pitt himself), and seldom doing things by halves, excited at last, by their exaggerated and foolish language, a panic so intense amongst all classes, that in January 1797, consols went down as low as fifty-four; and the sellers out at these ruinous prices, ran to the Bank *for gold*, to hoard it, in case of the invasion, which was now hourly expected.—In this seething state of alarm, irritation, and distraction, the public was kept, through the three weeks of February, when, on the 21st of the month, the telegraph having signalled that "a large fleet of French transports *with troops* and a squadron, were off Beachy Head," and this news being followed next day by the tidings of the actual "*landing* of French troops *in Wales*," the selling out of the funds, and the run upon the Bank became continuous, and such after-efforts as were made to explain away the causes of the panic, useless.

A situation of affairs like this could not last long, without producing some momentous change for good or for evil. The crisis in which the funds and paper currency were now placed, was one to which they naturally and inevitably tended. The impending shock was one which the system was *a priori* doomed to encounter; nor was it now within the compass of human power to avert it, nor to evade it, even for a day. The way in which it was to be met, was therefore the only consideration for those concerned,—at the head of whom stood the minister who, by his infatuated course had certainly been the proximate cause of all. How Mr. Pitt *felt* when, on the 21st of February, the existence of the peril in which the Bank was placed was, for the first time, divulged to him: or how he felt when, on the 24th of the same month, it was announced to him, that the sending Goldsmid and Eliason for gold to Hamburg, was "too late," and that the "safety of the house" was gone, and "stoppage" at the door, —it is difficult to conceive. I can liken his feelings best to those of the Cherokee chief, when he woke from his drunken sleep, and found himself, in his canoe, in the midst of the rapids, within a bow-shot of the falls of Niagara. The very sound of the word "stoppage" must have been, to *his* ears, mingled with the distant roar of the cataract, over which he and his fortunes, and the fortunes of his country, were now fated to go. Whether, like the chief, he, too, *went over with the bottle at his head*, cannot be known; though, from his previous habits, it is probable he did! He took the plunge, however, with better auspices than did the Indian,—though, as to the tremendous nature of the peril to be undergone, the cases are not very dissimilar. We must not, however, run before the events which we have undertaken to narrate.

I have already stated, that the intimation of their situation was made to Mr. Pitt, by the Bank Directors, for the first time, on the 21st February, 1797. On that occasion, he undertook to try to quiet the alarm, by some statement in the House of Commons; and at the same time urged the directors to purchase gold abroad. On the 24th, however, he was told *that it was too late*, and that all that could be done was to take the advice of a private meeting of bankers at his house next day, which was Saturday the 25th February. Through that day, the selling out of stock and drain of gold continued to increase; and it seems, therefore, that at this meeting was *really determined* the desperate step which ensued, of a refusal to pay in gold or silver at the Bank. This refusal was authorised by an "Order in Council," and was termed a "Restriction," upon the Bank from paying any more gold or silver. The order was signed on *Sunday* the 26th of February; and on Monday the memorable 27th of February, 1797, the eyes of the crowd, which had assembled at the doors of the Bank in Threadneedle Street, in order to get gold for their notes, were greeted with the following most original document, in which shame seems to have so far mastered the writers, as to have actually debarred them from saying in so many words that they meant no longer to pay their creditors. In truth, were it not for the order in council, a copy of which was appended to the notice, the document would only amount to an assurance to the public of the wonderfully flourishing state of an establishment which at that moment could not have paid half a crown in the pound upon its promissory notes in circulation! The notice is as follows:

"*Bank of England, February 27th* 1797.

"In consequence of an order of His Majesty's Privy Council, notified to the Bank last night, a copy of which is hereunto annexed, the governor, deputy governor, and directors of the Bank of England, think it their duty to inform the proprietors of bank stock, as well as the public at large, that the general concerns of the bank are in the *most affluent* [!] and *prosperous* situation, and such as to preclude every *doubt* as to the security of its notes. *The directors mean to continue their usual discounts* for the accommodation of the commercial interest, paying the amount in *bank notes;* and the *dividend warrants* will be *paid in the same manner.*—Francis Martin, Secretary." To this piece of cool originality was appended the Sunday order in council, which "required" the directors not to issue any more cash until the "sense of parliament" could be taken.

Thus, and after this fashion, on this memorable Monday morning, was the system of funding and paper money subjected to the most trying ordeal which it had yet encountered: and strange to say, it survived. In no other country, on the face of this globe, could it have so survived. In France it would not; in Germany it would not; in Holland, even, it would not; nay, the bearded Barbarians of Muscovy would have been too much for this; as the Empress Catharine could witness. In England it only succeeded from the excessive gullibility of the national character; from the habits of traffic, which led the people readily to pin their faith upon all sorts of paper securities; and from the extreme cunning with which the public mind was worked upon by the press and the parliament. To persuade the people that the Bank directors had been compelled, against their will, to cease paying their notes in gold and silver, lying and falsehood of the most elaborate and solemn character, amounting morally to the most deliberate perjury, were resorted to both by Pitt and by the Bank directors; and in the meantime, no time was lost in obtaining meetings of the influential classes, who signed *declarations of their faith* in the inconvertible bank paper, and of their determined resolution to take it in payment. At a meeting of merchants at the Mansion House, on the very morning of the stoppage, this was done. The magistrates at quarter sessions followed the example; and numbers of the members of both Houses of Parliament backed out the merchants and the magistrates. To this last document, Pitt himself had the inconceivable front to affix his own signature! All this was, however, outdone at a meeting of the proprietors of bank stock at the Bank itself; at which two directors of the names of *Thornton* and *Bosanquet*, declared, in a manner the most solemn, that "the measure was *not* adopted at the instance of the bank-directors," that it was "a great state measure"; and that "he *earnestly hoped* that the bank *which was quite able*, should *soon be permitted* to pay its notes in cash as formerly!" To crown all, the proprietors passed "a vote of thanks" to the directors, for their "*acquiescence in the order in council*"; and some fault was found with the House of Commons for appointing a *committee of enquiry*, which was declared to be "quite unnecessary!"

This tissue of enormous lying was repeated in the House of Commons, who, however, persisted in the farce of causing a committee to inquire into the state of the Bank affairs. Into the proceedings of this committee it is useless now to inquire. Suffice it to say, that in the progress of their examinations, they hit upon "a minute of the proceedings of the Bank Directors," in which it was recorded, that the deputy-governor, *Thornton*, and the director, *Bosanquet*, who had solemnly affirmed that the Bank restriction order was the sole act of the government, had actually been part of the deputation which waited upon Mr. Pitt on the 21st and 24th of February, to lay before him the state of their coffers, to ask "how far they were to go" in paying away their gold, and when he meaned to "interfere." Another curious circumstance is, that the Bank attempted to conceal, even from Parliament, the exact amount of money which remained in their till on Saturday night, the 25th of February. In the statement of their affairs, it will be seen that they lump together "bills and notes discounted, cash and bullion," into one *item* or entry. To show the decline in their strength, they merely gave certain *numbers*, which were intended to divulge only the rate of the decrease at different periods. From these numbers, however, Mr. Allerdyce, a member of the committee, contrived to discover the real amount of cash left when they stopped and published it. It is now known, that his statement was deduced from correct *data*, and that the amount of money left on the evening of Saturday, the 25th February, was £1,272,000 only, from which a sum of nearly £200,000 seems to have been abstracted on the 28th of February! Yet knowing this, the deputy-governor, Thornton, had the face to hope, on the *second of March*, that "they might *soon be permitted* to pay their notes in cash again as formerly"! This is surely unmatchable in the annals of hypocrisy and fraud! The following is the statement submitted to the "Secret Committee"; and I beseech the reader to look well at it.

FINANCIAL STATEMENT OF THE BANK ON FEBRUARY 25th, 1797.

Debt Account.		*Credit Account.*	
Drawing account	£2,389,600	Bills and Notes discounted - Cash and Bullion	£4,176,080
Exchequer Bills -	1,676,000	Exchequer Bills -	8,228,000
Unpaid Dividends -	983,730	Lands and Tenements	65,000
Do. in Bank Stock -	45,150	Money lent India Company - -	700,000
Do. in India Annuities	10,210	Stamps - -	1,510
Sundries unclaimed -	1,330	Navy and Victualling Bills - -	15,890
Due of Loan of 1797	17,060	American Debentures	54,150
Unpaid Irish Dividend	1460	Petty Cash in House	5,320
Do. on Imperial Loan	5,600	Sundry Articles -	24,150
	£5,130,140	5 per Cent. Annuities	795,800
Notes in circulation	8,640,250	5 per Cents., 1797	1,000,000
	£13,770,390	Treasury Bills paid	1,512,270
Balance -	3,826,890	Loan to Government	376,000
	£17,597,280	Bills discounted unpaid	88,120
		Treasury and Exchequer Fees -	740
		Interest due from Government -	554,250
			£17,597,280

This statement, it is to be observed, does not include (at least not as a whole) the *great standing debt* which the Government owed the Bank, which at that time amounted to £11,686,800, so that *upon paper*, to those who looked no further, the whole seemed a very flourishing affair. If, however, the credit account be sifted, it appears that, save and except the first, third, fourth, and eighth *items*, the whole consists of securities dependent altogether on the taxes. If, then, the bank-notes had shared the fate of the French assignats, it is clear the Bank must have been totally ruined, because in these worthless notes alone would or could taxes have been paid, and the Government could only pay the Bank what itself received. Nay, even the private debtors of the Bank would of course have paid their debts in the same worthless medium as long as it was to be had; so that, in all this account, the only solid things were the cash and bullion, and the petty cash really kept in the house, the rest being no better than empty air, and resting merely on public credulity. To suppose that the Government could, in case of the total extinction of these notes, have collected taxes *in coin alone* sufficient to pay the dividends, the current expenses of the nation, and, at the same time, to replace the *eleven millions* borrowed of the Bank, would be mere insanity. The attempt must have brought every thing to a stand-still. Thus the fate of the whole system of the Government really depended upon the inclination of the people to give credit to the inconvertible notes; and the refusal of that credit must have inevitably overset the whole.

In parliament, a system of delusion was maintained,

which, to persons unaccustomed to unravel the tricks of corrupt Governments, seems almost incredible. The assertions made out of doors, that the Bank Directors were restrained, against their will, from paying in cash, were boldly repeated, from Pitt, the prime minister, down to the lowest jackal of office. It was confidently held out, that the stoppage would be merely temporary: and after the Secret Committee, as it was called, made its report, Pitt proposed, that an act should be passed to authorise the "restriction" being continued until the 24th of June ensuing, being a period of *fifty-two days*, after which he calculated that the Bank would be able and willing to be "permitted to pay their notes in gold and silver, as formerly"! Thus were the minds of the people gradually accustomed to the idea of a Bank that could not pay in money; and led forward, as a horse is, by sticking a wisp of hay at a short distance before his nose, by the holding out of periods for gold payments, which were never intended to be attained. Mr. Fox, and others in the House of Commons, certainly saw the true state of the case, and said what they believed; their warnings, however, were as usual attributed to "faction," and went for nothing; though some of the words were hardly uttered ere fulfilment followed! The 24th of June rapidly drew near, and people again began to prick up their ears at the sound of cash payments. Alas! this very anxiety frightened the minister, and the poor Directors were again disappointed of being "permitted to pay their notes in gold and silver, as formerly." On the 22nd of June, another Act was passed to continue "restriction," until one month after the commencement of the *next* session of parliament. Well! In the October of the same year, 1797, parliament met again "for despatch of business," and this of the bank they "despatched" out of hand! In short, they passed, on the 30th of November, a third act to continue "restriction," until one month after the conclusion of the then war, by a definitive treaty of peace! Thus, step by step, was a complete system of paper-money established, which, at first, was to last *fifty-two days*, but which ultimately lasted *twenty-two years!* During the short peace of Amiens, which lasted a few months only, from 1802 to 1803, two acts were passed to continue the restriction; and when, in 1803, hostilities were re-commenced, a sixth act was passed on the 15th of December, of that year, to carry on the paper currency, until six months after the next definitive treaty of peace, which act was continued forwards until the year 1819. In our next letter, we shall examine some of the many consequences of this memorable transaction, which in a few years made more changes in the frame-work of society, than had before taken place during the lapse of centuries. In conclusion, however, it will be proper to see how "the debt" stood at the period when this change was effected. It stood as follows:—

	Principal.	Interest.
Debt at the war of 1793 .	£257,213,043 .	£9,669,435
Added in 1793 . .	6,250,000 .	252,812
	263,463,043	9,922,247
,, 1794 . .	15,676,525	773,324
Carried over .	£279,139,568	£10,695,571

Brought over .	£279,139,568	£10,695,571
Added in 1795 . .	25,609,897	1,227,415
	304,749,465	11,922,986
„ 1796 . .	41,303,699	1,850,373
	346,053,164	13,773,359
„ 1797 . .	67,087,668	3,241,790
	£413,140,832	£17,015,149

Here we see, that, in the short space of four years, the debt had gone far again to double itself. That it did not proceed at the same rate of increase, is to be attributed to the change in the currency, which enabled the people, amongst other strange things, to pay more taxes in proportion within the year; especially the Income Tax, which raised large sums, directly. To this, and the other effects of the inconvertible paper, we shall now turn.

LETTER VIII.

ISSUE OF NOTES FOR ONE AND TWO POUNDS.—PAPER-MONEY MADE VIRTUALLY A LEGAL TENDER.—EFFECTS OF THE PAPER-MONEY.—EXTENSION OF THE MANUFACTURING SYSTEM.—GREAT ADVANCE IN PRICES.—EFFECTS OF THE RISE UPON LANDLORDS.—UPON ANNUITANTS.—CIVIL LIST, AND PAY OF ALL GOVERNMENT OFFICERS OF THE ARMY, AND OF THE NAVY RAISED.—COMPARATIVE TABLE OF THE PRICES OF GRAIN.—OF THE PRICES OF COMMODITIES.—THE EFECTS OF THE PAPER ON THE PRICE OF GOLD.—THE DISAPPEARANCE OF THE COIN.—STATE OF THE BALANCE OF TRADE.—THE RATES OF WAGES COMPARED WITH THE PRICES OF PROVISIONS.—WAGES IN 1785 AND IN 1805, COMPARED.—THE COMMON LANDS.—THEIR ORIGIN.—INCLOSURE BILLS.—THEIR NUMBERS.—EXTENT OF COMMON LAND ALIENATED.—AUGMENTATION OF THE POOR-RATE UP TO 1803.—RETIREMENT OF PITT.

In the course of the many topics discussed in our last letter, we have seen, that, after all the triumphant boastings of Mr. Pitt as to the solidity "of the national resources," and after all his scorn of the "French assignats," which he certainly helped to discredit and destroy, he was, himself, forced on to a course of those very instruments at which, when they were issued in France, he had so eloquently railed; the only alternative being a total destruction of the Bank, and of all Bank paper-money, and (in short) national bankruptcy. That he escaped the last alternative, in the long run, can only be ascribed to the wonderful "luck," which in more than one desperate difficulty, has attended the system in England; to the cunning with which Pitt went about the gradual establishment of his paper currency; and to the disgraceful and slavish gullibility and subservience of the English as a nation, and their readiness to swallow any disgusting trick, which it may answer the purpose of their rulers to palm upon them.

This grand "hocus-pocus" was not to be performed, however, without giving birth to various other strange changes and transactions; and to some of these this appears to be the proper place to advert. Until 1797, the bankers had, after the acts of 1775 and 1777 against notes or bills for small sums, fabricated no notes for any sum *below five pounds;* but now when the great parent Bank was "restrained" by cruel Mr. Pitt, as the directors swore, *so much against their will*, from the payment of any more guineas, or even seven shilling-pieces, until six months after the end of a war that seemed as if it would have no end, something was to be provided, as a substitute, for the poor directors to pay with; and this substitute was *one and two pound notes*, with which the country was speedily deluged, and upon which the trade of "country-banking" grew, throve, and flourished, apace. Another point to be weathered, was the making the paper of the Bank of England *a legal money;* that is to say, a money which no saucy nor squeamish creditor could *refuse* as payment of a debt; and about this the minister went with his usual cunning. He avoided, as far as possible, the appearance of making this paper *a forced money*. He steered clear of enacting it, according to the *letter* of the law, to be "a legal tender." But he protected from *arrest* every person who offered these notes in payment of any debt; and left the creditor to get better payment, if he insisted upon it, by an action at law. He also, of course, protected the Bank itself from any suit for non-payment of its notes, for which it would give *other notes;* and if any person lodged cash in the Bank, specially even, only *three-fourths* of the cash lodged was permitted to be repaid. Hence, though Bank of England paper was not *in law* a legal tender, it was virtually so. Where gold was never seen nor heard of, no one dreamed of suits at law to obtain it; and before this, it had begun to become a rarity. It must not be forgotten that, though the act of 1777 for the regulation of notes and bills for small sums, admitted the issue of bank-notes for *five pounds*, the Bank of England did not avail herself of this privilege until the war-loans forced it upon her in 1794. The country-bankers, however, had taken care to exercise the privilege all along: and, as in 1797 they had risen in numbers to *two hundred and thirty-two* (despite the devastation of 1793), the country was, even then, tolerably well saturated with paper. As soon as the first panic caused by the stoppage of February was over, its growth went on with accelerated rapidity, as that of grass does when thunder-showers fall after a drought. Of the progress and consequences of that growth, we are now to treat.

From and after the crisis of 1797, which ended in establishing an inconvertible paper-money in England, the war against France went on, if possible, with double virulence. It continued, save and except two short intermissions of peace, in 1802 and 1814 (which will be noted in the proper place), until the year A.D. 1815, when the memorable conflict at Waterloo terminated it. During this long period, the issues of paper were enormous; and the effects caused by the consequent depreciation of the circulating money, and by the events of the varied conflict that was going on, were so multiform and extraordinary, that even heads used to such details are liable to be puzzled by their multiplicity and singularity.

The first phenomenon to be noted is, perhaps, the part which the discoveries in machinery, adapted for the spinning and weaving of cotton, woollen, linen, and silk fabrics, enabled us to play, during the many vicissitudes of the long contest. Through many periods, the entire Continent of Europe was shut against us: and yet, strange to say, this only added to our commercial resources. We preserved all along the mastery of the seas: and this gave the power of so effectually shutting the Continent out from all supplies of every sort of raw or manufactured produce coming from abroad, that, distracted as they were with the conflicts raging upon their own soil, they were compelled either to forego almost entirely the use of colonial produce, and the manufactures in ordinary consumption, or take them from their enemies! Hence, during the entire war, strange to relate, the whole Continent was, by means of neutral flags, supplied with colonial and manufactured articles through England, and her colonies: and as fast as the depreciating paper sent the precious metals *out* of the country, the state of the Exchanges, always in favour of England on the balance of trade, sent them *back again.*

In the mean time, as the expense of one fruitless expedition, added to the debt, necessarily augmented the expenditure of the next; and as the outlay for taking one sugar island from the French inevitably rendered more costly the capture of the succeeding one; the notes of all denominations were pushed out by the parent bank, and her illegitimate progeny, the country-bankers, who multiplied apace: and, as this went on, a general rise in the prices of all commodities followed. Under these circumstances, so great were the nominal profits made by traders of every grade, and so lavish was the expenditure of government, that the paper-money soon began to be popular amongst all the commercial classes, who, satisfied with the first effects of this delusive system, were unconscious or reckless of its more distant consequences. As most of the land was, at this time, also, let upon long leases, the farmers reaped double harvests from the steady advance in every sort of grain, the prices of which the seasons conspired with the paper-money to raise; and hence began to spring, and insinuate their roots throughout the surface of society, those strange and anomalous notions as to money, which afterwards showed themselves in the guise of pamphlets, with such titles as "Guineas shown to be a Useless Incumbrance"!

In the midst, however, of this apparent prosperity, though some classes of men were enabled to get together sums of money that were enormous, it must not be supposed that there were not many sufferers. There were many, both rich and poor. Such landlords as had let their estates upon long leases suffered considerably; for whilst the fortunate tenant was, by the great advance in the prices of all sorts of grain, and all descriptions of live stock, enabled to realise a fortune, the money, in which the lessor received his rents, was rapidly, year after year, diminishing in value. This was especially the case with the vast tracts of grazing land in the north and west of England, which were let on leases for lives. Other annuitants, having fixed incomes, suffered in the same manner; and before many years had elapsed, it became necessary to add to the pay of every one in the employment of Government, from the king himself down to the lowest tide-waiter or excise runner. The civil list was augmented; the salaries of the judges were increased: the pay of the army and navy, from the general and the admiral, down to the line and the foremast, was added to; and all the minor functionaries of the Government received an increase of nominal remuneration, in the same ratio. The old fundholders, however, and other private persons having annuities, or any sort of fixed incomes, had no such help or refuge, and they smarted accordingly. What was worst of all was, that the working population, and the poor were sufferers also; and in more ways than one. In spite of all the confident asseverations to the contrary, it is palpable enough, that this issue of paper-money was injurious, all along, to the toiling and industrious classes, as well as to the very poor. The wages of labour, in the mass, never rose so as to keep the remuneration of industry upon a level with the depreciation of the money in which the wages were paid: and the poor, in the course of it, lost the greater part of such hold as they had upon the soil, and upon the surplus wealth of those who had thriven under the system which helped to create them.

In order to attain to some definite idea of these things it will be necessary to look at the documents which go to prove them. Let us first look at the range of the price of wheat and other grain, from about this period to the end of the war in A.D. 1815.

AN ACCOUNT OF THE AVERAGE PRICES OF ALL SORTS OF GRAIN, FROM 1792, TO 1815 INCLUSIVE, LAID BEFORE PARLIAMENT.

	Wheat.		Rye.		Barley.		Oats.		Beans.		Pease.	
	s.	*d.*	*s.*	*d.*	*s.*	*d.*	*s.*	*d.*	*s.*	*d.*	*s.*	*d.*
1792	42	11	30	8	26	9	17	7	31	6	32	8
1793	48	11	35	11	31	9	21	3	37	8	38	4
1794	51	8	37	9	32	10	22	0	42	6	46	8
1795	74	2	48	5	37	8	24	9	46	8	53	4
1796	77	1	47	0	35	7	21	9	38	10	43	6
1797	53	1	31	11	27	9	16	9	27	6	33	5
1798	50	3	30	11	29	1	19	10	30	1	33	11
1799	67	6	43	9	36	0	27	7	44	7	45	2
1800	113	7	76	11	60	0	39	10	69	3	67	5
1801	118	3	79	9	67	9	36	6	62	8	67	8
1802	67	5	43	3	33	1	20	7	36	4	39	6
1803	56	6	36	11	24	10	21	3	34	8	38	6
1804	60	1	37	1	30	4	23	9	38	7	40	10
1805	87	10	54	4	44	8	28	0	47	5	48	4
1806	79	0	47	4	38	6	25	8	43	9	43	6
1807	73	3	47	6	38	4	28	1	47	3	55	11
1808	79	0	52	4	42	1	33	8	60	8	66	7
1809	95	7	60	9	47	3	32	8	60	9	60	2
1810	106	2	59	0	47	11	29	4	53	7	55	9
1811	94	6	49	11	41	10	27	11	47	10	51	6
1812	125	5	75	11	66	6	44	0	72	8	73	7
1813	108	9	70	7	58	4	39	5	76	5	78	6
1814	73	11	44	6	37	4	26	6	46	7	50	0
1815	64	4	37	10	30	3	23	10	36	1	38	10

This table, which was extracted by Mr. Tooke, from returns laid before parliament, I take to be a near approximation to the truth, and a better guide than the Eton, the Oxford, or the Windsor, accounts of prices, which are always above the average of the whole country, though accurately true, with regard to the rates at these places. I must take the opportunity also to impress the important fact, that the price of grain, especially in a country that is insulated, is the best criterion of any change that may be made in the currency of that country as to value, whether towards less or more. It is so, because the article is of such magnitude that its value cannot be materially altered, except by the seasons; and, therefore, any *long continued change in the average prices of grain*, whether upwards or downwards, for which the seasons will *not* account, must be ascribed to alterations in the value of money, and to that alone.

That the prices of merchandise generally, throughout the whole period of the Bank restriction, exhibited the same evidence of the depreciation of the money of the country, I consider to be, however, quite undeniable. It is only more difficult to be shewn, because the high prices always, *at length*, by stimulating speculation, caused a greater supply of the article, which in part neutralised the effect of the lower value of money upon the price. If, however, we look at two or three commodities, the quantities of which are least susceptible of very sudden or very excessive augmentation, we shall see in the range of their prices abundant evidence of what was going on. Let us take, for instance, tin, lead, tallow, and foreign wool of some particular growth and fineness, and we shall find, in their prices, the same evidence of the action of the depreciated currency that is afforded by the markets for grain, taking the rates every second year.

YEARS.	TIN.	LEAD.	LEONESA WOOL.	TALLOW.
	Cwt.	Fodder.	per lb. per lb	Cwt. Cwt.
	s. d.	£	s. d. „ s. d.	s. s.
1792	92 6 103 6	20 5 18 0	4 6 to 4 10 3 7 „ 4 10	42 to 43 46 „ 47
1794	103 6 100 6	20 5 18 0	3 8 to 4 0 3 6 „ 3 10	38 to 39 50 „ 51
1796	101 6 102 6	21 10 20 10	3 8 to 4 3 3 8 „ 4 0	68 to 70 58 „ 60
1798	102 6 100 6	19 10	3 10 to 4 4	49 to 50 56 „ 57
1800	104 0 110 0	22 10 24 0	4 0 to 4 9 4 7 „ 5 4	58 to 59 66 “ 68
1802	114 6 115 6	28 0 33 10	5 9 to 6 0 5 10 „ 6 3	63 to 64 64 „ 66
1804	115 6	33 0 33 10	6 6 to 6 9	68 to 69 70 „ 71
1806	128 6	41 0 38 0	6 7 to 6 9	66 to 67 54 „ 55
1808	118 6 120 6	38 0 43 0	6 7 to 6 9 10 0 „ 10 6	70 to 71 110 „ 112
1810	128 6 174 0	38 0 33 0	13 0 to 14 0 7 0 „ 8 0	83 to 84 64 „ 65
1812	139 6 131 6	30 0 29 0	8 6 to 10 0 8 6 „ 9 6	72 to 73 88 „ 90
1814	174 6 168 6	30 0 32 0 34 0	8 0 to 9 0 7 0 „ 8 0	107 to 110 87 „ 88
1815	148 6 152 6	28 0 25 0	7 6 to 8 0 6 0 „ 7 0	81 to 82 59 „ 60

The vicissitudes of the war, no doubt, from time to time, affected the markets for these articles; but the average rise caused by the pouring out of the paper money is evident enough all through.

After the bank stoppage and restriction act, the price of gold and silver bullion, as a matter of course, immediately rose; but *never to an extent commensurate with the depreciation of the paper.* Of this important fact due note ought to be taken. The causes, which kept the prices of gold and silver bullion down, were two-fold; and were as follows. In the first place, the advance in price caused, in spite of the severity of the law to restrain it, the melting or exportation of the *whole of the coin.* My own opinion is that the greater part of it was melted secretly, and sold to the goldsmiths in bars. There were penalties by law against persons who sold the coin of the realm, (if not light), for more than its nominal value: and a Jewess of the name of *De Yonge* was tried for this offence; although it was known that the government was obliged, in order to pay their troops abroad, secretly to buy guineas at twenty-seven shillings each! There were also penalties for melting the coin, or exporting it, and persons who sent *bars of gold* or *silver abroad* were made to *swear* that it was *not* melted coin. To sell the coin, however, required *two* parties; to melt and sell it in the shape of bars, *one* man only was required. Consequently the lesser risk was preferred, and the guineas melted; the persons who exported the bars taking the oath in any sense they chose. The second cause, was, that the balance of trade was, during the whole war, in favour of this country; and this caused gold and silver to be perpetually sent from the continent and elsewhere. This fact, as well as the other, was distinctly proved before the famous bullion committee of Mr. Horner, in 1810; the custom-house calculations giving the balance of trade in favor of this country, as follows:—

In 1805 about	- - - -	£ 6,616,000
1806	- - - - - - - -	- 10,437,000
1807	- - - - - - - -	- 5,866,000
1808	- - - - - - - -	- 12,481,000
1809	- - - - - - - -	- 14,834,000

These combined causes made gold and silver bullion so much of "a drug" in England, at this time, that there were actually no *open* sales of these metals *for several years together*, as was proved by *Aaron Asher Goldsmid* before the committee of 1810; and thus were the prices of gold and silver kept down, though not low enough to save the coin, which, with the exception of a few plain shillings, totally disappeared, whilst worthless "tokens," coined by the bank, as well as private persons all over the country, were used as change. In this strange state of affairs, it came to pass, that *light guineas* which could be *openly sold*, were worth more than those of full weight, *five pounds* in paper being eagerly given for three and a-half of them, at different periods; and yet, in the face of all this, the government had either the incredible ignorance, or incredible hardihood, to *deny* that the paper was depreciated or at a discount; and this they did, whilst secretly buying guineas at twenty-seven shillings each or more; and whilst they were openly ordering dollars, worth *four and sixpence* before, to pass for *five and sixpence*, in order to keep them in circulation!

Whilst every thing else was thus enhanced nominally in price, where it was practicable, in order to keep pace with the falling value of the inconvertible paper money, which was now being poured forth, from hundreds of flood-gates, all over the kingdom, the wages of labour lagged behind, and the temptation to rob the poor was increasing. The landlord and the farmer, the manufacturer and the tradesman, at once took advantage of what seemed to them a spring-tide of prosperity; but they were slow to raise the wages of the labourer and the artisan. It was not until the general dearness, as it seemed, of all commodities and articles of every-day consumption, had been established for some time, that the necessity for a rise also *in wages* was generally felt, seen, and acknowledged; nor was that rise, when accomplished, commensurate with the advance in prices, that preceded it. The sufferings of the poorer classes ever come first, their blessings and benefits last; and at ample proof of this we are now about to arrive.

I insert here an accurate statement, delivered on oath by Mr. Josiah Easton, to the lords' committee, in the year 1814, of the progress of prices, rates, and wages in the parish of Bradford, from A.D. 1773, to 1812. By this it will be seen, how the *wages* and *poor-rates* lag behind the augmenting cost of provisions and the advancing rate of landed rental. The poor-rates are given in gross with church and highway cess; but still the result is generally instructive.

PARISH OF BRADFORD.

Years.	Wheat per Bushel.		Beef and Mutton.	Poor, Church, & Way Rates.		Rent per Acre.			Men's Wages.		Women.		Boys.		Tithes. Great.	Modus. Small.
									Day.		Day.		Day.			
	s.	d.	lb.	£	s.	£	s.	d.	s.	d.	s.	d.	s.	d	£	£
1773½ to 1782½	5	11	$2\frac{1}{4}$	200	10	0	19	6	1	2	0	6	0	3	105	45
1783 to 1792	6	2	$3\frac{1}{4}$	210	0	1	0	6	1	3	0	6	0	3	120	50
1793 to 1802	9	5	$7\frac{1}{4}$	315	15	1	11	6	2	0	0	7	0	4	184	80
1803 to 1812	12	6	$8\frac{3}{4}$	430	0	2	1	0	2	4	0	9	0	5	232	100

The following statements published in 1830, by Mr. Potter Macqueen, bear witness to the same truth, that, in all advances in the prices of necessaries, whether such advances be owing to natural, or to artificial cause, the poorer classes, who live by the wages of labour, are sure to suffer. The *datum* upon which Mr. Macqueen sets out is, that, *when taxes were low*, *one-fifth* of the *quarter of wheat* was *only fair weekly* wages for an able-bodied man. Thus, as far back as 1742, the price of wheat, per quarter, being *twenty-nine shillings and sixpence to thirty shillings*, the week's wages of the rural labourer was, at least, *six shillings*. Now then, let us mark, with Mr. Macqueen, the progress of prices and of wages, and the difference between the rates of each. In 1790, wheat was at *fifty three* shillings the quarter; but wages, instead of being *ten shillings and sixpence*, were only *eight shillings* a week. In 1801, wheat reached the enormous nominal price of *one hundred and fifteen shillings the quarter*. Yet in 1801, wages, instead of reaching *twenty-three shillings*, only averaged *ten shillings* per week. In 1812, wheat touched the extraordinary price of *one hundred and twenty-two shillings and eightpence* the quarter! But did wages ever approach to *twenty-four shillings and sixpence?* Nothing of the kind. They only averaged *eleven shillings* per week; and as wheat fell, they fell with it. In 1826, wheat fell to *fifty-eight shillings*, and wages were not long in going down to *nine!*

If, however, we glance at the increase of taxes through all these periods, the rates of wages given by Mr. Macqueen show still heavier injustice.

In 1742, the taxes were about	.	£9,000,000
In 1790	,, ,,	16,000,000
In 1801	,, ,,	40,000,000
In 1812	,, ,,	64,000,000
In 1826	,, ,,	49,000,000

Part of these taxes, the poor labourer was to pay in imposts upon the articles he consumed; and yet see how his remuneration lags behind both prices and taxes.

The most direct proof, however, of the real effect upon the *working-man* of the rise in all commodities, caused by the augmenting issues of fictitious money, and of how small a part of the pretended prosperity, asserted to be created by those issues, fell to *his* share, is to be found in the following "*comparative statement*," which I believe to be very correct. It shows the wages and particulars of expenditure of mechanics and working artizans in London, at two different periods before and after the "Bank Restriction." The results cannot be misunderstood.

Expenditure in 1785.	£	s.	d.
Butchers' Meat, 8 lbs., 4d. to 6d.	£0	3	4
Bread, 4 Quartern Loaves -	0	2	0
Butter, 1½ lbs. -	0	1	0
Potatoes, 6 lbs. -	0	0	1½
Sugar, 1½ lbs. -	0	0	7½
Tea, 2 Ounces -	0	0	6
Beer, 7 Pots -	0	2	0½
Coals, 1 Bushel -	0	0	10
Candles, 1 lb. -	0	0	7
Rent per Week -	0	1	6
	£0	12	6½
Wages in 1785 -	0	18	0
Leaves - -	£0	5	5½

Expenditure in 1805.	£	s.	d.
Butchers' Meat, 8d. to 11d.	0	6	4
Bread, 4 Quarterns	0	5	0
Butter, 1½ lbs. -	0	1	9½
Potatoes, 6 lbs. -	0	0	4
Sugar, 1½ lbs. -	0	1	1½
Tea, 2 Ounces -	0	0	10
Beer, 7 Pots -	0	2	11
Coals, 1 Bushel -	0	1	8
Candles, 1 lb. -	0	0	10½
Rent per Week -	0	3	0
	£1	3	10½
Wages in 1805	1	6	0
Leaves - -	£0	2	1½

So much for the "prosperity" of a people under a constant outpouring of fictitious money!

Whilst the condition of humble industry was thus being insidiously sapped, undermined, and deteriorated, an underhand and furtive robbery of the very poor was commenced and gradually perpetrated, to an extent enormous, and, up to this time, known to or thought of by few. I do not here allude to the forcible reductions of the rates for the relief of the poor, nor to the cruelties attempted to be or actually inflicted upon them, under the various schemes which were laid or hatched from time to time for "amending," that is to say, abrogating the provisions of the original poor-law of the *forty-third of Elizabeth.* To these more open spoliations, and more barefaced cruelties, I shall afterwards have occasion to revert. At present, I have to treat of that more subdolous and furtive deprivation of the resources of the poorer classes, which was hatched soon after the birth of the paper-money and the debt, and which has gone on from that time to this with more or less of rapidity, as the temptations seemed greater or less, under the specious title of the "Inclosure of Common Lands." The first of these spoliation-bills, called "Inclosure-Acts," passed in the reign of Queen Anne. To come to a proper idea of the extent of the robbery thus begun, we must glance first at *the history* of these common lands; and in that history, as it respects their origin, we shall find evidence of their value, and of the purposes to which they ultimately came to be applied.

I have already explained, that under the feudal system, which was established by the Norman conquerors, the lands of the country, which were not actually retained by the king as royal estates, were divided and parcelled out amongst the barons, who became lords of the manors, holding of the monarch in virtue of certain services; and who subdivided their lands again amongst their vassals or followers, who held of them in virtue of other services, under various names, to denote the nature of the service. The real estates of the church were, after this period, held under similar conditions, which holding was in those days called by the general name of "Frankalmoigne," which generally denoted a tenure under the church; *Frankalmoigne*, in its *original* signification, being "lands given for God's service." Those tenants who held land, parcel of the *crown-estates*, directly under the king, were called holders "*in capite*," the king being here in the place of manorial landlord;

and thus, in these various ways, were the lands of England held for some centuries. Under this system, the early divisions of the lands, for the purposes of *cultivation by tillage*, were very imperfect, and so, for a long period, remained. The genius of the country then, and for many centuries afterwards, was *pastoral*. The *farming*, up to the Reformation, was in fact "grazing," animal food being the diet of the people, and grain, except for purposes of brewing and the fodder of cattle, comparatively neglected. Out of this neglect of tillage arose this custom, in which is to be found the origin of the common lands, that persons, allowed by their landlords to inclose and till land, used, for their husbandry-cattle, *one large common pasture*, into which the oxen or horses employed at the plough were turned every evening. As, by degrees, the manorial lords lost their hold of the lands when the feudal system began to decay, and to yield to the blows which the church, then the people's ally, liberally dealt it, and the different freeholds and copyholds, as they began to be termed in more modern times, grew into distinct and independent properties, these "common pastures" formed an exception. The whole face of the country was covered with them. The portion of land, which now constitutes a "township," was sure to include one or more of these common pastures. Hence, as barring the original Norman landlord, nobody could set up, or pretend a distinct title to these tracts, they of necessity remained "common property"; and hence the derivation of the word "common," which by no means denoted *a moor*, or a *barren piece of land*, but included, under that term, some of the best grassland in the kingdom. During what may be called the "time of transition" from the feudal system to the modern tenures of landed estate, this was the position of these "common tracts." As, however, tillage supplanted grazing, and as land became more minutely inclosed, these commons were gradually abandoned by the richer proprietors as inconvenient holdings. At last they became the joint property of the poorer sort, and a *village* or *town* naturally rose upon the verge of each, which was the origin of the "townships," into which the parishes came to be divided. From this statement, it is easy to deduce the great extent and value of these lands, and the immense resource which they must, through some centuries, have afforded to the poorer part of the population.

Such, up to A.D. 1509, which was the date of the accession of the grand robber, Henry VIII., was the state of the less wealthy portion of the people, as regarded these lands. After that epoch, events gave rise to causes, and these causes alternately to other events, which, at last, in their effects, produced a wresting of these lands from the poor, under colour of law. The real "tap-root" of the whole mischief may undoubtedly be traced up to those fatal acts of Henry VI., which arose out of the succession dispute, and which limited the parliamentary elective-franchise to a narrow class, the "forty shilling *freeholders*." Out of the supineness and general corruption of these electors, came the slavish and corrupt parliaments who truckled to Henry VIII.; and in the poverty just created by the seizure of the church-lands under the pretence of "reformation" by this monstrous tyrant, lies the germ of the loss of the common lands by the poor. This was the *first* cause; a *second*, still more powerful, was the rapid rise in prices caused by the opening of the American mines, and the *rapid diffusion of gold and silver* at this period. This wonderful advance in prices was one of the helping causes of the extension of tillage, and the decay of grazing and pasturage which ensued, arising out of the more rapid returns which tillage afforded. The change in the diet of the people, consequent upon this, and upon their greater poverty, gave a stimulus to the growth of population which has continued down to this time.—Thus it went on. As the population grew and swelled, the necessity of recurring to the cheaper diet of grain and potatoes instead of butchers'-meat, grew, as a matter of course, along with it. After the funding-system commenced, the pressure of taxation aggravated all these causes, still more and more. At last, the stoppage of the bank, in 1797, let out *the paper money in full swing;* and as the prices of produce rose, the profits from tillage appeared so rapid and so constant, that the landlords and their tenants, not content with ploughing up the old pastures in their hands, waxed insatiably covetous of the bulk of the common lands that up to that time remained in the hands of the poor; and in a few years, by means of "inclosure bills," the poor were bereaved of the whole! The first blow was certainly struck in the reign of Queen Anne; but the following brief return of the numbers of the "inclosure bills" passed at different periods, proves that the grand confiscation was caused by the issues and the taxes of 1797, which made the temptation of such acquisitions as these, to be irresistible by the land-owners of that period.

ENCLOSURE ACTS.

In the reign of	Queen Anne - - - - - -	3
	George the I. - - - - -	16
	George the II. - - - -	226
George III.	up to A.D. 1797. - - - -	1532
	afterwards - - - - -	2287
		4064

The number of acres inclosed from 1760, through the agency of these confiscating acts, are stated by Mr. Porter, as follows. The amount is enormous; but, for the reasons before adduced, I am of opinion the statement is not far from the truth.

AMOUNT OF COMMON LANDS INCLOSED

(From Porter's Progress of the Nation).

from 1760 to 1770 - - -	704,550 acres.
1770 to 1780 - -	1,207,800
1780 to 1790 - - -	450,180
1790 to 1800 - - -	858,270
1800 to 1810 - -	1,550,010
1810 to 1820 - -	1,556,990
1820 to 1830 - - -	375,150
1830 to 1834 - - -	133,590
Total	6,836,540 acres

As this does not include the two hundred and forty-five bills passed before the year 1760, the whole number of acres, so taken, must probably exceed *seven millions* which, at *fifteen shillings per acre*, would be, in round numbers, worth *five millions sterling per annum*.

The manner in which this swindle was effected, was in substance, this. It was assumed that the landlords, whose estates bounded these commons, were the owners in chief. In each act a clause was inserted, to enable the commissioners to pay such poor persons as claimed stints by prescription certain sums to "alienate." This they were compelled to take; and then the whole common was divided by the landowners of the vicinage, who could set up anything in the shape of claim. That these landowners could have no valid equitable claim is clear enough. If we trace back for titles, we must come to the feudal barons and manorial lords, who got these lands by conquest under the Norman. Barring them, the equity clearly resides in the inhabitant poor of the townships, whose rights rest on the usage and prescription of centuries. In them, however, there could be no power to *alienate;* because the possessors at any one time of the usufruct of these lands could have only a life-interest. They neither did nor could pretend to the power to devise away these lands from their posterity: and if they could not devise, they could neither sell nor mortgage. The law, however, was in the keeping of parliaments, chosen by landlords almost exclusively, and chiefly composed of them; and they passed the bills without "lett, hindrance, or molestation."

Whilst this process of bereavement was in rapid progress, it cannot be a matter of wonder that the poor-rate should rapidly increase. In the year 1803 it had reached the large amount of £5,348,204: a sum equal to Queen Anne's entire revenue, when Marlborough and his allies were beating the armies of the haughty Louis XIV. It is equally as little to be wondered at, that the public mind should now begin to show symptoms of change. In addition to the discontent naturally caused by the now enormous burthens upon the nation, all the minister's schemes had been productive only of a series of disappointment and disaster. Napoleon Buonaparte, under the title of "first consul," was now, not only virtually the autocrat of France, but of Europe. The war seemed to be totally hopeless as to results; and the minister Pitt, the ostensible cause, at all events, of this desperate position of affairs, was at length obliged to retire, and yield his place to a successor who might, peradventure, negotiate a peace with the victorious French people, and their extraordinary ruler. The events which followed this change we must reserve for another letter.

LETTER IX.

ADDINGTON SUCCEEDS PITT AS MINISTER.—NEGOTIATES THE PEACE OF AMIENS.—STATE OF THE EXCHANGES CAUSED BY THE DEPRECIATION OF THE BANK NOTES.—RENEWAL OF THE BANK RESTRICTION ACT UNTIL MARCH, 1803.—ADDINGTON'S SINKING FUND, ITS ABSURDITY.—BANK RESTRICTION ACT RENEWED A SECOND TIME.—WAR BREAKS OUT AGAIN.—PITT AGAIN MINISTER.—BATTLE OF AUSTERLITZ.—DEATH OF PITT.—PERCEVAL BECOMES MINISTER.—THE POLITICAL ECONOMISTS IN PARLIAMENT.—BULLION COMMITTEE APPOINTED.—ITS MEMBERS.—ITS REPORT; WHICH ASSERTS THE DEPRECIATION OF THE PAPER.—VANSITTART'S RESOLUTIONS.—LORD KING'S NOTICE TO HIS TENANTRY.—STANHOPE'S ACT.—PERCEVAL SHOT.—END OF THE WAR.—DEBT AND POOR-RATES UP TO 1815.

When the minister Pitt, fairly cowed, as it were, by the splendid success of that wonderful general Napoleon, now first consul of France, retired from office, in 1801, in order to allow of peace being negotiated with the victorious French nation; he was succeeded by Addington, a man destitute of talent, contemptible in influence, shallow in acquirements, and on the whole, only fitted for that, for which he was really intended, a "*locum tenens*," to keep the place warm for him who had just quitted, and who meaned soon to resume it. Before entering upon the detail of the extraordinary financial deeds, or rather pranks, of this man, it is proper to note that Pitt, immediately before resigning, had perfected the measure of the union between Ireland and Great Britain. This act, however important politically as completing the slavery of the Irish, was a financial move of small account. The landlords of that ill-fated country had ever resisted the introduction of poor-laws similar to those of England. Free from this check upon their rapacity, they had, long before the union, reduced the mass of the Irish people to the condition of paupers. Where the millions are destitute, taxes cannot be paid. Where the landlord swallows all, the government must go without. The union, therefore, only united an empty exchequer to that of England, and saved nothing but the keeping of separate accounts.

Addington succeeded Pitt as minister late in the year 1801; and, in 1802, the short-lived peace of Amiens was concluded with France. In a state of affairs like that of England, however, peace itself could be only a fountain of fresh troubles; and so the new premier quickly found it. The last "bank restriction act" of Pitt, had provided that the directors should begin to pay their notes again in gold and silver, "within *one month* after the signature of a definitive treaty of peace." Peace had now come; "definitive treaty" and all; but with a country over which were now floating untold millions of bank-notes, of all sorts and sizes, for which specie *might be* demanded. This was no experiment to be rashly ventured; and the first care of the new minister was to invent, and get the nation to swallow, some sleeveless excuse, or juggling pretext, for putting off the evil day. The necessity for this Addington, dull and empty as he was, had instinct enough to see or feel; and he lost no time in setting about it. On the 9th of April, 1802, the minister accordingly proposed that "the bank restriction act" should be continued, until March 1st, 1803; which bill, after some ineffectual remonstrances, passed on the 30th of April; being a continuance of ten months to the inconvertible paper.

With the very breath in which he made this proposal, the minister asserted, in terms the most unqualified, both "the ability and willingness of the bank to pay its notes on demand;" but he added he feared it would be "inconvenient" to do so, because "the *exchanges* were against this country, which, in case of gold payments at the bank, might cause the guineas to be exported abroad." Astounding as it may seem, this was, in reality, a lie; though perhaps a sort of "*white lie.*" The truth was, that, upon the balance of trade, the exchanges were *not* against this country, though, to persons uninitiated in the trickery of finances, the contrary might seem to be the case. The deception was this. In taking the ordinary exchanges, the currencies of the two countries are always supposed to be measured by a metallic standard; and the *par* of exchange is supposed to exist when a bill, on *Paris*, for instance, for a certain number of Louis or Napoleons, sells in England for the exact number of sovereigns that will balance the French coin, gold against gold, according to their relative fineness. When this is not the case; and when gold appears to be more valuable in Paris than in London, by the bill on Paris selling for more sovereigns than the *par* of exchange requires, then is the balance of trade against England as well as the exchange, because it is only a *scarcity of bills on Paris*, arising from our having *a balance to pay to France*, that causes this advance in the price of the bills. When, however, the currency of one of the countries is *depreciated* by issues of an excessive quantity of inconvertible paper, as was the case here, then, be the balance of trade what it may, the rate of exchange must always *appear* to be against that country. It must be so, because, bills of exchange on the other country being payable in gold or silver, no one will sell such a bill if he is to be paid in paper, except he gets as much paper as the gold would be worth for which the bill is drawn. A bill on Paris for a dozen Louis d'ors would, at that time, command about *three ounces, troy, of gold;* but gold in England at that period being probably about *fine pounds an ounce*, if bought with paper, such a bill would sell for about fifteen pounds in Bank notes, which was then the only money, except a few bad shillings, circulating in England; and, hence the exchange was sure to be, in appearance, against England, be the balance of imports and exports what it might. As, before the depreciation of the British currency, the guinea and the Louis d'or were not very different in value, Addington was right enough in supposing, that, if the bank began to pay in guineas, under such circumstances, the coin was sure either to be melted or sent abroad. The extremity of folly and ignorance was, in supposing that time could cure this, or that it could be remedied in any way, other than by drawing in such a quantity of the paper as would have made the English currency of its former value when gold was in circulation. The event showed this; for when the first of March,

1803, came, "the exchanges" were as awkward as ever, and the sage house had to pass another bill to "continue" the restriction until after the next meeting of that august assembly! Before that happened, war broke out again; and the house, without more ado, passed a bill to continue "restriction" until "six months after the signature of a definitive treaty of peace"—a period at that time nearly equivalent to "to-morrow come never";—and so the affair ended for the time.

When the premier had got the ticklish affair of the resumption of cash payments staved off, he found time to commence and perfect one of the most absurd financial ideas that ever struck root in the diseased compost of mortal brain; and which, if it had been found in the pages of Rabelais, would have been deemed extravagant even there! This was the never-to-be-forgotten Addingtonian "sinking fund," or, a scheme to *pay off* the national debt by means of *borrowed money*—a scheme unmatched even in "the academy of Laputa." How this monstrous piece of folly ever found its way to the heads of the ministry, it is difficult to imagine—(Dr. Price's calculations as to the powers of a system of compound interest have been quoted as the moving cause); but how a folly so enormous should have been believed by nine-tenths of the educated classes, including Lords and Commons, is absolutely inconceivable, unless we are to consider English gullibility as a sort of epidemic national fatuity.

Conceivable or not conceivable, however, the House of Commons of 1802, was brought by Addington, assisted, as it is correctly asserted, by Pitt, whose intellects must then have been getting obscured, to sanction this preposterous scheme. At this time, there were one or more loans contracted for every year; and portions of these were put into the hands of commissioners, who bought up old debt by means of new, and went on receiving the interest, adding to the succeeding loans for the purpose of further purchases of the old debt. Incredible as it may appear, people were taught to believe that by this process, the national debt might be cancelled in the course of a few *(forty or fifty)* years; and to *doubt this* was esteemed a sort of treason, or at all events "jacobinism" of the blackest dye! The concoctors of this precious fund, forgot that "compound interest," in its abstract and extended meaning, in which the interest is supposed to accumulate day by day, is a mere "mathematical chimera," incapable of being realised. They forgot the expenses of the commissioners; the effect of their purchases in raising the price of the old stock, and the loss to be incurred by negotiating the new loans in the midst of reverses and defeats. All this they forgot; and this contemptible *hocus-pocus* was permitted to go on, the debt growing, during the greater part of the time, larger and larger, until the accession of George the IV, in 1820, when the ministers, tired of paying the interest, cancelled, as a beginning, £12,000,000 of stock in the hands of the commissioners of the juggle. By another act passed the same year, they cancelled fifty millions more; and so went on, until the whole "fund," as it was called, was annihilated in reality; though an act still exists which directs one fourth part of any *surplus revenue* (if there be any) shall be applied to the reduction of the debt:—that is to say the act of the 9th of George IV., cap 92; hitherto an almost dead letter; or in strict truth quite so, so far as "surplus revenue" is concerned.

The shortness of Addington's administration made this freak of a "sinking fund" made of *borrowed money*, the only one of magnitude which he found time to play. As soon as the war recommenced with France, Pitt again became minister, and expended his few remaining energies and enormous sums of money in getting together that coalition against her, which Napoleon, now emperor, crushed at the decisive field of Austerlitz. The miserable minister sank under the blow. He had, for some years, been accustomed to lull the gnawing stings of chagrin and remorse by copious vinous libations, which, together with wearing anxiety, now brought him to the grave, a debilitated dropsical, imbecile, old man, at a period of life when other men are mostly in the pride and prime of their intellect. He expired in a small house on the edge of Wimbledon common, whither he had retired from Downing-street to die: a sad proof how one false step could ruin for ever the peace, the fame, and the name of a man born of illustrious parentage, educated in every good principle, and virtuous intention, trusted by both sovereign and people, and, though over-rated, of talents far from contemptible and acquirements far from mean. From the time of his death, the war went on under various administrations, first of the Whigs, then of Perceval, and then of Lord Liverpool; every year adding to the debt, and every year, until 1812, seeming to render the conflict more and more hopeless. When Pitt expired, he died with an exclamation in his mouth, which proved, that, whilst destroying himself, he felt he had, also, been perhaps the destroyer of his country; and for some years after, events certainly seemed to conspire to convince the survivors that he had "harped his fear aright." It is, however, with the financial events of these years that we have to do; nor were they devoid of interest.

In the first place, however, it ought to be observed that from and after the death of Mr. Pitt, in 1806, public opinion as to the disastrous contest that was raging, underwent a change that continued to grow until the end of the war. The writings of Major Cartwright, as to a reform of the parliament and its necessity, as well as justice, began to attract attention. The famous John Horne Tooke had exposed many of the insidious evils of the system. But, above all, the powers of the celebrated and unrivalled William Cobbett, whose Political Register was now widely circulated, produced an impression upon the national mind that could never be effaced, and the happy effects of which we are feeling to this day. It now began to be generally seen, that we had been plunged into a disastrous and bloody war, not for any really national purpose, but to prevent the high-spirited and brave French people from choosing, as they had an undoubted right to do, their own form of government; and that this war, amongst other evil results, threatened, in its ultimate consequence, to place the financial affairs of the country in a position of hopeless and irretrievable confusion and ruin. These opinions found their way by degrees into the House of Commons. The total disappearance of the coinage, and the high price of gold and silver bullion, were noticed and commented upon. The debased and depreciated state of the paper currency was asserted and deprecated; until, at last, in spite of all the efforts of the government to stifle this sort of discussion, the "political economists," as they were now called, forced the appointment of a committee of inquiry, which was known by the name of "the bullion committee," to whose deeds we shall shortly have to advert. It was in vain that the adherents of the ministry argued, that because a one-pound note and a shilling would, in the open market for commodities, purchase as much as a guinea, the paper *could not be depreciated.* It was replied, and most justly, that the paper, to use the words of Mr. Paine "pulled down the coin along with it" in the open market; but that, as in spite of all penalties, guineas secretly sold at the rate of twenty-eight shillings each, when paid for in paper, here was ample proof of the real depreciation of the paper currency, as compared with the currencies of other countries to which the coin so bought was sent. Under the guidance of Mr. Vansittart, the secretary of the exchequer or treasury at that time, the house was, even, at last, induced to pass a resolution which formally negatived the assertion of the economists. The men of the "bullion committee," however, resolutely stuck to their own opinion; and to their proceedings and the report which they, at last, when formed into a committee, presented to parliament, we shall now turn.

The "bullion committee" was appointed, and sat in the year 1810; and amongst its members, whose number was twenty-two, were included those members of the House of Commons, who had the reputation of being most learned and sage in the recondite matters of circulation, exchanges, and all the various mysterious money affairs with which this famous committee was to deal. Amongst the most prominent names are Francis Horner (chairman); Spencer Perceval, chancellor of the Exchequer; George Tierney; Henry Parnell; Alexander Baring; Wm. Manning, bank director; Pascoe Grenfell; and last, though not least, Mr. Huskisson. This last gentleman, who afterwards played a distinguished part amongst the political economists, was a man of singularly supple talents and address. He began life as a democratical politician, and was at one time, it has been said, a member of the "Jacobin Club," at Paris, in company with Robespierre, Danton, and the rest of the extreme party, then called "The Mountain." From this ticklish position, he soon found it advisable to remove himself; and making his way over to England, he contrived by some means or other, not exactly known, however guessed at, to get introduced to the notice of Mr. Pitt, who, in due time, found him a useful tool. He had, of course, by this time "put away" as the scripture phrase is, his jacobinical theories, as no longer either agreeable or useful; but, in lieu of them, he took to free-thinking in political economy, and the *vexata quæstio* of the currency. He made his way quickly into parliament; and being an eminent dealer in shallow, but nicely and cleverly constructed plausibilities, he became, naturally, a star in the sky of the new economy, and, next to Horner, the chairman, the "great gun" of the committee.

It was in the year 1811, that the report of this

famous committee was laid before parliament and printed. In some respects, it is a rather able document, although the measures recommended in it were, to a wonderful extent, rash and absurd. The evidence got together by the committee, and their reasoning from that evidence, established the fact of the depreciation of the paper money, to the satisfaction of all sensible men capable of understanding the question; notwithstanding the sophistries of Perceval, the Chancellor of Exchequer, and the preposterous resolution of his egregious secretary, Vansittart. The absurd position, that it was gold which had *risen*, and not bank notes which had *fallen* in value, they effectually negatived, by the production of witnesses, who proved that there had been no alteration upwards in the value of gold on the continent or any where else; and they showed that the coin had disappeared because it was worth more, when melted, than when circulating as coinage, in company with the depreciated and degraded paper-currency. Had they stopped here, their report would have done credit to their sagacity and to their wisdom; but here they unluckily did not stop. After proving to their hearts' content that the depreciation of which they complained, was owing to the enormous issues of the Bank of England and of the country banks, which were at this time beyond all precedent as to extent, they went on to recommend, without the addition of any preparatory measures to smooth the way for such a step, that these issues should be in a great measure withdrawn, and the Bank of England compelled to resume cash payments in the short space of *two years!* Had this suggestion been hazarded in the midst of a profound peace, it would have been *wild* enough, unaccompanied as it was by any auxiliary measures: but in the midst of an almost hopeless war, which, carried on as it was by huge half-yearly or yearly loans, rendered these extended issues inevitable, the recommendation seemed to smack of a degree of fatuity, that looked like political insanity. The funded debt, putting Exchequer bills out of the question, had by this time reached the enormous sum of *five hundred millions sterling!* The circulation of the Bank of England, from *eleven millions*, which was its full extent in 1797, had grown to *twenty-one millions*, and the circulation of the country banks, which were now fully *seven hundred* in number, probably, could the truth be got at, exceeded a good deal that of the Bank of England. Yet, in the face of all this, with war raging round them, here was a set of men, presuming upon their peculiar wisdom and knowledge of national affairs, rash and mad enough to call upon the bank to draw in these issues by one half, and then pay the remainder in gold and silver! The houses of parliament had too much caution and common-sense to adopt, at this period, such a precious piece of counsel; but the tendering it did no good to the credit of "the new-light," which, after this, was little heard of, until the conclusion of the war some few years after.

In the mean time, the depreciation of the bank-notes, as the quantities in circulation were augmented year after year, went on at a rapid pace, producing all the appearances that attend such a state of the currency; an enhancement in the prices of every thing that is bought and sold, and an ever-craving, never-satisfied itch of speculation and gambling, in the place of wholesome and natural trade. The period, however, was not without symptoms, that distrust as to the stability of this state of affairs had begun at times to exert an influence on the public mind; and that men, at length, began to bethink themselves of asking what might be *the end* of all this? In the September of the year 1810, a loan of fourteen millions was taken by the rich Loan-mongers Baring and Co., and Goldschmidt and Co., and suddenly fell to a discount, in consequence, it was thought, of the "*sudden death*" of Sir Francis Baring. Panic ensued: and such was the distrust abroad, that the discount upon the "omnium," or "scrip," was as much as *six per cent.!* The end of Goldschmidt soon ensued. His "scrip" was mostly unsold; and the loss was more than his means would stand. Forsaken of his god, gold, he retired in a state of despair to a "water-closet," and there shot himself, after, it was said, a vain attempt to cut his throat. The deed, the place, and the martyr, were worthy of each other, and afford hints for an epitaph by which his executors failed to profit. His tomb is therefore unrhymed upon! It has been said of this man, that, not many days before his catastrophe, he offered a young lady, who pleased him with a song, a "*slice of the loan*" as a complimentary and jocular recompense. Alas! Fate was in the strain; and, in a week's time, it was *at a discount*, and *not* "worth an old song!" "*Sic transit gloria.*"

This was tragical enough, as far as it concerned Goldschmidt the Jew: but the extraordinary "notice" which, during the following year, 1811, an influential and sagacious nobleman, Lord King, issued to his tenantry, had like to have become much more so to the paper-money itself. Determined to escape, if possible, from the loss which the rapid depreciation of the paper-money brought upon him, Lord King issued a notice to all his tenants who held *old leases*, declaring to them that, in consequence of the depreciated state of the paper circulation, he could no longer accept of Bank-notes in payment. That he did not wish to give unnecessary trouble, nor to exact any payment of any other value than that stipulated for in the lease. That he was willing to receive payment, therefore, in three different ways, as each might be convenient. 1st. By payment *in guineas*. 2nd. By payment in Portugal gold coin, equal in weight to the guineas requisite to discharge the rent. 3rd. By a payment in *Bank-notes* of such a sum as would, *at the then market price of gold bullion*, purchase gold enough to *equalise this with the two former payments*. This was the substance of the famous notice of Lord King, which was, at first, misunderstood and despised by the stupid ministry of the period; but which, had it been carried into execution, would have put the paper ultimately, at an *open discount*, all over the kingdom, and, in the end, have established *two prices* for all commodities whatsoever; a *paper price*, and a *gold and silver price;* thus striking at the very credit, nay, the very existence, of the debased paper! Strange to say, this peril was not seen by Perceval, at that time prime-minister, nor by his stolid cabinet; but it was immediately perceived by another member of the House of Peers, Lord Stanhope, who, forthwith, on his own responsibility, brought before the Peers a bill prohibiting, under penalties, Bank-notes from being covenanted to be taken at *less* than their *nominal* value, or coin being passed at *more* than *its nominal value* in paper. When this bill came to the second reading, the stupid ministers had become awake to the necessity of hurrying it through the Houses, and, under their adoption, it was passed at once. Had it not been so passed, all the landlords in the kingdom would soon have followed Lord King's example, and the open discount, *once established*, could not have been cured by after-legislation, which it would have become easy to evade, so profitable would have become this general traffic of coin for paper. As amongst his other measures, Lord Stanhope, had introduced a clause protecting from *distress for rent*, any tenant who tendered it in notes, of the Bank of England, there wanted now only one step to make the paper-money compulsory in law, as it was virtually in fact; and this step was to *formally bar all suits at law* for any other sort of payment. To this, however, the ministers were not driven to resort. The sudden fate of Perceval by the pistol of Bellingham, and the change of affairs brought about by the Russian Campaign of 1812, turned public attention into a totally new channel and direction; and the paper-money went on, unquestioned, to the end of the war, and the grand crisis of Waterloo, in June, 1815.

It is, of course, foreign to the purpose of these

letters to detail the various vicissitudes of that warfare, which raged from 1811 to Waterloo's "crowning carnage." I shall not even enlarge upon the probable motives which induced the English Government to wink at the sailing of Napoleon from the Isle of Elba to the Bay of Juan! That they did so there is strong reason to believe; and certainly unindebted, untithed, and almost untaxed France, must have appeared, to their vision, a more deadly and rankling thorn in the side in peace, than she had even proved in war! The conflict of Waterloo, however, as the third mortal peril through which the system was doomed to pass, must not be passed over in silence. It was, indeed, a crisis! Had the Prussian allies, on that eventful evening, failed to find, by some strange accident, that onward road which General Grouchy so unaccountably lost, and the event of the dice been reversed, even then might we have bid "good night!" to our funding and our paper. A great victory gained by Buonaparte, at that critical period, must, inevitably, in its consequences, have added *another brace of hundred millions* to the debt; and *this*, in conjunction with the measures which would have equally followed in that case, as they did follow the event which actually came to pass, would (as Mercutio says) have been "enough." Eight millions *additional* of annual interest, with the currency bill of Peel in their wake, would have swamped all: but it was ordered otherwise. Grouchy lost his way, and Blucher found it: and England, after a quarter of a century of war, was once more at peace. That quarter of a century had, however, changed the face of England more than two preceding centuries had changed it. That 18th of June, 1815, on which the conflict of Waterloo was won, may be fairly noted in the calendar as the top of the spring-tide of the modern English system; and that peace which followed it as the beginning of troubles. This was, in truth, its last real triumph: but before we examine the theory of effects which immediately followed that triumph, it is proper that we should note *first* the precise and actual financial and monetary position of the country, as it was left by this great event; and *next* the multiform and astounding changes which had been scattered over the entire surface of society, in the course of the long and desperate struggle of which this battle was the "grand finale." First, then, as to the money-matters.

It has been well remarked by Mr. Samuel Wells, the author of a luminous view of "The Revenue and Expenditure of Great Britain," that, such is the state of confusion and intricacy in which the public accounts are kept, it is almost impossible for any one to be sure of the real amount of the enormous debt which succeeding Governments have contracted. The following, however, appears to me to be a tolerably accurate statement of the position of the debt as it stood at the conclusion of the war in 1814. It is certainly accurate enough for all *practical* purposes; and he who is not satisfied by it as to the situation into which his country has been plunged, by a series of misgovernment unmatched in the annals of this world, must be hard to please upon such subjects.

GOVERNMENT DEBT.

As it stood on the 1*st of February*, 1815.

	£	s.	d.
Bank of England and Annuities, 1751 -	12,686,600	0	0
South-Sea Annuities, old and new -	25,984,684	13	11½
Consolidated Annuities - - - -	362,928,558	4	5¼
Reduced Annuities - - - - -	168,794,022	0	1
4 per Cent Consolidated Annuities -	74,077,744	2	2
5 per Cent. Consolidated Annuities -	106,062,254	13	7
Annuities 1797 and 1802 - - -	1,438,938	14	0
English total Debt - - - - -	£751,973,002	8	2¾
Irish unredeemed Debt - - -	120,862,338	14	5
Total Great Britain and Ireland - -	£872,835,341	2	7¾

UNFUNDED DEBT.

Exchequer Bills and Demands notpaid, 5*th January* 1815.

	£	s.	d.
Exchequer Bills, provided and unprovided for	57,941,700	0	0
Treasury Bills, etc. etc. - - - -	2,287,597	10	5
Army, Navy, Ordnance, Civil List, and Barracks	8,351,226	19	11¼
Irish unfunded Debts - - - - -	2,737,018	6	8
Total Unfunded - - - - -	£71,317,542	16	0¼

With a mixed account like this to deal with, it is impossible to say the exact amount of annual interest entailed by it upon the country; but the interest, *at the moment*, could not be under *thirty-three* or *thirty-four millions sterling*. The great reduction in the current rate of interest of money, which ensued when the war was concluded, enabled the Government afterwards to reduce this interest very considerably, the very immensity of the plunder thus tending, in some degree, to counteract itself. At the period of the close of the war, however, the enormity of the burden which it had laid upon the nation, astounded the few who deigned to reflect at all upon such topics, and ought to have damped the silly and short-sighted braggings and boastings to which the apparent triumph gave rise all over the country. The "collapse," however, had hardly then begun to be felt.

As the burden of the debt and taxes went on in its march, it is needless almost to say, that the burden of the poor-rates naturally and necessarily joined and kept step in that movement. There are no returns of the annual amounts of this rate to be relied upon, extending throughout the period of the war. The following, however, are in the main correct, and are sufficiently instructive as to the point of inquiry now before us.

POOR-RATES.

A.D. 1801	-	£4,800,000	
1803	-	5,348,204	
1812-13	-	8,640,842	(scarcity.)
1813-14	-	8,388,974	
1814-15	-	7,457,676	
1815-16	-	6,937,425	

Such were the direct monetary effects of this war, carried on by means of loans upon loans, and these borrowings transacted by means of an inconvertible paper-money, every year depreciating in *actual*, though bearing the same *nominal* value. The other varied and lamentable changes produced by this dreadful process, continued over the long period of *twenty-two years*, must be the subject of another letter. I shall only remark here, that these changes may be naturally and usefully divided into two distinct classes:—*first*, there are those which actually took place betwixt the years 1793 and 1816; and, *secondly*, there are those for which the foundation was laid during that period, but which showed themselves more palpably after the close of the war. Amongst the first, may, for instance, be classed the extraordinary advance in all rentals and profits, an advance partly nominal and partly real, and its consequences and effects upon society. Amongst the second may be placed the inroads upon the rights of the poor, the increase of crime, and various other phenomena, which shall be treated of in their proper places. To this salutary *exposé*, I shall devote our next Letter.

Before we take our tenth Letter actually in hand, however, it is necessary to note, that the short hostilities which ended in the battle of Waterloo, did not, upon the face of the account, much alter the Government debt as it stood in January, 1815. During the short interval of peace which intervened betwixt the return from Elba of the emperor and his original forced retirement thither, considerable sums, in the shape of "Exchequer bills due," had been run off; and this enabled the ministers to provide, by immediate issues of new bills, for much of the *immediate* expense which the short war in 1815 entailed upon them. This famous battle, nevertheless, in its after-effects, added enormously to the burdens of the people, in the shape of half-pay and military pensions, owing to the great promotions in rank which followed it, and the reckless profusion and extravagance with which pensions of all sorts were, during the madness of the period, granted by the Government. These imposts were afterwards put together under the odd title of the "Dead-weight," of which we shall see more hereafter. In the meantime, we turn to those equally curious topics, which are to form the subject-matter of our Tenth Letter.

LETTER X.

EFFECTS OF THE ENORMOUS LOANS AND INCONVERTIBLE PAPER.—RAPID EXTENSION OF COTTON FACTORIES.—PROFITS OF THE LOANS, MATERIALS FOR MORE.—THE DRAWING UP OF MONEY INTO HEAPS IN THE HANDS OF THE MIDDLE CLASS.—THE EXTRAORDINARY INCREASE IN THE LEGACY AND PROBATE DUTIES.—DETERIORATING CONDITION OF THE WORKING CLASS.—SCHEMES AGAINST THE POOR-LAWS, MATURED BY THE POLITICAL ECONOMISTS.—THE SYSTEM OF MALTHUS FIRST PUBLISHED.—PATRONISED BY THE ECONOMISTS.—CHAPLIN'S SPILSBY POOR-BILL, DEFEATED.—STURGES BOURNE'S POOR-BILLS, CARRIED IN 1818.—RAPID INCREASE OF CRIME.—ANNUAL COMMITMENTS FROM 1806.—STRIKING CHANGE IN MANNERS.—EFFECTS ON DOMESTIC COMFORT, ON MORALITY, AND ON SCIENCE AND LITERATURE.

WE are now to make a pause in the course of our inquiry into the tissue of strange events, and still stranger schemes and notions, amidst which this history conducts us, in order to note and examine some of the most striking of those changes, which were necessary consequences of the extraordinary transactions which took place during the twenty-two years that elapsed between Pitt's declaration of war in 1793, and the peace of 1815. It is true, that many of these changes did not develop themselves, to their full extent, during the period I have mentioned. But it was during these twenty-two years of war, loans, and paper-money, that their seeds were sown. I deem it best, therefore, to put them upon record, and to describe them now; reserving to myself the power to revert to them, if necessary, at some later stage of my narrative.

The first of these phenomena which attracts attention, is the birth and growth of the system of manufacturing by machinery; and more especially that portion of it respecting which we have heard so much under the name of "the Cotton Trade," with all its effects, moral and physical, upon the welfare and happiness of society in this country. The reader is already aware, that the *germ* of the system of superseding manual labour by means of machines, began to appear at the end of the American war, when the weight of the taxes and the distress caused by the sudden diminution of the issues of the Bank, at the conclusion of that disastrous conflict, put men upon drawing upon their ingenuity to find cheaper methods of making fabrics, which the people now began to be unable to buy at their ancient prices, with the additions which the heavy taxation of the country of course laid upon those prices. When the spinster, and the knitter, and the weaver, and the bleacher, and the dyer, found the cost of their living enhanced by the taxes upon the articles which they consumed, they, as a matter of necessity, laid that added cost upon the prices of the articles in which they dealt. But as the cost of these things rose, the means of the people to buy them were decreasing. Hence, the necessity of new and strange devices to "cheapen labour," as it was termed; which means, either to compel him or her who toils, to toil for less; or, to supersede that human toil altogether, and get it performed by machines made of iron and wood, which, when set up, can work, in a great measure, independently of the human hand, and without much cost beyond that of their setting up, and setting in motion. The machines which worked these changes, were the steam-engine of Watt, the spinning jenny, the mule, and other apparatus of Arkwright, and of Crompton, and the power-loom of Dr. Cartwright. They were to be sure backed out by a host of minor contrivances; but these were the principal; and, amongst the first fruits, they, for the most part, brought their inventors fortune as well as fame. Under a proper system, the employment of machinery cannot be an evil; but where the value of every thing is measured, as in England by money, and by money alone;—where the consequences of things, as respects national morality, or national happiness, are put aside as unworthy of notice, amidst the calculation of profits and the summing up of pounds sterling; these inventions may, and do bring with them, many evils. So it was in this instance. No one deemed the labourers, who were thus deprived of employment, worth a thought. Instead of being cared for, they were left to the comfort of a metaphor, and told to open out or seek "new channels of industry."

If little thought was bestowed upon the labourers displaced; still less was wasted upon those who under the new dispensation suddenly obtained places. These machines, although they rejected the aid of man, sought that of women and of children. Under due regulations, this might not have been a great disadvantage; but regulation was not thought of. The consequence was, that first hundreds, and then thousands, of these unfortunate creatures were torn from the pursuits natural to their sex and age, and shut up in the newly-invented mills, to spend a short, over-toiled, and diseased life, amidst heat, dust, and smoke, under circumstances not only destructive of all morality, but destructive of all their real usefulness as members of a civilised and rational society, where human beings are of more account than mere beasts of burthen. To shut out, however, thousands upon thousands of human creatures from the means of learning any of those duties which accountable and civilised beings ought to know—to doom them to an utter ignorance of even the commonest arts and services of life—to destroy, not only their physical utility, but their moral culture—in short, to steep them in one sickening stew of ignorance, disease, and vice—was held as nothing, when profits were to be calculated, and custom-house returns summed up; and whilst the work went on, amidst the applauses of selfish and mercenary economists, and the delight of unscrupulous ministers of state, parish pauper children were ransacked from all parts of the kingdom, and sold, as slaves are sold, by hireling overseers, to propagate a race of slaves more stunted in health, mind, and body than themselves, and end a short and miserable life beneath the wheels of the "Juggernaut" of the spindle, now the god of English idolatry. Such are the abuses, not the uses, of machinery.

That this violent and unnatural change in the habits of numbers, intended by Nature to be rationally industrious and moral members of society, has, in conjunction with other changes, made fearful havoc with much of the comfort of society in England, cannot be doubted. But there were other evils still in reserve, to be overlooked or despised as the former had been. It was obvious enough, from the beginning, that the cupidity of trade, once in possession of a power of production, such as is given by almost self-acting machines, was sure, if unchecked by salutary laws, to push production, in the end, to an extent that must ultimately recoil upon itself, and upon the unfortunate beings whose very existence was involved in its undisturbed continuance. Circumstances seemed, also, to conspire to bring about this consequence. In due time it followed: and when the continent of Europe had been deluged with the cheap and flimsy productions which, in spite of war and its prohibitions, were forced throughout its marts, not a habitable spot in the globe, where a market might be found, was left unsought, and Asia, Africa, and America, seemed too narrow for the *avalanche* of stuffs that was prepared for them. The revolutions that, in the sure course of time, beset the progress of this attempted monopoly, we shall have to contemplate hereafter. In the meantime, to get some idea of the strides with which the manufacturing system went forward, we may examine the following table of the quantities of raw cotton worked up at different periods. They would seem incredible to any one who was ignorant of the means employed; and when he was told that the spinning of wool, flax, and silk, are only second to that of cotton, the whole would seem a dream, or a miracle, rather than a matter of sober reality. One part of the delusion in which the whole of this strange process is steeped, is certainly betrayed by this view of them. We see in the quantities consumed, the real flimsiness of the articles substituted for the home-made fabrics worn by our ancestors; and are at once led to detect the truth, that the cheapness of the produce of machinery is in a great degree *apparent* rather than *real*; and that we often actually lose in strength and durability double of all that we seem to gain in price.

CONSUMPTION OF RAW COTTON.

				lbs.
In 1785 the Cotton wrought up was			-	17,992,882
1801	"	"	-	54,203,433
1805	"	"	-	58,873,163
1810	"	"	-	123,701,826
1815	"	"	-	92,525,951
1820	"	"	-	152,829,633
1825	"	"	-	202,546,869
1830	"	"	-	269,616,140
1835	"	"	-	333,043,464

During the greater portion of the war, the part which this manufacturing power, combined with her mastery of the seas, enabled England to play, was certainly an extraordinary one. She was apparently, for years together, shut out from the whole continent of Europe, or nearly so. She had, however, within her reach or power, the raw cotton of America, the flax of Russia, and the sugar and coffee of the West India islands; and within herself, she had the means of manufacturing this flax and this cotton, together with her own wools, to an extent before undreamed of. Thus provided, she was enabled, in spite of hostile decrees and Custom-house prohibitions, by means of neutral colours, forged papers, and counterfeit licenses, to deluge the continent both with manufactured stuffs and with colonial produce; and from the enormous profits reaped in this way, came many of those taxes, which by paying the interest of loans already made, gave the Government courage to contract more.

Whilst this extraordinary process was going on in manufactures, trade, in general, was going through a course very similar. The continued advances in the prices of all sorts of merchandise, caused by the rapid and progressive depreciation of the paper-money, of which fresh bales were every year poured out, occasioned, with some few interruptions, an appearance of growing and perennial prosperity amongst every class, but the class of those who toil. No branch of industry escaped the delusive effects produced by this *plethora* of paper-money, and the enormous extravagance of the Government. Ships were taken up for the transport-service, at tonnage rates which absolutely in some cases cleared the prime cost of the vessel in a period of two years. The rates of insurance paid by both ship-owners and merchants were so high, that many of these companies, who were compelled by their charters to make "a reserve-fund" of all profits which accrued beyond a certain amount, accumulated surplus millions. Enormous fortunes were made by contracts with the Government for the supply of stores and provisions, which were executed with articles of the very worst quality, and the official clerks bribed to "pass" them. Above all, the profits upon some of the loans were so great, that the gains of one might be almost literally said to be capable of affording the means for the next: and this is fully admitted by Sir John Sinclair, who in his History of the Revenue, is honest enough fairly to acknowledge, that it is impossible to account for the existence of the means for supplying the inordinate extravagance of the Government, except by supposing it to be created by means of the depreciating paper, which enabled the fruits of one fraud or peculation to be applied as a foundation for the next. "There is reason to believe, says Sir John (History of the Revenue, vol. ii. cap. 3, p. 138), that out of the *eighteen millions* now annually paid to the public creditors on the debt, funded and unfunded, a sum little short of *one-fifth part* is annually re-invested in the funds; more especially (continues the baronet) in time of war, when the *profit* is *so considerable!*" This was written about 1803; and thus, without an idea of blame, or a breath of reprehension, are a pack of harpies, in rapacity far beyond those fabled by the poets, encouraged to extract compound interest from their country, to a height of usury that must have seemed inordinate even to the conscience of a Jew—if Jews have a conscience.

The great and ultimate effect of this career of pillage and gigantic fraud was, that all men who dealt in produce, farmers, merchants, manufacturers, and traders of all descriptions; all who dealt in money, capitalists, bankers, discounters, loanmongers, stock-jobbers, and speculators of every conceivable kind; and all shipowners, shipbuilders, or persons connected with maritime carriage, as well as speculators in canal shares; and all persons owning the instruments of land carriage, were suddenly put in a position in which profit and wealth flowed in upon them; for as the paper money swelled, the prices and rates of everything grew and rose apace; whilst the receivers of wages, the labourers both agricultural and commercial, were gradually depressed, the rates of wages, generally, not keeping pace with the advance in prices; and hence, whilst the poor-rates grew and increased, money was drawn up into great masses, in the hands of saving persons of the trading and farming classes; whilst, by the inclosure bills, the poor were losing their last hold upon the soil, and were turned over solely to the protection of the poor laws. This source of protection for the unfortunate poor, was not long, it will be seen, in being sapped and mined; but we must, before contemplating the beginnings of this sapping and mining, take a look at the workings of the funding and paper money, in drawing that money together in heaps, in the hands of the trading middle classes. I know no way to exhibit this effect so completely, as does a view of the amount of the "probate and legacy duties," paid on the transmission of *personal property* by will, during the period of the grand swing of the paper system. The increase of these duties tells a tale not to be mistaken nor misunderstood; and this increase the following return fully exhibits. It will be seen, that it is constant and gradual; and, if we contrast this with the advance in the poor-rates, we have this part of the effects of the system fully before our eyes.

TABLE.

Shewing the amount of capital paying Legacy Duty yearly, from 1797 *to* 1835.

	£.		£.
1797 . . .	1,116,180	1817 . . .	33,118,281
1798 . . .	2,504,812	1818 . . .	30,178,613
1799 . . .	2,939,365	1819 . . .	29,411,662
1800 . . .	4,122,111	1820 . . .	31,245,274
1801 . . .	3,541,931	1821 . . .	33,023,060
1802 . . .	4,107,514	1822 . . .	34,922,682
1803 . . .	5,109,655	1823 . . .	32,735,674
1804 . . .	5,301,533	1824 . . .	35,852,824
1805 . . .	4,450,984	1825 . . .	34,801,851
1806 . . .	7,039,031	1826 . . .	31,024,593
1807 . . .	9,515,724	1827 . . .	34,058,313
1808 . . .	10,238,077	1828 . . .	39,099,523
1809 . . .	16,395,582	1829 . . .	39,667,277
1810 . . .	14,301,564	1830 . . .	31,219,324
1811 . . .	14,757,420	1831 . . .	39,532,397
1812 . . .	16,622,585	1832 . . .	43,334,508
1813 . . .	20,118,508	1833 . . .	41,974,429
1814 . . .	27,299,806	1834 . . .	41,574,628
1815 . . .	28,200,994	1835 . . .	41,092,660
1816 . . .	24,073,456		

Upon this striking statement, there is only, as it seems to me, one single remark needed to be made. It is, that, from 1797 to 1819, during which time the accumulations from the effects of the loans must naturally have been greatest, the increase is from *one* to *thirty*. After that time, the loans having ceased, and the currency bill commonly called "Peel's bill," having passed, the accumulation languishes and moderates, and the increase is only from *thirty* to *forty*. This needs no comment. It speaks for itself.

Whilst these enormous accumulations were going on, those who do the labour of the country were gradually and silently being stripped of all hold upon a soil, which, were it not for them, would be worthless. We have already seen what was the origin of the townships and of the common lands. In that origin we behold evidence irrefragable, that, when these townships were constituted, the rural population that resided without the walls of the cities and borough towns, were, as a matter of course, possessed of house and land, according to their degree; and that, unless by accident or imprudence, such a thing as "destitution" did not, and could not, exist in England. If any reasonable doubt could exist as to this matter, we have ample confirmation of its truth in the military codes of those times. In all those codes, up to the reign of Henry the VIII, *the minor military offences* are universally punished by *fine* of so much money, because, as Captain Grose observes in his Military Antiquities, "common soldiers in those days all possessed property." It may be true that, in certain cases, the men who served were *substitutes*, and the mulct for irregularities might be levied upon the principal; but this could only be true of the smaller number. These military codes, however, assume that every man in an army was capable of paying in some cases a somewhat weighty pecuniary fine; and there can be no doubt that either in themselves, or their parents, they were all possessed of some property. The reformation, by the seizure of the church lands, and by the ejection of all the holders under the church who would not conform to the new order of affairs, changed the aspect of the country somewhat in this respect. Still, however, it is certain, that up to the accession of George III, in 1760, many of the rural population retained their freehold or copy-hold cottages and gardens. After that, the increasing difficulty of living caused them rapidly to disappear. The cottage of the grandfather was sometimes sold to provide maintenance for the pauper grand-children; and at the end of the war, in 1815, little of this property of the industrious poor was left.

All this bereavement, under the colour of law, and of law pretended to be enacted by the people's representatives, might, one would have supposed, have sufficed. But the maw of pillage and corruption was not yet gorged nor glutted; and whilst this was going on, schemes were also hatching for depriving the unfortunate poor of their last miserable, remaining stay,—a recourse to the poor-rate for relief. I have already remarked,—and I repeat the observation with deep and bitter feelings of shame and of sorrow, that, from the time of Queen Elizabeth, when it was enacted, to this hour, the landlords of England have been the secret enemies of the poor-law. They have not often dared to speak out their wishes and their feelings; but of the melancholy fact I cannot entertain a doubt. They have, from first to last, strenuously resisted the extension of "the forty-third of Elizabeth" to Ireland; and as a certain consequence, they have reduced that unfortunate country to a state shocking to humanity. Until, however, they were aided and abetted by the "philosopers" and "political economists," they did not, as a body, dare to attempt any "overt act" against the English poor law, which, to use the words of Blackstone, had become "interwoven with the constitution of the country." In Scotland, the existing poor-law had, indeed, been suffered to become almost a dead letter; but, in England, until after the death of Mr. Pitt, who was fully sensible of its value, the law of Elizabeth remained in full force, as it does in the United States of America, at this hour.

Mr. Pitt died in the year 1806; the administration of Mr. Fox and the Grenvilles was broken up, by the death of the former, in the latter end of the same year. Mr. Perceval succeeded to power, after another desperate struggle of the Whigs for pelf and place; and under his *régime*, and that of Lord Liverpool, the "political economists" became a party in the House of Commons, possessing some power. They formed the main ingredients of the celebrated bullion committee, under the guidance of Horner; and thenceforward, that under-current of ill-will, which had long been setting in against the noble law of Elizabeth, a law which has been, not more emphatically than truly, termed the "Magna Charta of the industrious classes," appeared in open day, and found voice and channel. The enemies of the poor-law made their first appearance under the cloak of "philosophy,"—and the Paul, or rather Gamaliel, of this new sect, strange to relate, was found in the person of a clergyman of the church of England! The reader will almost start and shrink incredulously back at this announcement; but it is not more sad than true. It is impossible to set any bound to the extremes to which a desperately vicious and mistaken theory may carry speculative men, of intentions by no means bad; and we have here arrived at perhaps the most melancholy instance of this truth upon record: a grave proof how insufficient a guard, when the heart is torpid, or the imagination cold, the mere intellect may be against error the most dangerous; and how careful we ought to be of listening to it, when opposed to those feelings, which God, doubtless for wise as well as merciful purposes, has implanted in human bosoms.

About the beginning of the century was put forth by the Reverend Mr. Malthus, a clergyman of the church of England, but till then unknown as a writer, a moderate-sized octavo volume, entitled an "Essay on Population." Until the publication of this book of Malthus, population was a subject hardly thought about, or deemed worthy of thought. In the better days of England, as in most other prosperous and happy countries, a man who had been the parent and bringer up of a large family, especially if in an humble rank of life, was generally looked upon as a particularly meritorious citizen of the state. Large families were rare; and he who could boast of seven grown-up sons, fit for their country's service if needed, was esteemed an uncommonly good subject, and a proper object of royal favour and notice. Beyond this, population had not been, in modern times, a matter for general discussion of any kind. In the fifteenth and sixteenth centuries, the population of England had, indeed, exhibited such unequivocal symptoms of *decay*, that, for a series of years, beginning at about A.D. 1480, and extending into the reign of James I, which began with the seventeenth century, great alarm was excited, and many acts passed by the legislature to remedy, if possible, the consequences of the decline in the numbers of the people. After the commencement of the civil wars of Charles I, however, this alarm wore off, and the symptoms of decay which had excited it were no more seen. Up to the period of the publication, however, of the Rev. Mr. Malthus, the notion of *danger* from "*over*-peopling" had not entered into men's heads; and no proverb was more esteemed for its truth than that which affirms that "when God sends mouths he always sends meat!"

The essay of Malthus was, I believe, intended by its author principally to be an answer to those extravagant fancies of the "perfectibility" of the human species, in which Mr. Godwin and other democratic writers of that period had indulged. These democratical philosophers held that society, and of course the art of government, might be brought not only to a high state of excellence, but to *absolute perfection!* This seemed, in common parlance, certainly, "too good news to be true;" and to stop the expectations likely to spring from this extravagant supposition, the Rev. Mr. Malthus wrote his book. His theory was at all events a very pithy one. It asserted, in broad terms, that if they had full swing in breeding, the human race would increase far faster than provisions could be made to increase. Consequently, that, govern as you might, vice and misery of all kinds must arise, and thus check the march of population; unless some other moral check could be made to do the office of the crime, vice, misery, and starvation; and the *gist* of the whole was, that, unless

Mr. Godwin could find out some such check in his philosophy, "perfectibility" was mere moonshine even in idea! These notions of Malthus were by no means new, though they were new to the public. An author of the name of Wallace had, in a work "On the Prospects of Mankind," printed many years before the essay of Malthus, adopted the same fancy; and the well-known Dr. Benjamin Franklin had, in an essay written in Pennsylvania in 1751, and published in the "Universal Magazine" in 1768, advocated somewhat similar opinions, from observing a greater increase amongst the American settlers than was then seen in the old country. These notions, however, at that time did not attract the slightest attention. They were held to be fantastical and odd speculations, of no practical use; and as such were neglected, and very naturally neglected. The people were at that time comparatively prosperous, and the government fairly popular. Ministers of state, consequently, did not lack philosophical excuses for national miseries or depravities; and the population-theories of Wallace and Franklin remained in quiet on the shelves to which they had been very unceremoniously consigned.

When the book of the Reverend Mr. Malthus appeared, the position of affairs in England was very different. The poor-rate, following the march of government taxation, step by step, had, from a few hundred thousand pounds a year, grown into millions. As pauperism increased, crime had increased; and despite the building of churches, the spread of ascetic sectaries, and the adoption of new-fangled systems of education, the commitments for felonies increased, year after year; executions became frightfully frequent, and a gradual hardening of the laws against offences of a criminal nature was induced, which, although latterly marked by pretences of "improvements in the criminal code," has gone on to this hour, and is at this moment in full progress, as we shall see hereafter. In a state of affairs like this, the theory of Malthus, monstrous as it was, both in its alleged foundations and its consequences, was a perfect "god-send" to a government, conscious that the nation it governed was daily becoming more and more wretched under its sway, and that every year was producing an enlarged crop of national discontents and national sufferings. Here was a system that not only asserted, that, despite the best of government, vice, crime, distress and misery, of all sorts, must necessarily exist; but which charged the existence of these crimes and that wretchedness upon the improvidence of the people themselves, in obeying the laws of nature rather than the calculations of political economists. Doctrine like this was invaluable to profligate governments in want of excuses; but this system went further still. It not only taught the necessary existence of vice and misery as long as the people were permitted to marry at will, but it taught, also, that all charity, this including, of course, all laws imposing rates for the relief of the poor, were not only useless but actually pernicious, inasmuch as they encouraged men and women to have families without having at the same time an absolute competence in order to support these families. This doctrine was pretty sure to be popular amongst all those, whose mercenary and inhuman natures led them to grudge the rates, out of which the infirm and destitute poor had been kept since the act of the forty-third of Elizabeth; and it was received, accordingly, with a shout of applause. Inhumanity could now walk openly abroad in the vesture of philosophy; and no time was lost in commencing the work of sapping and mining the laws for relieving the unfortunate poor. It seems almost incredible that tenets like these could be broached by a man who not only professed to believe that gospel which says, "but *above all*, charity," but who avowed himself "called upon by the Holy Ghost" to preach that gospel. Such, however, is the inconsistency of human nature, and such the danger of a shallow and false philosophy, that these doctrines, merciless enough in form and effect to have been hatched by the devil himself, were absolutely promulgated by a Christian pastor, in other respects and up to that time of no unexemplary life and character! That to this inconsistency he should add another, and, after denying the propriety of all charitable donations, accept *a pension*, to be paid by the very people to whom he denied relief, is no matter for wonder.

Having published a volume in which I have demonstratively shown what "*the true law*" which regulates population really *is*, it cannot be expected of me to enter, in this place, into any reasoning to prove the utter falsity of the assumptions of Wallace, Franklin, and Malthus: suffice it to say, that the theory of these men is the reverse of the truth. Nature only causes an increased productiveness when a species is put in danger, and in the *ratio* of the danger. This law runs through the vegetable and animal creation. A plant or animal that is starved as to natural aliment is prolific in proportion. Hence whilst all rich aristocracies *decrease*, all poor communities increase. Nature, by this beneficent law, causes luxury to be barren to stop the progress of disease, and poverty to be prolific to save the species from extinction. Hence all richly fed nations, who use animal food or rich food of any kind, are of moderate numbers; whilst nations that live on rice, potatoes, or other meagre diet, like the Irish, Chinese, Hindoos, and Japanese, are over-populous. Hence the House of Lords and all nobilities are only kept up by new creations, whilst the poor never want a superabundance of heirs. And hence the true way to keep a people from being over-numerous, is to feed them richly and well; the very reverse of the ideas of Malthus, who fancied that the more the food, the more the population. It is with the *effects* of these fallacies, however, that I have now to deal; and they were not long in beginning to show themselves The Malthusian doctrine having been adopted by many men of weight and influence in both houses of parliament, eloquent complaints of the folly and evil of the existing poor laws were now perpetually made; and all sorts of abortive schemes for an alteration or abolition of them, laid and hatched. It would be superfluous, had I the means, to particularise these schemes; but as a sample, I may allude to one of the earlier ones brought before the House of Commons, by a Mr. Chaplin, in the session of 1811. This atrocious scheme was embodied in a bill called the "Spilsby Poor-bill;" and the experiment was to be tried upon twenty united parishes. This bill proposed to give to the magistrates a power to compel to go into workhouses or bastiles, all the poor *who applied for relief* and also *all* "VAGRANTS" *whether asking for relief or not!* In the magistrates was also to be vested the power of *deciding* what constituted a man "a vagrant;" and, to crown all, it vested in the overseers of the workhouses or bastiles, a power to inflict "*moderate*" *personal correction* for misbehaviour on the poor prisoners in their keeping: in other words, it authorised the arbitrary *flogging* of the poor, at the will of a gaoler! That such a bill as this could have *passed* the House of Commons or of Lords, even at that period, I will not affect to believe; but it got to *a second reading* in the Commons, when it was destroyed by the indignant opposition of a good-hearted as well as clever man, Sir Samuel Romilly. When men, however, are fairly besotted with a theory, and especially with a theory that squares well with their temporal interests, they are not to be baffled by a repulse or two. The political economists in the house had swallowed, as it were, the Rev. Mr. Malthus and his doctrine whole, much as a boa constrictor is said to swallow a tiger; and having snuffed their game, they ran it like blood-hounds. In seven years after this repulse, they succeeded in striking their first great blow at the noble act of Elizabeth, the root of which the axe now fairly reached. This axe was the series of enactments called "Sturges Bourne's bills," from their proposer "Sturges Bourne;" and this blow was the passing of these bills, in the year 1818. To describe minutely their provisions is not within the compass of this work; suffice it to say, that they took the power of providing for the wants of the poor from the overseers of the parishes, in whose hands, subject to an appeal to the magistrates, the law of Elizabeth had placed it, and put it into the direction of a set of men called "a select vestry," being a sort of committee of rate-payers, set up to control the overseers. But these men were not fairly chosen by the body of the rate-payers; a preponderance of votes being given to the rich by means of these enactments, which regulated the votes by the amount of the property of the voter. Thus the power of dispensing relief was actually in the hands of a minority of wealthy men, who had neither feelings nor sympathies in common with the poorer classes: and to enable them to carry their privilege of pinching the parish-pauper into practical effect, these insidiously tyrannical enactments gave to the select vestries the power of *hiring* overseers, if they chose, from a distance, who thus became their creatures, and treated the poor as they were directed to treat them, without shame and without compunction. The consequence was, that deeds from which a native overseer, standing alone, would have shrunk, were perpetrated, under the sanction of these bodies, by their hired creatures, and the unfortunate poor browbeaten, insulted, and starved with comparative impunity. The appeal to the bench was, to be sure, still remaining; but the fear of the "perpetual overseer," effectually over-awed the poor from resorting to it.

The march of crime, a sure consequence of growing poverty, had long been going on in England; but after the passing of these acts, offences against the law became, as might naturally be expected, more dreadfully numerous than ever. So must it ever be. Human nature, on the average, will only endure the ordeal of a very limited amount of temptation and trial. General comfort is the only security for general morality. Take away that comfort—steep a people in pauperism and difficulty—and from that hour, in the exact *ratio* of the destitution, will offences against property and general morality spring and flourish; despite the gaoler and the clergyman, and their denunciations of punishment for evil-doers in this world and the next. The following tables of annual commitments will abundantly demonstrate to the reader this important truth; and if, as he proceeds with the narrative, he will, from time to time, recur to them, he will find them indicate the periods of the greatest pressure, with all the nicety of a barometer. In due time we shall also see new species of crime follow new sorts of punishment. We shall see England almost rival unhappy Ireland in abundance of agricultural outrage; and incendiary fires, night after night, begin to illuminate the sky in half the counties of England.

COMMITMENTS OF ENGLAND AND WALES, FROM 1806 TO 1834, INCLUSIVE.

(Extracted from the Official Returns.)

1806	1810	1811	1812	1813	1814	1815
4,346	5,146	5,337	6,576	7,164	6,390	7,818

1816	1817	1818	1819	1820	1821	1822
9,091	13,932	13,567	14,254	13,710	13,115	12,241

1823	1824	1825	1826	1827	1828	1829
12,263	13,698	14,437	16,147	17,924	16,564	18,675

1830	1831	1832	1833	1834
18,107	19,647	20,829	20,072	22,451

In the meantime, the consequence of this state of society was, first, a hardening of the laws; and, next, a disuse of juries, and an increase of the summary and arbitrary powers of the magistrate. From the very frequency of them, men at last shrunk from the open and direct punishments inflicted in the face of day;

and, as a substitute, secret torture in prisons, tread-mills, solitary cells, insufficient food, and various other inflictions, came gradually to be resorted to—punishments unknown in the better days of England, secret in their nature, and contrary to every notion of proper security for the prisoner, or responsibility on the part of those carrying the sentences of the law into execution. Thus, under the pretexts of a spurious "humanity," and of "improving the criminal code," the number of felonies were greatly increased, the summary powers of magistrates augmented, juries disused, and the prisons calculated to give the means of carrying on a system of ingenious torture, under the specious name of "regulating and improving prison-discipline." At a future stage of this melancholy narrative, I shall adduce ample proofs of the truth of these general assertions. That in former times, prisons were often neglected, and the state of their inmates too little inquired into, is too true. The reader, however, will easily distinguish between the want of due inquiry into a disgusting subject on the part of the community, and refined modes of secret torment under the name of "regulation;" and not confound a culpable, but natural apathy, with a sickening ingenuity in the production of prison-infliction, by which the mind and body of the prisoner are at once racked, and ultimately, perhaps, destroyed.

The most striking and pernicious change of all, however, produced upon society during the inflation of the paper-money, was, perhaps, apparent in the new and strange ideas as to education which sprung up, and which remain to this hour. As to this vital topic, the ideas of our ancestors were plain and practical. They were, in this department at all events, true Utilitarians; and the groundwork upon which they set out was, that every man and every woman should be accomplished in that calling which was to be most useful to them through life. Hence the handicraftsman looked mostly to a thorough knowledge of his trade; the countryman studied the labours of the farm; the merchant, trade; the dealer and chapman, the changes of markets and the qualities of that in which he dealt; whilst females, even of the highest ranks, were expert in all that relates to domestic economy, and the management of the house, from the castle or hall, down to the cottage. In this state of society, science, art, and literature were studied by the few, whose genius was really adapted for them. Publications were few, but elaborate, and well digested; and hence men's knowledge, as far as it went, was sound and good. The clergy were the great instructors; men's leisure was great; and we learn from Chief Justice Fortescue, that, in the fifteenth century, the "Frankelayne" and the "Yeoman," generally possessed a fair knowledge of the law and constitution of their country, besides being well skilled in such useful parts of knowledge as their pursuits in life required. In the hands of the females was placed the whole domestic economy of life; and it was then varied as well as valuable. The mistress of the mansion was not only the instructress of her servants in the ordinary household avocations, cookery, confectionary, wine-making, and brewing; but many arts and manufactures were carried on under her guidance and inspection. The wool and the lint was both carded and spun; and when it had passed the loom of the weaver, was dyed or bleached at home, if not of the finer woofs.

The manufacture of worsted was carried on in the same manner; and when it was fit for use, it was knit into stockings during the winter evenings. Family medicine was not neglected, nor were the various culinary comforts for the sick. Thus every mansion was a school, and every dame of a family a schoolmistress of the most valuable description. No servant existed who could not knit, spin, bake, and brew, as well as cook, conserve, and manage pastry. Many of the ordinary habiliments were made at home; and simple was she who did not add some of the craft of the tailor to the art of the spinster and sempstress. Here was a true "society for the diffusion of useful knowledge;" and excellent were its fruits. This manner of life not only conduced to instruction, but begat a friendly feeling between the teachers and the taught. Domestic servants were humble friends. They seldom left a house until they married from it; and this amiable intercourse often continued through life, each taking an interest in the prosperity of the other. The mutations made in society by the taxing and paper-system extended, in time, to this also; but up to the reign of George III., much of it remained. His insane reign was destined to be the end of it; and what the convertible paper began, the inconvertible paper and the manufacturing system finished.

We have already seen what were the effects of the pouring out of the inconvertible paper on prices. Amidst the artificial rise in all commodities, and the expenditure of the money borrowed by the Government, fortunes were rapidly accumulated, and an appearance of prosperity created amongst the middle classes totally unlike anything that had appeared before. One of the worst effects of this was a total change of manners amongst these classes—a reckless profusion—a disdain of homely and prudential living—and a disgusting and soul-degrading aping of aristocratical manners and ways of life, pernicious in the highest degree. At former periods, the abundance of diffused wealth had caused symptoms of this malady to appear in England; but it now spread like a pestilence, and changed all the wholesome usages of society. Education was totally changed. Forgetting that the business of life must be carried on by men and women, with the partial exception of a very few, indeed, of the very highest rank, a rage for showy and superficial accomplishments seized upon the middling classes of society. All the useful arts of life were to be despised and thrown aside as vulgar and degrading. Common sense seemed to have fled the land. Quackery and affectation be-devilled every thing. All young men were to be linguists and fine gentlemen; and all young women musicians, painters, and heroines of novels. The pianoforte, and the pencil, and colours, found their way into the farm-house and the back-shop; and from that hour the really useful domestic sciences became obsolete. What the middle classes had ceased to learn they could not teach; and a domestic revolution was effected, the uncomfortable effects of which we are feeling at this hour. The manufacturing system, by taking thousands of young females from their homes, and shutting them up amidst the heat, ignorance, and vice of those demoralised dens called "factories," completed the work; and domestic comfort, as it formerly existed in England, is unknown. The parlour-tables are loaded with degraded and silly novels and albums, and still more contemptible music-books; whilst ignorance of the real arts of life, affectation, recklessness, vice, and dishonesty, too often occupy the rest of the house. Such are the effects of essentially vicious systems. Their diseased ramifications reach every class. They afflict society as "the dry-rot" does the mansion; sparing nothing, and affecting every thing, from the garret down to the cellar, until a nation becomes one corrupt and crawling mass of degradation, vice, affectation, ignorance, misery, and mischief.

In the midst of all this mutation, literature also suffered like the rest. The graver and higher departments of inquiry became gradually neglected. Moral philosophy and the science of mind, the grave studies of history, and the more abstract mathematics, gradually yielded to shallow physics and trifling annals; and a muster-roll of plants and flowers, or a list of stones, with Greek and German names, constituted science; whilst the trifling chronicle of a court-parasite, or the notes of some butterfly diplomatist passed for history. In the belles lettres the same depression of standard taste took place. The drama, once the pride of England, was sunk in contemptible farces, or more contemptible melo-dramas. The buskin was banished from the stage, and Thalia in hourly dread of an irruption on the part of Punch and Judy. Fashionable reading was confined to flimsy novels, too trifling to be as pernicious as their writers would have made them; and crudely constructed tales, crammed with distorted history and mawkish sensibility. Literature, once wrested from the hands of those really qualified by nature to exalt and adorn it, sunk, as in such cases it ever does, into a gulf of puerility and conceit. The books and the manners became worthy of each other; and the diseased state of society became evident, from the very crown of the head to the sole of the foot.

Such were the effects of a national surfeit of iniquity, extravagance and paper-money. In our next, we shall resume our view of the current of events, as it continued to flow forward after the year 1815. We shall now begin to trace retribution succeeding profligacy; doubt stealing in upon hitherto triumphant villany; and diseased weakness following artificial strength. We shall begin to detect the sinking of the pulse of corruption, and to see, at length, the system begin to ebb from that full spring-tide, which it had now reached, of insolence and folly.

LETTER XI.

CHANGE OF CIRCUMSTANCES AFTER THE WAR.—THE DISAPPOINTMENT OF THE PEOPLE.—DIFFICULTIES OF LIVERPOOL AND CASTLEREAGH.—PRICES FALL RAPIDLY.—EXPORTS FROM FRANCE OF CATTLE, POULTRY, ETC.—ALARM OF THE LANDLORDS.—AGRICULTURAL COMMITTEE.—THEIR PROCEEDINGS.—MR. ARTHUR YOUNG'S CALCULATIONS OF THE EXPENSES OF TILLAGE AT VARIOUS PERIODS.—ITS RESULTS.—THE CORN-BILL OF 1815 PASSED AMID AN ARMED FORCE.—SOON FOUND INEFFICIENT.—ESTIMATE OF THE DEPRECIATION OF THE PAPER UP TO 1815.—EXPOSÉ OF THE BANK CIRCULATION.—THE COUNTRY BANKS.—WILD OPINIONS ON THIS SUBJECT.—GENERAL DISTRESS.—BANKS BEGIN TO STOP.—FALL IN PRICES CONTINUES.—PRICE OF BULLION FALLS.—PROCEEDINGS OF THE ECONOMISTS.—THEIR COMMITTEE—"PEEL'S BILL" PASSES IN 1819.—ITS ENACTMENTS.

We are now arrived at the finish of that profligate and wonderfully eventful war, which, beginning in the year 1793, ended on the memorable 18th day of June, 1815; and before the bell-ringings, the thankings, the pension-votings, the cheerings, the bonfire-makings, the illuminations, the ox-roastings, the serpentine-river sham sea-fights, the addressings, the crammings and the guzzlings, in which all the corrupt, ignorant, stupid, silly and half-cracked portion of the nation were at that time engaged, were well concluded, it began to be evident to the few well-informed, sensible, virtuous, and cool-headed men, who were left, that "the top spring-tide" of the system was now passed; that the ebb had commenced; that the day of imaginary triumph, like that of Napoleon at Moscow, was only the beginning of national trouble; and that, thenceforward, might be looked for that downward course in the march of affairs, which Mr. Paine had, many years before, well designated as "the Decline and Fall of the British System of Finance." Amongst others, this downward progress was distinctly foreseen and predicted by the sagacious mind of the late Mr. Cobbett, who, in a letter, dated Botley, 12th September, 1815, just three months after the "triumph" at Waterloo, thus speaks:—"It is now hoped by some persons, that the restoration of the Pope, the Inquisition, the Jesuits, and the Bourbons, will so far brutalise the people of the Continent of Europe, that we shall have no *rivals* in the arts of peace; and that thus we shall be left to enjoy a *monopoly* of navigation, commerce, and manufactures; and be, *thereby*, enabled to *pay the interest on our debt, and to meet the enormous annual expenses of our Government.* Without stopping to comment on the morality and humanity of this hope, entertained in a country abounding with Bible-societies, I venture to give it, as my decided opinion, that the hope is *fallacious*. *Russia*, Denmark, Sweden, Holland, Austria, *Spain*, the Italian States, and EVEN THE BOURBONS, will all push forward for their *share* of the benefits of the arts of peace. While our purse is open to them all, they will be subservient to us; but that cannot be for ever. It cannot be for many months longer; and, mark my words, as soon as we cease to *pay*, so soon shall we cease to have *friends* so *very* complaisant as our friends now are!" In the course of a very few years, we shall see this prediction amply fulfilled by the "restored Bourbons," who sent an army, in 1823, under the Duc d'Angouleme, to put down the "Constitution" which we had helped to establish in Spain, and to re-conquer the revolted Spanish colonies; a scheme which was only frustrated by the jealousy of Austria and Russia, who dreaded to see Mexico and Peru in the hands of France! Before, however, we advert further to this part of the subject, we must take a look at the more immediate consequence of the peace of 1814 and 1815, and at the amazing troubles and difficulties which that "transition" brought, without delay, upon the government of Liverpool and Castlereagh, now ministers, and inventors of that excusatory phrase for all evils, "the transition from war to peace!"

The first trouble, which the "triumph" of 1814-15 brought upon the heads of the ministers and their supporters, was of a somewhat singular nature, being the plague of "plenty and cheapness!" Cheapness and plenty had, hitherto, been esteemed as amongst the first blessings of a state of peace. Amongst the people, indeed, they were esteemed so still; for, amongst the illumination-devices, one of the most vulger was a great loaf, and a foaming pot of beer, with the mottoes of "I am coming down!" and "I am coming after you!" This vulgar view of matters did not, however, suit persons who had now contracted a "national debt" of *eight hundred millions of pounds*, and who were still paying taxes to the tune of *sixty millions per annum!* They by no means relished the "*mottoes*" attached to the "big loaf," and cauliflower-headed "pot of porter;" and when they saw them, in 1814, in the way of being realised with all speed, their inward consternation was tremendous. In short, when, after the opening of the ports, they saw French corn, French sheep, French cows, French poultry, and French pigs, besides butter, cheese, fruit, and vegetables, about coming over by ship-loads, and boat-loads, amidst rapidly falling prices, and universal difficulty, both commercial and agricultural, they were thunderstruck; and instinct, if not reason, told them that no time was to be lost before something was done. They felt at once, that a highly taxed and tithed country, as England now was, could not possibly carry on cultivation in competition with lightly taxed and untithed continental rivals. As early as the autumn of 1814, therefore, they had got together parliamentary committees to inquire into the state and prospects of agriculture; and these committees soon came to the conclusion, that, if the landed interests were to stand at all, it could only be by means of "protection," and a "corn bill."

That these committees were right in the abstract, I do not see how it is possible for any reasoning man to deny. The best way to demonstrate this, is, however, to contemplate some of the *evidence* on which their conclusions were based; and some of it was certainly of exceeding strength. I accordingly insert here a comparative table of the expenses of cultivating arable land, calculated upon one hundred acres, for the years 1790, 1803, and 1813, given in to the Lords Committee by that experienced and accomplished farmer, Mr. Arthur Young. To these years I have added a calculation, made for the year 1835, by a skilful and successful farmer of the county of Durham. From these tables it appears, that, even in the year 1835, when the taxes for the service of the year were reduced as low as, under the existing system, they can be permitted to go, these expenses were far more than expenses and rent altogether in 1790. With wheat then at the same price, and money of the same value, that ruled in the year 1790, it follows, of necessity, that the farmer could not pay rent, and make a living; and this was amply proved in 1821 and 1822, and in the three years ending in 1835, when wheat fell to the prices that existed prior to 1790, in spite of the corn-bill, and when agricultural distress, to a ruinous extent, overspread the country.

COMPARATIVE TABLE OF THE EXPENSES OF ARABLE LAND.

	1790.			1803.			1813.			1835.		
	£.	s.	d.	£.	s.	d.	£.	s.	d.	£.	s.	d.
Rent - - -	88	6	3¼	121	2	7¼	161	12	7¼	150	0	0
Tithe - - -	20	14	1¾	26	8	0¼	38	17	3¼	30	0	0
Rates - - -	17	13	10	31	7	7¾	38	19	2¾	30	0	0
Wear and tear	15	13	5¼	22	11	10¼	31	2	10¾	20	0	0
Labour - - -	85	5	4	118	0	4	161	12	11¼	180	0	0
Seed - - -	46	4	10¼	49	2	7	98	17	10	53	0	0
Manure - -	48	0	3	68	6	2	37	7	0¼	20	0	0
Team - - -	67	4	10	80	8	0¼	134	19	8½	120	0	0
Interest - - -	22	11	11½	30	3	8½	50	5	6	16	0	0
Taxes - - -	0	0	0	0	0	0	18	1	4	5	0	0
Total - - -	411	15	11¾	547	10	11½	771	16	4½	624	0	0
Deduct rent -	88	6	3¼	121	2	7¼	161	12	7¼	150	0	0
Nett expenses £	323	9	8½	426	8	4½	610	3	9¼	474	0	0
	Gold Money.			Paper £. worth 14s.			Paper £. worth 10s.			Gold Money.		
Price of wheat per quarter.	46s. per qr.			56s. 9d. per qr.			108s. 9d. per qr.			44s. 2d. per qr.		

Thus it is evident, that with an amount of taxation, such as existed in 1835, and such as must continue to exist as long as the interest of the debt is paid; the expenses of tillage, upon land of average goodness, must be far more than expenses and rent and altogether in 1790; and much greater than in 1803, when the average price of wheat was 56s. 9d. per quarter. And hence it is further evident, that, even allowing for improvements in the management of land since 1790, to make farming yield a fair rent, and a living for the farmer and his labourers, the price of wheat must be somewhere between the average of 1803 and 1813; and that to reduce wheat below the prices of even 1790, which a free admission of foreign wheat would now do, would be *ruin, immediate and inevitable*, to the landed interest, unless the interest of the debt ceased to be paid, and unless the annual amount of taxation was reduced to the level at which it stood in the year 1790, that is to say, to about *a fourth part of its present amount.*

This reasoning, at all events, convinced the legislature of the year 1815, that a prohibitory corn-bill to protect the land was absolutely necessary, if landlords were to continue to receive rents; and despite the natural unpopularity of the measure, the Liverpool and Castlereagh administration were compelled to pass "the corn-bill" of that year, which was done, whilst the houses were surrounded with soldiers to protect the members from the fury of the people, to whom this first taste of "the blessing of peace" was irritating in the extreme. It would answer no useful purpose to enter into any detail of the provisions of the bill so passed; for it was soon discovered to be short of its aim and purposed end. It was, in short, an act, the stringent clauses of which went to prevent foreign grain from being imported into England, Scotland, or Ireland, as long as the price of wheat averaged under *eighty shillings the quarter*. They, who passed it, stupidly imagined that by means of this enactment, wheat would be *retained* at about the price of eighty shillings per quarter, on the average. They were too ignorant to see, that, under the new circumstances which were about to render the value of *money* fully *double* that of the money of the latter years of the war, it was impossible, excepting in seasons of actual scarcity, that wheat could bring such a price as eighty shillings for a quarter. After a few years, however, it was discovered, that to double the value of money was to lower the average price of grain, in spite of prohibitory corn laws; and that to leave the landed interest to such prices as even the natural produce of the empire, measured by metallic money, would bring about, was in itself almost a sentence of ruin. Hence, it was found necessary to devise a means by which the price of grain might be artificially and easily forced up beyond its natural level, as ruled by the seasons and the value of money; and this was found in "a sliding scale of duties," which *lowering* as grain *rose* in price, acted as *a continual premium* to speculative persons, exciting them to "gamble up" these prices to the highest possible figure by means of false averages, false reports, combinations, false sales, and all that enginery, which clever but unprincipled men know so well how to employ. This "cunningly devised scheme" for giving and insuring an almost perpetual false value to

English grain, was hit upon in 1823. We shall hereafter see, that in seasons of extraordinary fruitfulness and plenty it is inoperative, and fails of its intended effect. In all ordinary seasons, however, it is successful; and the system of the "sliding scale of duties on corn" has therefore been continued, with some modifications, ever since its first invention. Corn-laws, however, in any shape, must ever be odious to a people; and the repeal of these and all other corn-laws has been often demanded. In the course of this narrative, we shall clearly see the consequences to which such a repeal as is demanded must surely lead us.

Such was the first step taken by parliament on the conclusion of the long conflict with France, in 1815. They imagined, that by means of the corn bill, which they then passed, they had secured an average price of *eighty shillings the quarter*, or *ten shillings the bushel*, for wheat; but events soon came to undeceive them. Scarcely had hostilities come to a close, when the paper money, which was now out in immense bales, began to feel the effects of what Castlereagh called "the transition from war to peace." Before we examine, however, into the causes of the distress and consternation which now took place amongst the issuers of the paper, and amongst all connected with them; we must endeavour to arrive at some rational and sober estimate of the amount of the paper-money actually in circulation in Great Britain, in the summer of this year, 1815, and during the war generally; because upon *this amount* hinges the grand question of WHAT the depreciation of money at this period actually and really was—a question of paramount importance; inasmuch as upon *this alone* we can again base our calculations of the actual effect of the famous "currency-bill" of 1819, commonly called "Peel's bill," and arrive at a clear explanation of the causes, remote and proximate, of all the troubles, mutations, and confusion, that have since followed.

In estimating the amount of money afloat from year to year, from the period of the Bank-stoppage in 1797, up to the month of June, 1815, we should have little difficulty to contend with, had we only to deal with the transactions of the parent-bank. These transactions are now certainly to be known; accounts the most minute with regard to all these transactions having been obtained, and published in a voluminous Report made to Parliament by the Secret Committee of 1832, a copy of which Report is at this moment lying before me. The amount of the Bank circulation, at any given time, affords, however, no *criterion* from which we can certainly estimate the amount of *Country Bank paper* circulating at the same period. Neither is it possible to discover the amount of *small bills of exchange*, drawn either by bankers or other private persons circulating from hand to hand, though in a limited way, at any given time; yet that these form *some part* of what may be properly called the circulating medium, and help to affect prices in general, can hardly be doubted. I do not lay much weight upon these bills, because they, at most, pass only through a few hands, and are generally drawn for sums much exceeding ten pounds. In a calculation of this sort, however, they are not altogether to be omitted, however unsafe it might be to lay much stress upon their effects as to prices of commodities. With these difficulties before us, the best way, as it seems to me, to ascertain, with a fair degree of probability, the actual value of the money of the last years of the war up to 1815, will be, *first*, to see what the circulation of the Bank of England was during these years; *next*, to try to estimate the probable amount of country paper of all kinds; and, *lastly*, to try how far these calculated amounts tally, in the gross, with the prices for commodities actually paid in these years, with the transactions of the Government, and with all other transactions which can help to throw a light upon the actual quantity and value of the circulating medium throughout this period. That this is the only way to arrive at anything like a correct conclusion I am well convinced. It has been, I know, absurdly held, that the price of gold bullion throughout the period we are examining, is a correct measure of the depreciation of the paper. There never was a more shallow nor more erroneous fancy than this. We have already seen, in part, the causes which tended to depress and altogether falsify the quotations of the prices of gold and silver bullion during the war. We shall discuss them fully when we come to the passing of THE BILL OF PEEL in 1819. In the mean time, with these remarks, we proceed with our present inquiry.

The following particulars of the gradually increasing circulation of the Bank of England I take from a minute account, printed by the Secret Committee of 1832, in the Appendix to their Report. It embraces all the particulars for each year, from 1778 to 1832, and is a most curious and instructive document.

CIRCULATION, DEPOSITS, AND SECURITIES OF THE BANK, FOR EACH HALF-YEAR IN 1797, 1800, 1805, 1810, AND 1815.

28th February, 1797.		£	28th February, 1797. Securities.		£
Circulation - - - -		9,674,780	Public	£11,714,431	
Deposits - - - -		4,891,530	Private	5,123,319	
					16,837,750
			Bullion - -		1,086,170
		14,566,310	Rest -	£3,357,610	17,923,920

31st August, 1797. Circulation.			31st August, 1797. Securities.		
Notes and Post Bills	£10,246,535	11,114,120	Public	£8,765,224	
Ditto under £5 -	867,585		Private	9,495,946	
					18,261,170
Deposits - -		7,765,350	Bullion		4,089,620
		18,879,470	Rest -	3,471,320	22,350,790

28th February, 1800. Circulation.			28th February, 1800. Securities.		
Notes and Post Bills	£15,372,930	16,844,470	Public	£13,975,663	
Ditto under £5 -	1,471,540		Private	7,448,387	
					21,424,050
Deposits - -		7,062,680	Bullion		6,144,250
		23,907,150	Rest -	£3,661,150	27,568,300

31st August, 1800. Circulation.			31st August, 1800. Securities.		
Notes and Post Bills	£13,448,540	15,047,180	Public	£13,586,590	
Ditto under £5 -	1,598,640		Private	8,551,830	
					22,138,420
Deposits - -		8,335,060	Bullion		5,150,450
		23,382,240	Rest -	£3,906,630	27,288,870

28th February, 1805. Circulation.			28th February, 1805. Securities.		
Notes and Post Bills	£13,011,010	17,871,170	Public	£16,889,501	
Ditto under £5 -	4,860,160		Private	11,771,889	
					28,661,390
Deposits - -		12,083,620	Bullion		5,883,800
		29,954,790	Rest -	£4,590,400	34,545,190

31st August, 1805. Circulation.			31st August, 1805. Securities.		
Notes and Post Bills	£11,862,740	16,388,400	Public	£11,413,266	
Ditto under £5 -	4,525,660		Private	16,359,584	
					27,772,850
Deposits - -		14,048,080	Bullion		7,624,500
		30,436,480	Rest -	£4,960,870	35,397,350

28th February, 1810. Circulation.		£	28th February, 1810. Securities.		£
Notes and Post Bills	£15,159,180	21,019,600	Public	£14,322,634	
Ditto under £5 -	5,860,420		Private	21,055,946	
					35,378,580
Deposits - -		12,457,310	Bullion		3,501,410
		33,476,910	Rest -	£5,403,080	38,879,990

31st August, 1810. Circulation.		£	31st August, 1810. Securities.		£
Notes and Post Bills	£17,570,780	25,793,990	Public	£17,198,677	
Ditto under £5 -	7,223,210		Private	23,775,093	
					40,973,770
Deposits - -		13,617,520	Bullion		3,191,850
		38,411,510	Rest -	£5,754,110	44,165,620

28th February, 1815. Circulation.		£	28th February, 1815. Securities.		£
Notes and Post Bills	£18,226,400	27,261,650	Public	£27,512,804	
Ditto under £5 -	9,035,250		Private	17,045,696	
					44,558,500
Deposits - -		11,702,250	Bullion		2,036,910
		38,963,900	Rest -	£7,631,510	46,595,410

31st August, 1815. Circulation.		£	31st August, 1815. Securities.		£
Notes and Post Bills	£17,766,140	27,248,670	Public	£24,194,086	
Ditto under £5 -	9,482,530		Private	20,660,094	
					44,854,180
Deposits - -		12,696,000	Bullion		3,409,040
		39,944,670	Rest -	£8,318,550	48,263,220

Thus, then, it is quite certain, that the paper circulation of the Bank of England was *tripled* between the memorable 27th February, 1797, and the same day of the same month, A.D. 1815: but then this must not be accounted as a tripling of the money of the country by the Bank to that full extent, because a considerable portion of the one and two pound notes then issued only replaced guineas and silver coins circulating when the Bank-stoppage took place. In short, for the purposes of a calculation of this kind, it would be unsafe to consider the Bank issues to be much more than a doubling of the portion of the circulation controlled by the Bank, which amounts to a depreciation of *fifty per cent.* upon the value of the paper, reducing the value of the *paper pound* to *ten standard silver shillings*, or half a gold sovereign, as now coined. But this is only one portion of the currency of the country. We are next to attempt to estimate the effect of the issues of the Country Banks; and this is a much less easy matter.

At the period of the crisis of 1797, the number of Country Banks has been stated at about *two hundred.* There were no licenses required for banking at this time, nor until the year 1808. In 1809, *seven hundred and two licenses* were granted to country bankers; and from that time they increased, year by year, to *nine hundred and forty* in the year 1814, since which period they have decreased. Thus, then, in the period between 1797 and 1815, the Country Banks have been nearly *quintupled;* an enormous increase, and startling even to a rash calculator. We must not, however, fall into the grievous error of imagining, that this increase implies a quintupled issue of country notes. We must, on the contrary, recollect, that a portion of the issues of these new Banks would only replace coin, or notes of the Bank of England, already circulating in these districts, as well as a portion of the circulation of existing country banks, which would be narrowed by the growth of increasing rivals. Making all allowances, however, for these "sets-off" against it, it seems impossible, not to conclude that this enormous vegetation of banks should not have been accompanied by a vast increase of the circulation. In fact, the circulation of the Bank of England was, by the issues of these banks, fairly cooped up within a circle of ten miles round

London; nor can I see that, upon the whole, we can set down the multiplication of this portion of the currency, at less than three times that of 1797. We must remember, that a portion of the notes set down as "circulation" by the Bank of England, are always lying dead, as it were, in the tills of private bankers all over the country, and forming no part of the active currency. This was not the case with the country notes, which were nearly all for one, two, or five pounds (notes for sums above ten pounds being rarities) and which were always in active circulation until returned to the bank which issued them. If to these considerations, we add the effect of the innumerable small bills of exchange drawn and negotiated during this period, by means of which the excise and customs duties were, for the greater part, paid throughout the country; these bills being discounted by the bankers for those purposes; we cannot but see, that the depreciation of the entire currency of the country, during the last years of the war must have been very great; and I, for my part, cannot believe that, in 1812, 1813, 1814, and 1815, the pound-note could have been worth more than *seven or eight standard shillings!*

This, on a first view, may appear an exaggeration: but after long consideration of all the bearings of this perplexing subject, I am convinced it is not so; nor are there wanting other facts to corroborate this conclusion. Amongst the rest, the average prices of grain directly indicate this truth. If we except the two years of excessive issue which caused and made part of the crisis of 1797, we shall find the average price of wheat, from the end of the war with the colonies in 1783 up to 1794, to be a trifle above *forty shillings* the quarter. If, however, we average the prices of the last seven years of the war up to 1815, we shall find the result to be *ninety-five shillings* a quarter; more than double those of the other. Rents, in many districts, rose in a proportion equal, or more than equal, to this: nor is it possible to account for the enormous nominal sum raised annually by the income tax (£14,000,000; of which the fund-holders paid £3,000,000), without supposing either that a large portion of the profits upon which the tax was levied never existed save in the imaginations of the payers, or, that the depreciation of the currency, during the last few years of the war, was so rapid, as to raise the nominal profits upon commodities to a pitch inconceivable under any other order of affairs. That both descriptions of delusion were at work, I do not doubt; for, putting the people's power to purchase and consume goods at the highest conceivable amount, and putting the profits upon the things consumed at the highest conceivable amount, and making every other allowance, still it seems impossible, even upon the supposition that the pound note was worth only *seven standard* shillings, to arrive at the result of an *aggregate national income*, out of *real* profits, so high as to pay an impost of *eleven millions*, with a levy of only *ten per cent;* especially when we consider, that the other taxes, at that time, amounted to more than *sixty millions per annum*.

The question of what the actual augmentation of the country paper really was as to amount, if that amount is to be stated as *a fixed sum*, I shall not attempt to answer. I have never met with any *data* for calculating the sum of country paper circulating at any given periods, which appeared to me deserving, in any degree, to be relied upon: and the statements, authoritatively put forth have been so conflicting and so wild, as totally to destroy confidence in such assertions, come they from whom they may. Before the committee on the currency, in 1819, the most widely differing amounts were assigned to the country paper. Alexander Baring (now Lord Ashburton), stated, if the *notes under five pounds* were withdrawn, "*forty* to *forty-five millions* of gold and silver coin would be absorbed." Mr. Lloyd, the banker, a much better authority, stated the amount of the *whole* of the country bank paper in 1815, at "from *forty* to *fifty millions*." Lord Lauderdale stated, that his opinion was, that the country bank circulation was only "about equal to that of the Bank of England!" The committee taking the stamp-returns, as their criterion, and *supposing* the notes to last three years on the average, made the amount in 1818, *twenty-nine millions, two hundred and thirty-two thousand, eight hundred and seventy pounds*, a larger amount than the same returns make the circulation of 1815! This was probably erroneous in all points of view; and yet the calculations of Mr. Sedgwick and Mr. Robert Mushet, made since that period, would considerably lower both these amounts. In plain truth, none of these statements are to be relied upon. The authority of Mr. Lewis Lloyd, the banker, I should esteem much the highest; but from what *data* he spoke he did not explain. My own conclusions I derive from relative and not positive amounts. Be the circulation of 1797 what it might, it is sufficiently clear in evidence that the augmentation, up to 1815, must have been such as to account for all the phenomena of prices that followed: and as to these last, there can be no doubt.

Such was the state of the paper-money in 1815; and hardly had the echoes of the cannon of Waterloo died into silence, when it began to be felt that this state could not continue longer. That monopoly of supply, which the extraordinary circumstances of the war had thrown into the hands of Great Britain, begun, forthwith, to fall to pieces. The seas were now equally open to all. The colonies which, during the long period of hostilities, had been wrested from the French, Spaniards, and Dutch, were now for the most part to be restored. We could not hold them in peace. Thenceforward the European nations were not only independent of us as to colonial produce, but, freed from the ravages of war and the obstacles of blockades, they began to manufacture for themselves. The woollens of Saxony and the Merino fleeces of Spain began to be felt clogging the wheels of our machinery. That machinery, despite of penalties and prohibitions, in due time found its way across the narrow seas, up the Baltic, and beyond the broad Atlantic. Russia established the cotton-manufacture. The United States did the same. The coal of Belgium began to work steam engines and mechanism unknown before. With all this, the expenditure of the government at home for warlike stores, recruits, commissariats, and transport-ships suddenly ceased. Prices fell, on a sudden, to a ruinous extent—banks broke—wages fell with the prices of manufactures; and before the year 1816 had come to a close, panic, bankruptcy, riot, and disaffection, had spread through the land. Vast bodies of starving and discontented artisans now congregated together, demanding a reform of the parliament, a repeal of the corn-laws, and a reduction of taxation. The discontents, the government, as usual, put down by an armed force, who with the constitution in their mouths, sabred the people *a la Cossaque.* The commercial distress they ascribed to "the transition from war to peace;" and contented themselves with the application of some palliatives, in shape of advances of money and Exchequer bills, through the Bank, hoping that affairs would gradually come round to a settled state. In this they were, after a time, partly gratified. The mercantile part of the community accommodated themselves gradually perforce to the new scale of prices after a "transition," which, in its progress through 1814, 1815, and 1816, rendered bankrupt no less than *eighty-nine country banks*, together with an enormous number of traders of all grades and descriptions. The reduction of wages, however, which, from that period, has never been stayed for any length of time, is naturally working its own effects; and now bids fair to arm nine men out of every ten against a system, which seems to exist for no other purpose than to plunder and oppress them.

In the midst of this turmoil, another grand cause of confusion remains to be mentioned; and this was *the new and ticklish position* of the grandam of so many years of villany and egregious folly; to wit, of the "Old Lady of Threadneedle-street," as she now began to be called; that is to say, of the Bank itself. The reader will remember, that throughout the various times when the acts for continuing Pitt's "Bank-restriction" were to be renewed or altered, one clause was always retained, and that was the clause binding the Bank to "*resume cash-payments*" within a few months after peace should come. It has been asserted, that Pitt never meaned this clause to be enforced, *at least as far as regarded the fundholders;* and that he intimated as much in Parliament on one occasion. This may possibly be true; but the clause, nevertheless, was adhered to; so that, before the Waterloo bonfires were well out, the Bank Directors, with this clause staring them in the face, began to bethink themselves, how they might most quickly lessen the enormous bales of their paper that were afloat, so as to give them some chance of paying the remainder in gold and silver "on demand." This was a new feature. During former revulsions, such as that in 1810, caused by the decrees of Bonaparte against the admission of British goods, the Bank had come promptly forward with loans and discounts to relieve the pressure. Now, however, the Directors scarcely dared to move an inch. They knew that "the political economists" were strong in the House, and that *they* were bent upon cash payments, at all risks. They knew that the Jews of Change Alley would secretly abet the same doctrine. Against a combination of usurers and theorists, one set all selfishness, the other all crotchets, there was no defence to be made. The country gentlemen, who were the dupes of the economists, were led to believe that cash payments were necessary for both the interest and security of themselves. Those who had the power were resolved; and nothing was left to the Bank but to narrow its issues, and look about for gold and silver wherewith to meet the storm. This was altogether a difficult business. In the year 1816 alone, *thirty-seven Country Banks* had become bankrupt. The commercial world, therefore, required additional propping. But the Government was in the same dilemma; and to it the merchants were sacrificed. Between February and August, 1816, the Directors lessened their discounts from *twenty-three millions* to *eleven millions;* and before February, 1817, to *eight millions;* and before August of the same year, to *seven millions:* whilst up to nearly the same period, they held of Exchequer-bills, etc. *twenty-five millions!* This reduction of private discounts answered two purposes of the Bank: it kept their circulation within bounds; and, if it slaughtered the merchants and manufacturers, it brought about another novelty; viz. *a reduction in the price of gold* down to *four pounds the ounce;* or nearly to the mint-price! This enabled them to get gold on easier terms, and to make a flourish, by the voluntary issue of a large sum in sovereigns; a measure absurd and premature to the last degree, for by this addition thrown into the currency, the prices of gold and silver bullion were again raised a little, and the whole of this new coin was exported!

This reduction of the Bank issues, and destruction and crippling of the Country Banks, had another and still more important effect, inasmuch as by causing the price of gold to fall to nearly the mint-price, it encouraged the political economists to press forward, and, at last in 1819, to pass an act, the most important in its consequences, and extraordinary in its circumstances, that ever was decided upon by any legislature, in any age or country. This was the celebrated Bill "for the Restoration of Cash Payments," passed in 1819, and since famous as "Peel's Currency Bill."

The great cause of the passing of the Currency Bill of 1819, was doubtless the extraordinary fall (as it seemed to most people) of the price of the precious metals; but another cause was also in operation; and this was the alarming increase of the forgery of Bank one and two-pound notes. The actual forgers of these notes could never be traced in almost any instance; but the "utterers," as the law terms them, were hanged in such numbers, that at last the juries shrank back, appalled at the shedding of so much blood as a holocaust to Threadneedle-street, and refused to convict upon the insufficient evidence adduced as to the actual fact of forgery. The convictions had generally taken place upon the mere oath of a hired "inspector of Bank-notes," who swore the note was not genuine, but refused to reveal the sources of his knowledge! This dreadful practice went on for years, until, at last, it began to be suspected that these men were not unfrequently *mistaken*, and the juries began to shrink from "a verdict of guilty" on such evidence. The convictions had in the mean time grown to so horrible an extent, that men hardly felt themselves safe in offering small Bank of England notes in payment, unless they could prove from whom they had had them. In consequence of all this, the credit of the notes began to be so shaken, that an alarm of extensive forgery, if cunningly gone about, might have made them share the fate of the French assignats. As no *inimitable note* could be discovered, nothing remained but the extinction of the smaller paper; and upon this the economists were now determined.

The Currency bill of 1819 was passed at the instance of a committee, amongst the members of whom were included all the parliamentary dabblers in political economy of any name or talent, and of whom Peel was chairman. Horner, the chairman of the bullion committee of 1810, was dead; but, in his stead, they had Ricardo, a rich Jew stock-jobber, who having made an immense fortune by this worst species of gambling, had also contrived to obtain a reputation by the publication of some books on political economy; ingenious in argument, but, in many points, of very questionable soundness; and frequently substituting an elaborate superficiality for wisdom and depth of reflection. Backed by the authority of this rich and arrogant man, the economists obtained on this occasion an almost entire command of the House of Commons. The ministry were led into the snare, with open eyes indeed, but, like somnambulists, with eyes of which "the sense is shut." They selected a young member of their own body, Mr. Peel, to bring the bill for the restoration of cash payments before the House of Commons; and hence the bill, much to his detriment, has borne his name. It is only justice to say that to Mr. Peel, now Sir Robert Peel, the obloquy of this greatest blunder that ever legislature committed, ought not to be given. He was but the mouth-piece, and the ignorant mouth-piece, of an ignorant and blundering House of Commons, led by the nose by a self-conceited but shallow junta of theorists. He was pitched upon for this unfortunate service, merely because he was a *young man* of aspiring pretensions, vast wealth, and of that sort of mediocre, but well-cultivated and accommodating talent, which recommends its possessor as likely to do what is expected to pass for a brilliant thing cleverly and showily. The fact was, the whole debate on this bill was a laughable farce. The mind of nearly every man in both Houses was made up to support this measure. That the finger of Providence was manifestly in it, I cannot doubt, until I doubt whether there *be* a Providence. *Quos Deus vult perdere, prius dementat!* The Houses made the plunge with one accord. There was hardly the semblance of an opposition. Ricardo had the enormous folly to tell the House that the bill was "not worthy of half an hour of even *their* consideration;" and assured them that the whole question was one of "three per cent.;" this being the *extent* of the *fall of prices*, which this man calculated would take place, after all the one and two-pound notes in the kingdom were burned, and the remainder, of five pounds and upwards, made "payable on demand in gold sovereigns, coined from metal worth *three pounds, seventeen shillings, and tenpence halfpenny the ounce*"!

In short, there was only one man in the Commons who really understood and opposed the measure; and this man was Mr. Matthias Attwood. The Bank directors had, indeed, said, they "feared the country could not bear the measure," but they dared not oppose it; and Mr. Attwood was prevailed upon to quit the House that the vote might be "unanimous"! In the House of Lords, Lord Grey alone ventured to dissent from the measure; but he only "washed his hands of it," as Pontius Pilate did before him, suffering the deed to be done, and drily saying, "he hoped it would produce the consequences which their lordships expected from it;" a significant sentence, and one of which their lordships must have, since that time, often thought! The Houses, however, for once, "were all in one accord." The Speaker and the Prince Regent congratulated each other on the completion of this monument of the legislative wisdom of the empire; and "the question of cash payments" was, in the flippant phrase of Mr. Canning, "set at rest for ever"!

As a bit of legislation, this ever-memorable act is remarkably brief, and to the point; consisting only of *thirteen* not very long nor wordy clauses. It repeals, in the first place, all the acts for restraining the Bank from paying its creditors, which had been passed from 1797 up to that time, the repeal going into effect "from and after the first day of May, 1823." This was a repeal of all Bank-notes on demand for sums *less* than *five pounds*. It then provides for a gradual return, in the mean time, by the Bank to cash payments; beginning with an issue of gold at *four pounds one shilling the ounce*, in 1820, and ending with the standard mint-price of £3 17*s.* 10½*d.* The concluding clauses repeal all the old statutes against the melting and exportation of coin or plate, and repeal also the *oath* required from exporters of bullion, that it was not melted plate or coin, or clippings of coin, as far as relates to the melting portion, retaining only the portion that applies to clippings of the coin of the realm. It also required, that the Bank should *publish*, every quarter, until May, 1823, an account of its average circulation, for the benefit of the lieges, who might doubt as to the prudence with which its affairs were conducted; an arbitrary and questionable step, but which was afterwards extended much further, on a subsequent occasion.

This was the substance of the celebrated bill to which the name of "Peel" has, unfortunately for his reputation, been wedded, after a fashion that admits of no divorce in future time. By all, except the few minutely acquainted with its history, he will be believed to be the originator and framer of an act, which, if, as is too probable, not only the present system, but the present form of government, be doomed to be in no long time swept away, will be found to have been one of the grand preparatory causes of the catastrophe. That Sir Robert Peel is, partly at least, of the same opinion, seems evident in the attempts which he has so often made to shake off his reputation for its exclusive authorship, and to place the *onus* of the deed upon the rightful shoulders. For these attempts, no man of common sense can blame him; and the only objection to them is, that they must be fruitless as to the result which he so palpably desires.

I must here conclude this Letter. In my next, I shall advert to some of the *warnings*, which the authors of the measure received as to its inevitable consequences; and we shall, as the periods arrive, see how completely these warnings were, in the ripeness of time, one after another, fulfilled and verified.

LETTER XII.

THE POLICY OF PEEL'S CURRENCY ACT DOUBTED.—MR. COBBETT'S LETTER TO TIERNEY ON THE SUBJECT OF CASH PAYMENTS.—HIS PREDICTION ON THE PASSING OF THE BILL.—THE PREDICTION GENERALLY LAUGHED AT.—THE EFFECTS OF THE BILL.—CRIME INCREASES.—EXECUTIONS FOR FORGERY.—BLOODY SCENE AT MANCHESTER.—THE SIX ACTS.—DIFFICULTIES OF THE GOVERNMENT INCREASE.—THE DEAD-WEIGHT SCHEME.—ITS FAILURE.—THE SAVINGS BANKS COMMENCED BY GEORGE ROSE.—HIS MOTIVES.—THE INJUSTICE OF THE SCHEME.—ITS PROBABLE EFFECTS.—SECRET ADDITIONS TO THE DEBT, BY MEANS OF THESE BANKS.—RECIPROCITY SCHEME, ITS CAUSES.—REPEAL OF THE NAVIGATION LAWS.—COMPARATIVE TABLES OF SHIPPING.—THE PRUSSIAN LEAGUE.—FOREIGNERS SEE THE WEAKNESS OF ENGLAND.—THE DUKE D'ANGOULÊME ENTERS SPAIN.—EFFECT ON EUROPE.—BANK DIMINISHES HER CIRCULATION AND DISCOUNTS.—GENERAL FALL OF PRICES, AND CONSEQUENT DISTRESS.

ALTHOUGH the Currency Bill of 1819, which was to set that much controverted question "at rest for ever," but of which we have since heard so much, was passed by a unanimous vote of both houses, this was not exactly the case out of doors. Throughout the country, there were many persons who disputed the justice and who denied the policy of the measure; and amongst these, were that steady and numerous class of thinkers, of whom the late Mr. Cobbett was the head and leader, and whose organ his "Political Register" especially was. In the pages of this celebrated publication, from the moment when this measure was first mooted, the government was emphatically warned of the consequences which must inevitably ensue, if it were carried into effect, as apparently intended by its partisans; and especially in the year 1818, when Mr. Tierney made a speech expressly to drive the ministers into the course which they eventually took, the author of the register, in a letter to that gentleman, dated from Long Island in the United States, on the 1st July of that year, fully demonstrated the effects that would follow, if, without accompanying measures, the bank was forced to resume metallic payments. In this letter, it was shown, with all that force and clearness, for which its author was remarkable, that it was impossible for the bank to begin and continue to pay its notes in gold and silver, without a great accompanying diminution of the quantity in circulation; that this diminution on the part of the bank must cause a corresponding diminution every where else; and these, united, a fall in prices, which must be ruinous universally, if the then amount of taxes was attempted to be collected; and which, in any case, would be ruinous to all who held stocks of goods, or who owed large sums, or who had heavy mortgages on house and land. The few who understood this question knew that the fall in the price of bullion, on which the economists laid so much weight, was only brought about by a state of distress, till then hardly known in England. But they knew this was not the worst; that had it not been the case that gold, owing to the state of the balance of trade and the secret melting of the coin, had been a sort of "drug" in England for years, this would not have happened; and that, if a further diminution of the floating paper were ventured, a further reduction in the price of commodities, not of *three* but probably of *thirty per cent*, would inevitably follow.

These warnings, I need scarcely say, were totally lost upon those to whom they were addressed. The conceited economists laughed them to scorn; and the press generally treated them as the effusions of disaffected or absurd persons. The bank directors disregarded them so far as to issue, whilst the prices of both gold and silver were above par, a large sum in coin, which was in a short time either melted or else exported. The economists, however, persevered; and in the year 1819, the memorable bill of Peel was passed, amid the loud cheers of a full House of Commons, and shortly afterwards became law. Upon the news of this event reaching America, Mr. Cobbett wrote another article on this subject, in which he had the boldness to say, that "before this bill could be carried into complete execution, a million of persons, at least, must die of hunger;" that it never would be completely carried out; and that, "if it were so, he would suffer Castlereagh to broil him alive, whilst Sidmouth stirred the coals, and Canning stood by to make a jest of his groans!" The audacity of this declaration unquestionably excited shouts of derision amongst the ignorant and rancorous many, whilst it somewhat astounded even the few, who generally agreed with the writer; for, at this moment, no man dreamed that the bill would be absolutely *prevented* from being carried into effect at the period determined on; that is to say, on May the 1st, 1823. Mr. Cobbett, who soon after returned to England, adhered, however, stoutly to his prediction. When, in the progress of our narrative, we touch upon this period, we shall see what the event actually was; but before making this step, we must notice one or two intermediate matters, which, though of minor importance, we cannot leave unadverted to.

Distress is the real parent of crime. Keep a people at ease, and their moral teachers must be at fault indeed, if the mass is not well conducted and honest. Plunge them into misery and desperation, and vice and criminality shall, forthwith, begin to stalk through the land. We have already seen, that from the increasing pressure of the debt and taxes, and from the ease with which it was effected, the crime of uttering forged bank-notes had grown, until the juries grew sick of blood; and executions, as a spectacle, even ceased to interest the strangely constituted minds that find a pleasure in such exhibitions. Well might this be, when we learn the appalling fact that in the single year of 1820, *one hundred and fifty-four persons* were tried at the Old Bailey alone for uttering false notes; and that, of these, *forty-six* suffered death; being at the rate nearly of a victim per week, through the twelve months! This, however, was only a part of the mischief of the time. The enormous distress caused by the breaking of the banks and the stoppage of the manufactories, produced its own peculiar fruits; and these were the bloody outrage at Manchester, and those infamous acts commonly called "the six acts." Into the details of the first, it does not accord with my plan to enter. They are well known, and must be remembered whilst England has a history. Of the second, I may say, that they completely swept away the little that was left having the semblance of freedom in England. They prevented even a dozen or two of people meeting in a room without a license. They gave the magistrates power to enter private dwellings and seize any arms found therein. They prohibited everything having the semblance of martial exercises on the part of the people. They gave the ministers power to imprison persons at their pleasure. They made political libels felonies, punishable by transportation; and lastly they surrounded the press with so many difficulties, publishers of newspapers being compelled to give security beforehand, to answer for any libel which possibly *might* be inserted therein, and to deposit at the stamp office a copy of every paper they published, that unless backed by one of the great political parties that ruled the state, to conduct a political journal became a matter of deadly peril; and freedom of writing was at an end. Every man who really opposed, in writing, the existing system of tyranny and deception, was sure of pecuniary ruin and the loss of liberty—perhaps of life. The few honest and intelligent public writers at that time existing were exiled or silenced; and, upon the whole, the most dismal and dark year of English history was perhaps that of 1819. That famous bill, however, which we have just seen the houses of parliament pass so unanimously, soon made amends for all. Some of "the six acts" were temporary, and expired. The laws concerning the press, however, remain to this hour;

but the changes produced by the workings of the bill of Peel, have enabled the people partly to overgrow them; and their sting is all but gone.

Such were the fruits of the revulsion of the paper-money, as far as respect for the maxims of constitutional law was concerned; but it produced more novelties than these. Amidst the doubts, fears, and general want of confidence, caused by appalling ruin which flowed from the sudden drawing-in of the paper, and by the bloody outrages and bitter persecutions, which again flowed from the effects of that ruin, it was felt necessary to attempt to draw, if possible, the ties that bound the middling classes of the nation to the funding and paper system still closer, and to add, if such a thing could be accomplished, to the strength and number of these ties. Close observers, and those especially behind the scenes of this strange drama, saw that the fabric was now beginning to show signs of dissolution. The people, amazed that a state of peace, instead of its usual blessings, had brought a palpable increase of difficulty and suffering, showed a marked and alarming impatience under their manifold burthens. In proportion as the discontent was strong, had the government, of a sudden, become weak. That strength which is derived from the power of lavishing immense sums of money was gone for ever. The eight hundred millions of debt were borrowed and expended. No increase could be made here; and those who carried on the government were, henceforward, bound by the bill of Peel to pay the interest of that debt in convertible money of the value of £3. 17s. 10½d., to the ounce of gold; and to raise all their taxes in money of the same value, which was (had they known it) a virtual bar to any future increase in the proportionate issues of paper, however desirable the ease obtainable from such issues might be. We shall, in due time, see the effects of their ignorance of their position in this respect; but, in the mean time, they could not help feeling that some strange change was come upon their state, and that more strength, if such could be, was desirable.

The scheme hit upon as the most likely to answer this purpose, that is to say, the erection by government of the institutions called " Savings' Banks," was first patronised, in or about the year 1816, by a pensioner and placeman, well known in those days as " old George Rose;" a favourite servant of Mr. Pitt, and a man who succeeded in amassing a large fortune " in the service of his country," under various administrations. In 1817, these institutions, under the force of an act of Paliament, were commenced in good earnest, and have gone on increasing ever since. That the whole was a plan for connecting persons of very moderate means with the funding system, I cannot for a moment doubt; for I do not believe that either Mr. Rose or the ministry of that period ever anticipated the use that succeeding governments have, in their extreme need, made of the funds of these banks. With the details of the plan of these establishments, most people are acquainted; and the *design* appears manifest enough in the details. Persons having sums of *two hundred pounds*, or less, to spare, are invited to deposit them in these banks for security; and at first, a rate of interest was paid them, rather above that which was yielded by the funds. This money, so deposited, is placed in the hands of government commissioners, who are empowered to invest it in various government securities, the balance of interest and expenses not obtained in this way, being made up *out of the taxes.* Thus a small advantage was given to these banks: *first,* by a higher rate of interest than the funds yielded; and *next,* in being secured from the loss which sometimes follows fluctuations in the value of stock. The temptation answered its end; and the sums deposited have so much increased, that government has been compelled to lower the interest, and to take stringent precautions against capitalists, who to a great extent lodged money in these banks in the names of others. It is curious, but, from first to last, hardly a word has been uttered anywhere against the injustice of this cunning scheme, which goes upon the principle of taxing those who cannot save, to take care of the money and pay the interest of those who can. Of late years, however, still worse uses have been made of these institutions. By a clause, in the act for *amending* the management of the Savings' Banks, the commissioners have (it is said), deemed themselves authorised to receive new Exchequer bills from government, in lieu of similar securities held by them, the minister re-selling or funding the old bills so obtained, or in other words creating new stock by some circuitous method, and thus surreptitiously adding to the amount of the already unmanageable debt. It is quite certain, that the government has been recently charged, in open parliament, with spending these moneys, so placed in the hands of their own commissioners, and by some indirect process increasing the amount of debt to a corresponding extent; nor was any *denial* ventured to be given of the truth of the accusation. Upon this part of the "saving-bank system" comment is surely unnecessary.

That the government really derives much strength from these institutions I am inclined to doubt. It is impossible to believe, that much of this money can belong to the active and toiling portion of the people, because, as the deposits have increased, the wages of labour, and profits of trades, have decreased; whilst the poor-rates have swelled, year after year. But it is from the strong hands and hardy spirits amongst a people, that a government, in its need, must look for succour, and these are not implicated in the hoards of these banks; whilst, in a state of national alarm, the very nature of these establishments would render them dangerous in the extreme. Let a panic of invasion, of European war, or of civil insurrection, once take place, and these banks might, in the course of a few weeks, be called upon to repay the millions deposited (now above twenty), in gold and silver; and this at a time when the irritation arising from the inability to perform their engagements, would be most dreadfully perilous to the government which invented them.

These banks were one of the many strange things that arose out of that debility in the Government, which sprang out of the reduction in the paper-issues which the peace of 1814 brought with it; but there were many more. It would be inconsistent with proper brevity to advert to many of these changes; but two or three of the principal innovations of the period I must mention; and as their foundations were laid between the period of 1819, and that fixed for carrying the currency bill into full effect, I shall advert to them in this place. The first is the scheme for lessening the weight of the half-pay, and naval and military pensions, commonly called "the dead-weight." The next, the relaxation of the ancient navigation laws, under the pretext of encouraging "free trade," and promoting our intercourse with foreign nations.

The "dead-weight scheme" which, in its end, was one of the most delusive bungles ever attempted and mismanaged by a minister of state, was a plan for lessening the weight of these payments upon the finances of the now impoverished Government, and pushing it forward for a few years upon another generation. It arose altogether out of national poverty; and in its failure, as such schemes mostly do, it rendered that poverty still more galling. The idea was this. Up to the year 1822, and at the commencement of that year, the naval and military pensions amounted, in round numbers, to the enormous sum of *five millions sterling;* a sum equal to Queen Anne's whole revenue! On calculating the value of the lives of the heroes and heroines who received these pensions, it was found that the whole might, by a gradual decrease, be expected to be extinguished in the course of *forty-four years*; and upon these two facts this scheme was based. In order to ease the existing Government of this tremendous weight, as it then pressed, the average or mean value of these pensions for lives was calculated and found; and the result was, that if any party could be met with who would pay yearly the sums to which these pensions were calculated *as being likely to amount*, in each and every year of the forty-four, such party would be *remunerated* if the nation paid to him an annual sum or annuity of *two millions, eight hundred thousand pounds* during the whole forty-four years; at the end of which, the pensions were expected to become extinct. By this plan, the burthens of the existing Government would have been lessened, and those of a future administration augmented; but, unluckily, no parties could be found ready to grapple with this extensive bargain. At last, however, the Bank agreed to purchase as much of the annuity as amounted to 585,740*l.*; but the scheme was varied, for instead of the Bank purchase-money being in payments spread over *forty-four* years, it was arranged that all paid by the Bank should be advanced in *six* years. Hence, the matter took this shape, that during *six* years, the commissioners, who were to manage the transaction, received out of the consolidated fund 2,800,000*l.* Of this they paid 585,740*l.* to the Bank, and the balance, together with the Bank's purchase-money, was paid into the Exchequer as a part of the ways and means! Thus, by this juggle, there appeared an accession to the revenue, to a large amount, for these six years; at which time it ceased; and the country had to go on paying 585,740*l.* up to the end of the "forty-four years," which will not expire until A.D. 1867. It was these six years' payments, lasting from 1823 until 1829, that created the apparent *surplus* which ended with the Duke of Wellington's administration in the following year; so that this entire transaction has been a "ruse;" the country being saddled with the payment to the Bank, and having the existing half-pay and pensions to discharge as before!

This strange and blundered transaction was one effect of the difficulties which now began to throng and surge round the Government; another was the necessity which now manifested itself for the altering of the famous and ancient navigation laws, which had existed intact from the time of their enactment under the powerful and wise rule of the Protector Cromwell; but which were now to be sacrificed to the embarrassments of an enfeebled and impoverished system. These laws were of a most stringent order, and secured to the British marine a complete monopoly almost of British transit commerce. Under these acts, no goods, the produce of Asia, Africa, or America, could be imported into England, unless in British ships, and these manned, all but one-fourth, by Englishmen. European goods, in foreign bottoms, were not prohibited, but were highly taxed; as compared with the same commodities by British vessels. It was the proud position of England, at this time, which, alone, enabled her to pass such laws. Her exports were of infinitely more consequence to the nations who took them, than to her who sent them. Her imports were chiefly luxuries, with which she could, if requisite, dispense; but her taking which was of vital consequence to the foreigner who dealt in them. At this time, too, the power of England was so great, that foreign statesmen trembled at the name of Cromwell; and a threat of war by England was quite sufficient to carry consternation into every European cabinet, from one end of the Continent to the other.

At the period at which we have now arrived, all this was reversed. It had become of vital importance to Great Britain, that Europe should continue to take her manufactures. She had reared an immense and poor population, nearly dependent for daily bread upon the uninterrupted transit of the stuffs which they wove or helped to weave; and, therefore, to ensure the continuance of this transit, foreigners were to be coaxed and bribed; for, with a debt of eight hundred millions sterling, it was felt by the ministers, that threats of *war* were out of the question! Foreign nations had now begun to manufacture for themselves; and when we complained of the restrictions which they laid upon *our* goods, their answer was, "Look at your own navigation laws, and the prohibitions which they lay upon goods *from us!*" This was thunder! This was an argument which an embarrassed and unpopular Government was in no condition to resist. The miserable ministers, therefore, "made a virtue of necessity," and unwillingly sacrificed the marine supremacy of England, in order to give a short respite, for it was no more, to her manufactures. To give a colour to this transaction, the economical system of "free trade" was adopted; and British shipping, loaded as it was, with its share of a taxation unparalleled in extent, was exposed to an unequal competition, by the repeal of these laws, with the comparatively untaxed vessel of the foreigner. The result has been ruin enormous amongst the ship-owners of this country, and a decline of our *carrying trade* between England and the States of Europe, which can neither be concealed nor glossed over. The following tables speak for themselves. They give the carrying trade, as it was before 1823, when the "reciprocity acts" were law, and after that period.

COMPARATIVE SHIPPING TABLE.

	1822. Ships.	1822. Tons.	1839. Ships.	1839. Tons.
British Shipping to Prussia	539	102,847	721	111,470
„ Denmark	57	7,096	49	5,536
„ Norway	168	13,377	21	2,582
„ Sweden	123	20,799	49	8,359
	887	144,119	840	127,947
Prussian Shipping to Britain	258	58,270	1283	229,208
Danish Shipping - -	44	3,910	1531	106,690
Norwegian Shipping - -	558	87,974	868	109,228
Swedish Shipping - -	71	13,692	272	49,270
	931	163,846	3954	494,396

These Tables relate to the carrying trade with the north of Europe. The following, however, shews the general effects of the "Reciprocity System" upon the commercial marine and transit trade of Great Britain. It there appears, that but for our increasing colonies, and for the United States, in whose favour the navigation laws were gradually relaxed after the peace which secured their independence, and whose cotton exports are of great consequence to both nations, the British marine would have probably declined upon the whole ere this. The future may be different.

ANALYTICAL TABLE,

Showing the Tonnage, at different Periods, between the United Kingdom and the Principal Geographical Divisions of the World.

Divisions.	1802. Tonnage.	1802. Centesimal Proportion.	1814. Tonnage.	1814. Centesimal Proportion.	1835. Tonnage.	1835. Centesimal Proportion.
With the States of Europe	1,034,517	63.28	1,126,152	65.06	1,615,563	48.59
British Dominions in Europe, without Ireland	60,275	3.69	84,755	4.90	165,233	4.97
With the United States	123,108	7.33	(war) 476	0.03	370,924	11.15
With *foreign* American Colonies	1,804	0.41	67,163	3.88	101,806	3.06
British American Colonies	268,463	16.42	348,188	20.12	803,596	24.17
With Africa -	44,070	2.70	15,945	0.92	48,586	1.46
India and *the Cape*	59,546	3.64	41,993	2.43	149,958	4.51
New South Wales	—	—	561	0.03	35,919	1.08
Greenland, and the Southern Fisheries	43,021	2.63	45,375	2.63	33,636	1.01
Totals - -	1,634,804	10.000	1,730,808	10.000	3,325,211	10.000

The above is from "Porter's Progress of the Nation." It certainly shows a small increase of our European transit trade up to 1835, taken alone; but a decrease as compared with our whole shipping trade. Since that date, a decline must have begun to take place. Mr. Porter states, that "the value of the exports to all Europe, in the five years from 1832 to 1836, were *less* by nearly *twenty per cent.*, than those during the five years after the war, from 1815 to 1820. Since then, however, and in spite of all these concessions, "the Prussian League," which shuts out our manufactures from eighteen millions of Germans, has come into active operation: nor will this league be prevented from extending itself, unless by the cannon of some coalition to prevent the Czar of Russia from planting one foot on the Danube, and the other on the Indus or Ganges, whilst he sets up the shrine of St. Nicholas in the Mosque of St. Sophia at Constantinople!

All these signs of the weakness of the once haughty and hectoring English Government could not exhibit themselves at home, without attracting the eager gaze of foreign powers, and being understood by them; and that they were both seen and rightly interpreted by our rivals abroad, the conduct of France, in the memorable year of 1823, gave ample proof. I need not remind the intelligent reader, that during the last years of the war, the French, who had occupied Spain and Portugal, were driven from both, chiefly by the exertions of an English army paid by English money, assisted by Spanish and Portuguese soldiers, also paid by England, and generalled by the Duke of Wellington. When peace came, the Spanish prince, Ferdinand VII., took possession of the throne under English auspices, and accepted of a sort of "constitution" which, during the war, the Spanish Cortes had manufactured, under the guidance of the English ministers. The king, however, soon showed his reluctance to govern by this constitution, one of the grand aims of which was, to sell the rich possessions of the Catholic church in Spain, and with the proceeds to clear off the *debts*, which, during the conflict, Spain had contracted with the Jews of London and Amsterdam! Ferdinand, who was a zealous Catholic, and many of his subjects, abhorred this spoliation, which really despoiled themselves as well as the church, a large portion of whose revenues are expended in supporting the poor. The end was a civil war, during which the Cortes were forcibly assembled at Madrid, and the king coerced by a body of troops under the command of Riego, who was the "Constitutional" general. This crisis aroused all the feelings of ambition and rivalry in the French Government, so recently the apparent vassals of England. They determined to strike *a grand blow;* to re-assert their power; to regain their influence in Spain; and, lastly, to re-conquer, nominally for Spain, but really for themselves, the rich Spanish colonies of *Peru* and *Mexico,* now in rebellion against the mother country. To do this, they entered Spain with one hundred thousand men, headed by the Bourbon Duc d'Angoulême, the French king's nephew, with the avowed intention of putting down the Cortes, and re-installing King Ferdinand in full power, under French protection!

Here was an insult to England, who stood in the eyes of the world as the protectress of Spanish "Constitutional Liberty," and who, besides that, was looking at the contest going on in Mexico and Peru, as the means of opening a new emporium for the advent of cottons, and the absorption of gold and silver into the coffers of the Bank; and upon England, accordingly, the eager gaze of all Europe and all America was now turned. No man expected anything but an immediate war. The idea that *Great* Britain could, for one moment, succumb beneath this worst of all indignities, was scouted from one pole of the earth to the other. All the cavaliers of Europe began to equip themselves to attend the lists, and witness this unhoped for "joust" between two such rivals, and for such a prize. Alas! they reckoned without their host! The French knew better. King Louis XVIII., (maugre the asseverations to the contrary), *had learned*, whilst at Hartwell, *one fact;* and that was, that the period predicted by Hume, the historian, had now arrived, when *the salvation of the dividends* would, and must be preferred to the honour and safety of the country.

The calculations, upon which Louis XVIII. and his cabinet so confidently proceeded, were substantially these. They knew that the *government debt* was, in round numbers, *eight hundred millions of pounds sterling;* that the *interest* was, taking funded and unfunded debt, in round numbers, *thirty millions of pounds sterling;* and the *fundholders*, who receive this interest, about 275,839 in number. They knew also that these receivers may be classed as follows.

	Numbers receiving.
Fundholders who receive not more than £200 a year	250,816
Fundholders who receive not more than £1000 a year	22,934
Fundholders who receive not more than £4000 a year	1,937
Fundholders who receive sums *above* £4000 per annum	152
Total Fundholders	275,839

			Sums received.
The 250,816	Fundholders	probably receive .	£9,000,000
The 22,934	" "	probably receive .	8,500,000
The 1,937	" "	probably receive .	3,500,000
The 152	" "	receive *all the rest* .	9,000,000
275,839		Totals	£ 30,000,000

This "estimate" was made some years after, by Mr. Cobbett, from some *data* printed in 1829, by the Wellington ministry, for heaven knows what purpose. The general truth, however, was known before by all who had access behind the scenes; and this was enough for Louis *Dixhuit*, and Messrs. Villèle and Chateaubriand! They knew perfectly well, that the Jew or money interest was now quite predominant in England: they knew that the hundred and fifty-two men, who received the "nine millions" yearly, must be at the head of this interest, and consequently the real rulers of the country; and they knew, that, happen else what might, these men would never suffer that to take place which must, in its first consequences, more than jeopardise the payment of these yearly millions. They knew, that this *must be*, unless human nature were changed. They knew, that, however "honour" or however "patriotism" might call upon them, these receivers of annual millions must, with the venom, have also the adder's deafness; and they determined to persevere. Events soon proved that they were right. The ministers soon discovered that if "negotiations" failed, they were not "bound" to maintain the powers of the Cortes by force and arms! They advised and besought the Spaniards to compromise the matter in some way; but this the Cortes refused. They then offered to "mediate;" but France, having both eyes fixed on Mexico and Peru, refused to temporise any longer. In parliament every one exclaimed against France; but no one had the hardihood to utter the word "War." At last, whilst Lord Grey was offering up a prayer in the house of Lords, that "God in his infinite mercy might deny the French success," and Canning, who had now succeeded Castlereagh as secretary, was doing the same in the Commons, the French marched, and in a few weeks dispersed the Cortes, who had taken shelter in Cadiz, and reinstated Ferdinand in his arbitrary power! The jealousy of the holy alliance here interfered, and the departure of a French fleet and army to Mexico was prevented. The eyes of all Europe were, however, thenceforward opened to the *real situation* of England; and this first insult and aggression was, in due time, followed by a plentiful crop of national degradations. These shall be adverted to at the proper period. Other matters at present demand our attention. The national difficulties and distresses, out of which all these disgraceful exhibitions sprung, went on increasing, as a matter of course; their intensity aggravating, as the period for the completion of the currency-bill of Peel approached. It was now at hand. The French were across the Bidassoa, on that very first of May, when and after which a bank-note for any sum "under five pounds" was to be seen no more, and, to repeat the phrase of Canning, "the question was to be set at rest, for ever!" No wonder that the ministers, who were now well-nigh suffocated by petitions about agricultural and commercial distress; no wonder, that the two hundred and seventy five thousand and odd fundholders, who were now to receive their dividends in gold and silver on demand; no wonder, that the bankers, who were not only to cancel their "one and two pounders" but pay all the rest in standard-mint-coinage, should tremble at the very idea of a war, at a crisis so interesting! As it was, that crisis produced some curious results;

but these we must reserve for our thirteenth letter, "sufficient for the day being the evil thereof!"

Before we close the present letter, however, it will be proper to look at the proceedings of the Bank, preparatory to extinction "for ever" of the notes for sums under five pounds, in accordance with the provisions of the famous bill of 1819; and at the effects upon the prices of grain, butcher's meat, etc., produced by these preparations. Having done this, we shall be, in some measure, prepared for that which followed, and feel less wonder to see the house of Commons, in a manner, overwhelmed with petitions from all quarters, all complaining of the deep distress, agricultural and commercial, the produce of an act not yet carried into effect, but to carry which into effect the most complete, the house was pledged as deeply as words could pledge any set of men, who were not actually sworn upon the gospels, or bound in penalties to do that which they had so unanimously and boastingly promised to do. The following gives the Bank's circulation, from February 1819, down to the same period in 1823, and also her discounts.

Circulation		£	Securities		Discounts
27th February, 1819.			27th February, 1819.		
Notes and Post Bills	£17,772,470	25,126,700	Public	£22,355,115	31,455,000
Ditto under £5	7,354,230		Private	9,099,885	
29th February, 1820.			29th February, 1820.		
Notes and Post Bills	£16,794,980	23,484,110	Public	£21,715,168	26,187,490
Ditto under £5	6,689,130		Private	4,472,322	
28th February, 1821.			28th February, 1821.		
Notes and Post Bills	£17,447,360	23,884,920	Public	£16,010,990	20,796,270
Ditto under £5	6,437,560		Private	4,785,280	

28th February, 1822. CIRCULATION.	£	28th February, 1822. SECURITIES.	DISCOUNTS.
Notes and Post Bills £17,290,500 Ditto under £5 - 1,374,850	18,665,350	Public £12,478,133 Private 3,494,947	15,973,080
28th February, 1823. CIRCULATION.		**28th February, 1823. SECURITIES.**	**DISCOUNTS.**
Notes and Post Bills £17,710,740 Ditto under £5 - 681,500	18,392,240	Public £18,658,829 Private 4,660,901	18,319,730

Here we see that the bank, between 1819 and 1822, reduced her circulation, nearly by *seven millions;* and that in the course of this violent operation, she reduced her discounts to merchants from *nine millions* to *four millions.* The country banks, under the stringency of this treatment, and with the prospect of cancelling all their notes under five pounds, as a matter of necessity followed the lead of the parent bank; and the terrible effects of this joint action as affecting both agriculture and commerce, the reader need not be at a loss to conceive. In fact, the universal fall of prices ruined thousands; as, when we look at the extent of it, is no matter for wonder. The following exhibits the rapid reduction in grain and in butchers' meat.

Dates.	Wheat, per Quarter.			Mutton, per Stone, 8lbs.					Beef, per Stone, 8lbs.				
	s.		*s.*	*s.*	*d.*		*s.*	*d.*	*s.*	*d.*		*s.*	*d.*
Jan. 1819	64	to	82	5	0	to	6	4	4	0	to	5	0
July, 1819	58	,,	80	4	6	,,	5	2	4	6	,,	5	4
Jan. 1820	54	,,	70	3	4	,,	4	4	3	4	,,	4	8
July, 1820	58	,,	81	4	2	,,	5	2	3	6	,,	4	6
Jan. 1821	40	,,	62	3	0	,,	4	0	3	2	,,	4	2
July, 1821	36	,,	63	2	2	,,	3	4	2	8	,,	3	8
Jan. 1822	30	,,	66	2	2	,,	3	2	2	0	,,	3	0
July, 1822	30	,,	56	1	10	,,	2	6	2	0	,,	2	10
Jan. 1823	30	,,	50	2	4	,,	3	0	2	4	,,	3	0
July, 1823	46	,,	67	2	8	,,	3	6	2	4	,,	3	0

These are the prices of Mark Lane and Smithfield. In the country, prices went still lower; and commercial articles all partook, more or less, of the same depression. Iron, for instance, went down from £12 10*s*. per ton, to £8 10*s*. per ton. Havannah sugar from 60*s*. per cwt. to 42*s*. per cwt., coffee from 158*s*. to to 110*s*. per cwt. East India cotton from 1*s*. 8*d*. to 9*d*. per lb. Tobacco from 1*s*. 1*d*. to 7*d*. per lb. Memel deals from £22 to £17 per load. The extensive distress and ruin caused by this depression spread consternation, as a matter of course, through the country. The wonderful effects of that distress, as laid before parliament, and the results of this extraordinary state of things, we shall examine, amongst other matters, in our next letter.

LETTER XIII.

THE SESSION OF 1823.—FALL IN THE PRICES OF GRAIN AND ALL COMMODITIES.—UNIVERSAL DISTRESS.—THE PETITION OF CHARLES A. THOMPSON PRESENTED TO THE COMMONS.—ITS EXTRAORDINARY ALLEGATIONS.—MR. WESTERN FORCES ON HIS MOTION OF AGRICULTURAL DISTRESS, DEFEATED, BUT THE HOUSE PASS A SMALL-NOTE ACT, TO RESPITE THE ONE AND TWO POUND NOTES FOR ELEVEN YEARS.—MR. WESTERN'S PROOF OF THE REAL EFFECTS OF PEEL'S BILL.—THE DUC D'ANGOULEME TRAVERSES SPAIN, UNOPPOSED, AND DESTROYS THE CONSTITUTION.—EFFECTS OF THE SMALL-NOTE RESPITE.—GREAT RISE IN PRICES.—SPECULATIONS.—ENORMOUS FOREIGN LOANS.—ROBINSON CHANCELLOR OF EXCHEQUER.—HIS IGNORANCE AND DELUSION.—THE EXCHANGES TURN, AND PRODUCE THE PANIC OF 1825.—ITS EFFECTS.—LORD LIVERPOOL AND CANNING DIE.—JOINT STOCK BANKS COMMENCED BY GODERICH.—WELLINGTON MINISTER.—EXTINGUISHES THE SMALL NOTES IN 1829.—THE AGRARIAN FIRES.—THE TORY POWER BROKEN UP.

When the two Houses of Parliament met for the session of the year 1822–3, to the eyes of intelligent observers, an extraordinary scene presented itself. There, on one side, were the two Houses, constituting "the Imperial Parliament," gaged and pledged, as deeply and solemnly as ever men were pledged in all this world, to set the currency question "at rest for ever," as far as extinction of all Bank-notes for sums under five pounds, and the payment of the remainder on demand, in sovereigns coined out of gold at the rate of 3*l.* 17*s.* 10½*d.* per ounce troy, could set it at rest: and there, on the other side, were Mr. Cobbett, and his readers, with their *grid-iron*, ready either to repeat upon the person of that extraordinary man, the sad story of St. Lawrence, or to be adopted as a type and token of the triumph of his principles, as to this grand topic, for ever and ever! At this period, however, Mr. Cobbett did not stand so much alone, as he did at the time of his hazarding the prediction, with all its penalties annexed to it. As the memorable first of May, 1823, drew near, the country-bankers, as well as the Bank of England, naturally prepared themselves by a gradual narrowing of their circulation, for the dreaded hour of gold and silver payments "on demand," and the withdrawal of the small notes. We have already seen the fall in prices produced by this universal narrowing of the paper circulation. The effects of the distress produced all over the country, the consequence of this fall, we have yet to see.

The distress, ruin, and bankruptcy, which now took place, were universal; affecting both the great interests of land and trade; but, amongst the landlords, whose estates were burthened by mortgages, jointures, settlements, legacies, etc., the effects were most marked and out of the ordinary course. In hundreds of cases, from the tremendous reduction in the price of land which now took place, the estates barely sold for as much as would pay off the mortgages; and hence, the owners were stripped of all, and made beggars. I was, myself, personally acquainted with one of the victims of this terrible measure. He was a schoolfellow, and inherited a good fortune, made principally in the West Indies. On coming of age, and settling with his guardians, he found himself possessed of fully forty thousand pounds; and with this he resolved to purchase an estate, to marry, and to settle for life. He was a young man addicted to no vice; of a fair understanding, and a most excellent heart; and was connected with friends high in rank, and likely to afford him every proper assistance and advice. The estate was purchased, I believe, about the year 1812, or 1813, for eighty thousand pounds, one moiety of the purchase-money being borrowed on mortgage of the land bought. In 1822–3, he was compelled to part with the estate, in order to pay off his mortgage, and some arrears of interest; and when this was done, he was left without a shilling, the estate bringing only half of its cost in 1812! Thus, without imprudence or fault of any kind, was this amiable man, together with his family, plunged in irretrievable and inevitable ruin, by the act of a legislature which ought to have protected both, and which was fully warned of the consequences of what it was about to do; but which, in requital, chose to laugh those who warned to utter scorn. My readers must not suppose that this was either an exaggerated or uncommon case. On the contrary, the country teemed with similar examples; and on the commencement of the session of 1823, the tables of both Houses were loaded with petitions, detailing scenes of hardship and destitution, appalling in the extreme. As a sample of the whole, I have selected one, which most fully exhibits the dreadful effects of this infatuated measure upon the welfare and happiness of the community; and of this petition I here insert as complete an abstract as I can frame. The substance of this very extraordinary document was as follows. It was presented to the Commons by Lord Folkstone, and to the Lords by Earl Stanhope.

It sets forth, —

1. That the petitioner, having contributed both in purse and person to the maintenance of the State, had a right to expect *protection* of person and property in return; but that, instead of this, he is ruined by an act of the parliament.

2. That he imputes no *intentional* wrong-doing, but grievous error to the Government; yet he hopes the Government will not change error into injustice, by persevering in it.

3. That the petitioner's ruin, as well as that of thousands of other persons, arose from Peel's bill for returning to cash payments; but that few cases can exceed his in hardship.

4. That petitioner and his father were wine-merchants, and made a large fortune; with part of which, in 1811 and 1812, they bought land.

5. That they bought the estate of Northaw, in Herefordshire, for £62,000, and laid out £10,000 more in improvements, investing in all £72,000.

6. That, in 1812, they bargained with John A. Trenchard, Doctor of Divinity, for the estate of Pontrylas, for which they agreed to give £60,000, paying £5,555, as a deposit. That the title not being satisfactory, the result was a suit at law, which was not decided until 1819, when judgment went against them, awarding a gross sum of £71,957 19*s*. 5*d*. to Dr. Trenchard, being purchase-money and interest.

7. That in the mean time petitioners had experienced heavy losses in trade, and could not pay this sum; and, therefore, gave Dr. Trenchard a mortgage on *both* the estates of Northaw and Pontrylas, for £65,000.

8. That after 1819, when the suit ended, petitioner and his father paid £5,000 in part of the debt, and £8,000 interest up to 1821.

9. That on the suit ending in 1819, they received up to 1821, out of the estate, for rent and wood, £3,410.

10. That in July 1821, the *two* estates were offered for sale, but *would not bring the sum for which* they were *mortgaged.*

11. That in 1821, petitioner and his father were *bankrupts.*

12. That Dr. Trenchard then got possession of *both estates*, and gave notice to *foreclose the mortgage.*

13. That petitioner and his father thus actually paid Trenchard £18,555, and have only received out of the estate £3,410; and they are now about to lose both the estates of Pontrylas and Northaw; the last of which cost £72,000.

14. That Trenchard, on the other hand, has received in cash £18,555, with all the rents of Pontrylas from 1812 to 1819, and that he is now about to get the *two estates*, with all arrears of rent from February 1820, in lieu of his debt of £60,000.

15. That petitioners' assignees are praying the Court of Chancery not to *allow this;* for that, if it be granted, the result will be, that Dr. Trenchard will have received all the rents and profits of Pontrylas estate, except for two years; £1,470 for timber; £18,555

in cash from the petitioner, and in addition to his own original estate of Pontrylas, *he will also have got the other estate of Northaw, which cost* £72,000.

16. That petitioner and his father had other estates in Middlesex, Essex, and Hampshire, which cost £36,000, but have now been sold for £12,000! That by the depression in trade they became bankrupts. That petitioner's father died, in 1822, of a broken heart; and that he is himself a ruined man, with seven children of his own, ten of his brother's, and seven of his sister's, all depending on him.

17. That petitioner, therefore, prays for an EQUITABLE ADJUSTMENT of this and all similar contracts.

This petition was that of Charles Andrew Thompson, of Chiswick, in the county of Middlesex; and is certainly calculated to tear in pieces, almost, the heart of every just and sensible man that reads it. What effect it produced upon Peel, Ricardo, and the Houses I cannot say; but the country throughout was in a state of deep agitation, and remonstrance after remonstrance poured in upon the legislature. At last Mr. Western, one of the members for Essex, a man of good talents, gave notice of a motion for "inquiry" into the state of the country, and into the distress that now seemed to threaten a convulsion. This notice probably decided the ministers. Mr. Western's motion could not be stopped. It was, therefore, met and negatived, after a long debate of three or four nights, in which a determination amongst the landed interest to have an equitable adjustment of *public* as well as private contracts (including of course the debt), was more than hinted at. The negative vote, however, was only obtained by a total virtual "throwing overboard!" of Peel's bill. A short act was hastily smuggled, in silence, through the Houses, which enacted a respite (as the Houses fondly deemed) of the *one* and *two pound notes for eleven years.* The rest of Peel's bill as to cash-payments, etc., was left in full force; but still the prediction of Mr. Cobbett was really fulfilled; for, without the extinction of the small paper, —this act was (as we shall shortly see), something much worse than a dead letter, and actually brought the whole system nearer to the very gulph of destruction than it had ever been, narrow as were some of its escapes.

In the mean time, the country generally, the country bankers particularly, and the houses of parliament especially, were profoundly ignorant enough to imagine that this, in a different sense from that intended by Canning, was "a setting at rest of the question for ever." A respite, for *eleven years*, of the paper, was held to mean an *entire reprieve;* and, with the exception of the Bank of England, who, *luckily for herself*, would not avail herself of the small-note-respite act, the bankers universally put out their paper again, as if this state of things was to continue for ever, unalloyed by reverses and unvisited by storms.

Before we survey the strange events which were produced by this most ignorant attempt of the legislature to escape from the consequences of the ruinous, suicidal, and unjust Currency Act of 1819, we must advert to one portion of Mr. Western's speech, on moving for a committee of inquiry, as it puts the shocking injustice of that act in a light so strong, even upon the mistaken principle of Ricardo and the rest of its principal active abettors, that it must not be omitted. The honourable member for Essex, like all other sensible persons, contended that the prices of *grain* on the average, and not the price of *gold*, which was a sort of drug in England from 1797 to 1816, formed the true measure and criterion of the depreciation of the paper. But he also showed that, even upon the bullionists' *own* principles, the taxes, though nominally reduced after 1819, were actually rendered *heavier* than they had been in any year (after 1809) of war and bank-restriction, save the years 1810, 1815, and 1816. This he did by the following table.

Years.	Price of Gold	Difference from mint price.	Nominal Taxes.	Amount in Gold Currency.
	£ s. d.		£.	£.
1809	4 10 9	$16\frac{1}{3}$ per cent.	71,887,000	60,145,000
1810	4 5 0	$9\frac{1}{10}$	74,815,000	68,106,000
1811	4 17 1	$24\frac{1}{2}$	73,621,000	55,583,000
1812	5 1 4	30	73,707,000	51,595,000
Sep. to Dec. 1812.	5 8 0	$38\frac{1}{2}$		
1813	5 6 2	$36\frac{1}{10}$	81,745,000	52,236,000
Nov. 1812 to March 1813.	5 10 0	41		
1814	5 1 8	$30\frac{1}{8}$	83,726,000	58,333,000
1815	4 12 9	$18\frac{8}{9}$	88,394,000	66,698,000
1816	4 0 0	$2\frac{1}{2}$	73,909,000	72,062,000
Oct to Dec. 1816.	3 18 6	under 1 per ct		
1817	4 0 0	$2\frac{1}{2}$	58,757,000	57,259,000
1818	4 1 5	5	59,391,000	56,025,000
1819 to Feb.	4 3 0	$6\frac{1}{3}$	58,288,000	54,597,000
1820	3 17 $10\frac{1}{2}$		59,812,000	59,812,000
1821	3 17 $10\frac{1}{2}$		61,000,000	61,000,000

This statement proves, clearly enough, that even upon the principle of those who proposed it, the currency-bill of 1819, made the subsequent taxes, though nominally reduced, really far heavier than the average taxation of the period of the French war. When we recollect, however, that, in truth, the £88,394,000, of 1815, were not worth more than about *forty millions* of the money of Peel's bill, as measured by the prices of grain as they ruled prior to 1793, and as they have been since 1819, whenever wheat was plentiful enough to neutralise the action of the corn-laws, we cease to wonder at the ruin which followed even the attempt to carry the bill into effect. In spite of all the efforts to arrest it, this ruin has never really altogether paused since 1819. Either in agriculture or commerce, it has been more or less apparent, excepting, perhaps, in the years 1824 and 1836, when it was neutralised by the excessive issues of paper-money; and it must continue its insidious progress until, in all human probability, it will end by plunging England in the fathomless abyss of a total revolution.

We are now to contemplate the effects of the attempt to escape from the enactments of the bill of Peel and its assured consequences, by the small-note-respite act of the year 1823. As soon as this act was in force, the joy of the public, and especially of the unthinking portion of that public, was excessive. Landlords, farmers, bankers, merchants, shipowners, and tradesmen all joined in the universal exultation; and they were not long in persuading themselves, and each other, that the sun of national prosperity was now risen, never to decline, never to be eclipsed again! The consequences of this most besotted confidence were not long in shewing themselves. The country bankers pushed out fresh bales of paper, "nothing loth." Speculation roused himself, and commenced building fantastical castles in the air, after a fashion rarely, if ever, seen before. The South-sea madness seemed again to have become epidemic amongst the people. As the paper became excessive in amount, and the currency swelled and bloated itself, prices rose; and as prices rose, speculation took new forms. The whole national business became like some monstrous balloon in the process of inflation, and people indulged in golden dreams of the most preposterous description. The disgrace inflicted by the entrance of the Duc d'Angoulême into Spain, and his triumphant march to Cadiz which now took place, were forgotten, amidst visions of "prosperity;" and such were the varied and delusive schemes afloat, that, to the few sober-minded and intelligent spectators, the country seemed little better than huge Bedlam!

It has always been a favourite topic with political economists to carp at the management of the Bank of England; and, on this occasion, the conduct of the directors was severely blamed. This blame, I must own, seems to me to be not a little unreasonable. The bank, in the first place, has the merit of not having availed herself of the power to continue the issue of notes for one and two pounds; and, if we look at the returns of her circulation, we do not find any great impulse given to the over-trading and speculation that ran through the country.

THE CIRCULATION OF THE BANK OF ENGLAND,

				£.
30th August,	1823	was	- -	19,231,240
28th February,	1824	,,	- -	19,736,990
31st August,	1824	,,	- -	20,132,120
28th February,	1825	,,	- -	20,753,760
31st August,	1825	,,	- -	19,398,840

Now in this there is no great stimulus to the strange

speculations that obtained footing in these years. That the bank, by interposing sooner than she did, might have checked the mad movements of the capitalists, country bankers, and paper-kite-flyers, of all grades, is true enough. Few people, however, were aware of the extent of the danger thus brought about, until it was too late; and of some want of foresight the bank-directors were, perhaps, guilty. If the directors were dim-sighted, however, the ministers were blind, stone-blind, sand-blind, and gravel-blind; and where a government could not see at all, we may surely forgive a set of directors for not being too far-sighted. What the bank actually did not do, however, the capitalists, money-lenders, country bankers, and town discounters did for her, and the speculative madness of these years, certainly almost exceeds belief. Nothing approaching it in sheer insanity, had been witnessed since the epoch of the South-sea delusion; and, in 1824, some wag, who to humour added wit, re-published one of the pamphlets describing the South-sea madness, as a warning to those engaged in the fantastical schemes then rife. It was of no avail; but the parallel between the schemes of the times past and present, was both close and amusing. It is impossible, in a work like this, to give the details of all the different fantasies, which in the shape of Mining Companies, Insurance Companies, Building Companies, Shipping Companies, Colonising Companies, Railway Companies, Washing Companies, etc. etc. etc., then inundated the public. The following summaries, however, have been published as authentic; and those relating to the foreign loans no doubt are so in the main, having been given in to "the secret committee" on the Bank Charter. The others are of more questionable authority.

A LIST OF FOREIGN LOANS CONTRACTED IN ENGLAND

*(those marked * continue to pay dividends).*

Countries.	Amounts.	Dates.	Contractors.
* Austrian	£2,500,000	1823	Rothschild.
* Belgian	2,000,000	1832	Ditto.
* Brazilian	3,200,000	1824	Wilson and Co.
* Ditto	2,000,000	1825	Rothschild.
* Ditto	800,000	1829	Rothschild & Wilson
Buenos Ayres	1,000,000	1824	Baring and Co.
Chili	1,000,000	1822	Hullett and Co.
Columbian	2,000,000	1822	Baring and Co.
Ditto	4,750,000	1824	Goldschmidt and Co.
* Danish	5,500,000	1825	Wilson and Co.
Greek	800,000	1824	Loughnan and Co.
Ditto	2,000,000	1825	Ricardo and Co.
Guatemala	1,428,571	1825	Powles and Co.
Gunduljava	600,000	1825	Ellard, Jun.
Mexican	3,200,000	1824	Goldschmidt and Co.
Ditto	3,300,000	1825	Barclay and Co.
* Neapolitan	2,500,000	1824	Rothschild.
* Prussian	5,000,000	1818	Ditto
* Ditto	3,500,000	1822	Ditto
Portuguese	1,500,000	1823	Goldschmidt and Co.
Peruvian	450,000	1822	Frys and Co.
Ditto	750,000	1824	Ditto
Ditto	616,000	1825	Ditto
* Russian	3,500,000	1822	Rothschild
Spanish	1,500,000	1821	Haldimand
Ditto	1,500,000	1823	Campbell and Co.

Here are twenty-six different loans, all to foreigners, amounting in all to a sum of £55,794,671, eighteen of which were made in the years, 1823, 1824, and 1825. When we consider that upon only ten of these loans interest has continued to be paid, and that the other sixteen are, consequently, a total loss, the ruin caused in this way, by the epidemic madness of these years, may readily be conceived. Mr. Canning, who, at this period, possessed great power in the government, was a grand instrument in all this ruin.

In order to revenge, by a side-wind, the aggression of France upon Spain, he advised the recognition of the independence of the Spanish Insurrectionary Colonies. Hence arose the republics of Mexico, Peru, Columbia, etc., and the schemes of raising money for them in England; and for being instrumental to all this delusion and mischief, a statue is erected to this man, almost at the very doors of the houses of parliament. Those who literally credited his flashy and shallow effusions, imagined that all the gold and silver of Peru, and of Mexico was about to be poured into this country. The actual consequence was the generation of a host of wild and unprofitable speculations, amongst which were these loans, which were the means not of *bringing* but of *sending* enormous quantities of silver (as we shall shortly see), from Great Britain to these very countries. So much for the loan-speculations of these strange years; let us now examine the other schemes.

It has been calculated, that there existed in this country, up to the year 1823, as follows:—

Canal Companies	63
Dock ditto	7
Insurance ditto	25
Water ditto	16
Bridge ditto	4
Gas ditto	27
Road ditto	7
Miscellaneous	7
Total	156

The following is a statement of the new associations that sprung up after the year 1823, and the nominal capital *subscribed* for their various undertakings:—

74	Mining Companies	£38,370,000
29	Gas	12,077,000
20	Insurance	35,820,000
26	Investment	52,600,000
54	Railway and Canal	44,051,000
67	Steam	85,555,000
11	Trading	10,450,000
26	Building	13,781,000
23	Provision	836,000
202	Miscellaneous	148,109,600
532	Total	£441,649,600

For the accuracy of this extraordinary statement I cannot vouch. It is certain, however, that in 1825, decided alarm was expressed, by some of the most observing members of both Houses of Parliament, at the extraordinary prevalence of schemes and speculations of all descriptions; and ominous forebodings as to the future began to be entertained by the most intelligent everywhere. All, however, was lost upon the ignorant ministry. Warning was useless. If the people were bad, their rulers were infinitely worse; and, in the Session of 1824, the Honorable Frederic Robinson, a shallow and superficial man, then Chancellor of the Exchequer, had the incredible folly and senselessness to allude exultingly to the unnatural rise in prices then going on, and to boast of the matchless prosperity of the realm, as an indication of the perfection and faultless excellence of its government! Never was gasconade so unlucky as this hapless *escapade* of this most silly and contemptible of all financiers. It drew down upon him the immediate notice of Mr. Cobbett, who, in the celebrated letter addressed to "Mr. Prosperity Robinson," again predicted the utter dispersion of all these visions of wealth, and assured him, that "within eighteen months from that time," his banks would be blown up, and his prosperity be dissipated in their explosion. This prophecy was again unheeded; and the people and their rulers went recklessly on in their career of schemes and self-gratulations.

Towards the autumn of the year 1825, strong symptoms of the catastrophe, to which all things were tending, began to exhibit themselves. Wheat, which, in 1822, together with butchers' meat, had been greatly depressed, rose apace. The following Table exhibits the progress of the advance.

Years.	Wheat, per quarter.	Beef, per Stone.	Mutton, per Stone, 8 lbs.
	s. s.	s. d. s. d.	s. d. s. d.
January, 1822	30 to 66	2 0 to 3 0	2 2 to 3 2
July, "	30 ,, 56	2 0 ,, 2 10	1 10 ,, 2 6
January, 1823	30 ,, 50	2 4 ,, 3 2	2 4 ,, 3 0
July, "	46 ,, 67	2 4 ,, 3 2	2 8 ,, 3 6
January, 1824	46 ,, 75	3 0 ,, 4 0	3 0 ,, 3 10
July, "	46 ,, 71	3 8 ,, 4 4	3 8 ,, 4 4
January, 1825	56 ,, 80	4 2 ,, 5 0	4 8 ,, 5 8
July, "	56 ,, 76	4 4 ,, 5 0	4 4 ,, 5 0

The same cause that raised wheat and meat; that is to say, the multiplication of bank-notes in circulation; soon raised every thing else. Mr. Tooke, in his

Treatise on the State of the Currency, published in 1826, states, that in his belief "not less than *fifty per cent.*" was added, during these years, to the circulating money of the country. The effects were inevitable. "It became (says Mr. Tooke) the business of speculators and brokers to look minutely through the general price-currents, with a view to discover any article that had *not* advanced, in order to make it the subject of anticipated demand. If a person, not under the influence of the prevailing delusion, inquired for what *reason* any particular article had risen, the common answer was, 'every thing else has risen, and therefore this *ought to rise!*'" This fictitious prosperity gave an impulse to speculative gambling, unprecedented in modern times; so much so, that "persons removed from all business, retired officers, widows, and single women of small fortune, risked their incomes, or their savings, in every species of desperate enterprise; and the competition and scramble for premiums in concerns which ought never to have been otherwise than at a discount, were perfectly astonishing to those who took no part in these transactions."

This high-handed gambling, adding, as it did, every hour, to the quantity in circulation, affected, more or less, all merchandise, and all commodities, though not of course to the extent to which it acted upon the prices of grain. In commodities generally, the immense imports, caused by the gradually advancing markets, kept the prices in some degree in check. In grain, the advance caused by the depreciating currency went on without hindrance or control, the corn-laws standing in the way of importation.

The following table shows the rate of advance in commodities; gold, alone, being kept at mint-price by law.

COMPARATIVE TABLE.

(Bonding goods in bond.)

	1823			1825		
	£	s.	d.	£	s.	d.
Brimstone, rough, per ton - - - -	6	10	0	10	0	0
Butchers' Meat, Beef, per lb. - - - -	0	0	4½	0	0	8
" " Mutton " - - - -	0	0	4	0	0	7½
Cochineal, Spanish, " - - - -	1	0	0	1	6	0
Coffee, British Plantation, per cwt. -	6	0	0	6	13	0
" St. Domingo - - - - - -	4	2	0	4	8	0
Cotton, Georgia, bowed, per lb. - -	0	0	8½	0	1	6½
" Bengal and Surat, ditto - -	0	0	6½	0	1	1½
Flour, Yarmouth, per stone, 14lbs. -	0	1	8	0	2	6
Indigo, East India, per lb. - - -	0	9	9	0	16	0
Iron, per ton - - - - - - - - -	6	0	0	13	0	0
Lead, per ton - - - - - - - - -	22	10	0	30	10	0
Rum, Jamaica, per gallon - - - -	0	2	9	0	3	4
Extra " " - - - -	0	3	2	0	3	8
Salt Petre, East India, per cwt. - -	1	4	0	1	16	0
Spices, Cinnamon, per lb. - - - -	0	6	8	0	13	6
" Mace " - - - - -	0	5	2	0	18	0
" Nutmegs " - - - - -	0	3	1	0	12	0
" Pepper, Blk. " - - - - -	0	0	5½	0	0	9½
Spelter, per ton (1824) - - - - -	20	10	0	41	15	0
Sugar, B. P., Gar., average per cwt.	1	10	0	2	5	2
Sugar, White Havannah, per cwt. -	2	4	0	2	17	0
Silk Reggio, per lb. - - - - - -	0	11	6	0	17	0
" China, " - - - - - -	1	0	0	1	8	0
Tallow, per cwt Y. C. - - - - - -	1	11	0	2	3	0
Tobacco, Virginia, ordinary, per lb. -	0	0	2½	0	0	6½
Tin-Block, per cwt. - - - - - -	3	17	0	5	1	0
Wool, per lb. - - - - - - - - -	0	6	6	0	9	6

This advance, and, as most people ignorantly deemed it, stream of prosperity, went on unchecked until the autumn of the memorable year of 1825. The enormous quantities of manufactures forced by speculators abroad, balanced, or nearly balanced, the imports, great as they were, up to that period. About the month of July, however, the exchanges became unfavourable; and these symptoms becoming still more virulent, the Bank directors became alarmed at length, and by means of private sales of Exchequer bills, began to draw in their notes. It was too late, however, to avoid a crisis, and perhaps the most perilous that the system had yet encountered. The enormous *surplus* of imported goods was to be paid for. For this surplus, bills of exchange could not, by possibility, be obtained. The drawers of bills by trade were soon exhausted; the bills drawn against exports were all remitted; and for the balance, GOLD, of necessity, was to go; for the foreign loans being in great part remitted in *silver*, the country was, in 1823 and 1824, pretty well stripped of that metal.

As soon as the demand for gold became marked, decided, and progressive, the Bank, in alarm, began with all haste to draw in her circulation; and to effect this, she threw her Exchequer bills in such quantities upon the market, that these ticklish instruments, instead of bearing *a premium* as usual, went to *a discount*, and were beginning to be paid into the Exchequer by persons who had duties or taxes to discharge. As Bank-notes became scarcer, the discounters of bills became terrified, and refused all accommodation to their equally terrified customers. This roused panic amongst the London-bankers, who, in their dismay, turned round upon the country-bankers, their customers, and bade them "rely upon themselves for obtaining discounts." Thus suddenly "taken a-back," the country-bankers, in their fear, refused all accommodation to their trading customers, and by December, 1825, all

Great Britain and Ireland was in one scene of confusion, dismay, and bankruptcy. In order to give the reader the best idea I can of the position of affairs, during this period of mingled folly, ignorance, and madness, I insert, first, a statement of the exports of *silver*, and then of *gold*, during these years. These figures explain, better than words can, the causes and extent of the confusion that ensued.

RETURNS OF SILVER EXPORTED.

Years.	Silver Bullion.		Foreign Coin.		British Coin.		Total.	
	oz.	dwt.	oz.	dwt.	oz.	dwt.	oz.	dwt.
1822	7,980,315	10	6,565,506	8	0	0	14,545,821	18
1823	1,511,331	15	10,056,922	5	0	0	11,568,258	0
1824	2,516,680	0	6,069,056	0	0	0	8,585,731	0
1825	1,313,762	0	4,134,462	8	118,175	0	5,566,399	8

RETURNS OF GOLD EXPORTED.

Years.	Gold Bullion.		Foreign Coin.		British Coin.		Total.	
	oz.	dwt.	oz.	dwt.	oz.	dwt.	oz.	dwt.
1822	57,218	17	97,478	2	147,555	18	284,252	17
1823	87,022	0	111,351	8	98,000	0	296,373	8
1824	241,840	4	128,403	7	764,109	12	1,134,343	8
1825	291,668	14	126,608	17	855,646	1	1,273,323	13

The panic may be said to have been commenced in good earnest, by a Mr. Jones, of Bristol, who, towards the end of 1825, having demanded gold of a Bristol banker for his notes, was *refused*, and *notes of the Bank of England* tendered instead! Mr. Jones immediately sued for a writ to hold the banker to bail, and petitioned the House of Commons as to his case. The fact could not be denied, as there was Mr. Jones ready to attest it at the bar of the House; nor dared the ministers to deny the liability of the bankers to an action for having refused legal payment. This exposure acted strongly on the whole community, showing, as it did, the unsoundness of the entire state of things; and a gradual run for gold spread over the country. This general distrust soon produced its effects. The first grand stoppage was of the London bank of "Godfrey Wentworth, and Co.," with all its country branches. From that moment, consternation and panic-fear went on, until it reached its acme. Several London banks were brought to the ground; and upwards of one hundred country banks suspended payment. In some cases, such was the want of confidence, that goods were obtained *by barter only!* Nay, the whole country was, confessedly, and in the words of the ministers themselves, "within twenty-four hours" of that consummation; the Bank of England being drained of coin, and only saved from ruin by one of those extraordinary interpositions, which seem intended by Providence to save the Funding System, until it shall reach the very rottenness of ripeness, and ripeness of rottenness, and afford mankind an example, not to be mistaken; not be misconstrued; and not to be forgotten.

The position of the Bank of England I shall give, as described in evidence, by one of its principal directors, Mr. Jeremiah Harman, to the secret committee of 1832.

"Was there a period in December, 1825, during which the Bank contemplated the probability of being entirely exhausted of gold?" "At the latter end of 1825, *decidedly*."

"Do you recollect the lowest quantity of gold which the Bank possessed during any period of December, 1825?" "I do not remember immediately; but it was *miserably low*."

"Was it under the £1,300,000 you have mentioned?" "*Unquestionably*."

"It was stated by the late Mr. Huskisson, that he, as a member of the administration at that time, suggested to the Bank, that, if their gold were exhausted, they should place a paper against their doors, stating 'that they had not gold to pay with, but might expect to have gold to recommence payment in a short period;' do you recollect such a suggestion?" "There *was* such a suggestion."

"What would, in your opinion, have been the consequence of that paper, placed against the door of the Bank, without preparation to support commercial and financial credit?" "*I hardly know how to contemplate it*."

"The Bank issued one-pound notes at that period. Was that done to protect its remaining treasure?" "Decidedly; and it worked wonders. And it was by *great good luck* that we had the means of doing it; because one box, containing a quantity of one-pound notes had been *overlooked*, and they were forth-coming *at the lucky moment!*"

"Had there been *no foresight* in the preparation of these notes?" "None whatever; *I solemnly declare*."

"Do you think that the issue of these one-pound notes *did* avert *a complete drain?*" "As far as my judgment goes, *it saved the credit of the country*"!

No words can go further than these do to portray the scenes then going on. The whole system, debt, dividends, dead-weight, half-pay, pensions, secret service-money, Exchequer bills, and all together, were within a few hours of total destruction and irretrievable ruin! It has been asserted, that Mr. Thomas Attwood, afterwards member for Birmingham, was the man who suggested the issue of the "lucky box" of one-pound notes. Be that as it may, it is evident that Providence, in its inscrutable purposes, had seen fit to bring the whole affair to the very verge and brink of the gulf, until it heard the very roaring of the fires, and yet continue it for a season longer. There is abundant proof (extraordinary as it may appear), that the whole catastrophe came upon the wretched and ignorant Government, without being foreseen almost for a single hour! When pressed by the horror-struck Directors to try to play, a second time, the trick of Pitt's "Bank Restriction," they had not nerve to move; and Huskisson's advice about the "paper on the door," was all the comfort they could give the Bank. In truth, the probability was, that all was put upon his shoulders. The empty Canning was, just before the storm burst, sailing in senseless security about the Cumberland lakes, and listening to flatteries as nauseous as they were undeserved. Lord Liverpool had no nerve left; and Robinson, the silly Chancellor of the Exchequer, never had any to begin with; so that, saving Huskisson, there was not a man of business to apply to. The result of the application we have seen.

The mass of ruin brought about by this terrible explosion of the paper system, it is not possible either to estimate or detail. The commissions of bankrupt issued against *Country Banks*, stand as follows:—

1825	January - -	1	
	September -	1	
	October - -	5	
	December - -	30	
		--	37
1826	January - -	12	
	February -	10	
	March - -	11	
	April - -	3	
	May - -	5	
	September -	1	
	November -	1	
		--	43
	Total - -		80

In London, where the bankers do not issue notes, the stoppages were fewer comparatively, and less disastrous.

When the imbecile ministers began to recover somewhat from their consternation, they got a perception of one truth; and this was, that cash payments and small notes are incompatible. Eager, therefore, to turn the current of blame from themselves, they foolishly, as well as basely, tried to shift the whole onus of national displeasure, and lay it upon the unfortunate country bankers, whom they themselves had applauded and encouraged. They stigmatised the small notes, in the very words of

Mr. Cobbett, as "worthless rags," and hastily passed an act, to abolish them for ever, in the year 1829. Even this, however, they could not do, without being guilty of gross inconsistency. In order to neutralise the powerful opposition made to this measure by the great Scotch Banking Companies, headed by Sir Walter Scott, who had himself been ruined by the explosion of December 1825, they continued the small-note circulation to Scotland, whilst they extinguished it in England—a measure at once weak and futile in all points of view—the value of money in Scotland being, of course, governed by that of the English currency, of which it forms a part. The clamourers in Scotland, however, understood nothing of the subject as to which they clamoured. The bankers looked merely at the profit of the one and two-pound circulation which they retained, heeding nothing of the effect of the measure upon the country; so that this silly concession satisfied everybody for the time, though the ultimate withdrawing of the English small notes was felt, in its effect on prices, just as severely in one country as in the other.

Such was the memorable paper panic of 1825-6; which, in reality, destroyed both Lord Liverpool and his ministry, though both lasted for a few months after the crisis. The growing difficulties of government had for some time terribly shaken the nerves of the former; who declared before his death, that, "for years, he trembled to open a despatch!" He was finally stricken with paralysis in 1827, and died a wretched wreck, both in mind and in body. To him succeeded the empty and flippant Canning, who also soon died, a striking example of that "vaulting ambition which o'er-leaps itself, and falls on the other side." He was followed by the incapable Robinson, now metamorphosed into Lord Ripon: and he, after passing an act embodying some favorite crotchets of substituting "joint-stock banks," for the old country banks of six partners, soon grew terrified at his situation; and under some shuffling pretences of ill health, absolutely slunk away from the responsibility of managing that which was fast (as even *he* saw) becoming unmanageable.

It now almost seemed as if the post of prime minister was "going a begging," when the Duke of Wellington, placed there rather by George the Fourth's hatred of the Whig party, than from any merits of his own, accepted the reins of a miserable power. The unthinking part of the community looking only at the Duke's stern and arbitrary character, imagined that they had now obtained that favorite thing to most minds, "a strong government." Alas! the difficulties which now environed the government were not such as could be put down by a field marshal's "word of command." As the time for the total extinction of the small paper drew nearer and nearer, the bankers began to decrease their already diminished circulation, and the prices of all sorts of produce gradually to fall. As prices slowly fell, distress, disaster, and discontent increased, and once more a cry began to be raised for another respite of the paper. This cry was commenced in the North of England principally, and was supported by the ordinary sophisms, current amongst paper-money-mongers, one of the principal of which is the very strange fallacy of the superior *cheapness* of paper as money. The idea of a "cheap" money, if by a "cheap money" is meant a money of no intrinsic value, is in itself sufficiently absurd. If, however, by this term is meant a money that costs little, never was fallacy more flagrant. People who talk in this way, seem not to be aware that gold bullion is obtained by means of a profitable trade just as other commodities are. English cottons, for instance, are sent across the Atlantic and sold for a profit. The returns are partly, say, in bullion, and partly in tobacco. Upon both the profit is equal to the trader; and the only difference is, that the weed is smoked or snuffed away by idlers, whilst the gold or silver bullion, being coined, answers a valuable purpose, in addition to being a part of the staple in a profitable trade. The expense of coinage is paid by an allowance termed a *seigniorage* upon the coin, so trifling as not to be noticed in its value: and the *wear and tear* of metallic money is, in reality, very small. Mr. Jacob, in his very curious and excellent treatise on money, states the loss of weight on three hundred and fifty sovereigns, which had been in circulation *nine years*, say from 1817 to 1826, was at the rate of *four shillings and sixpence farthing* on *each hundred*. This is *five shillings per cent* in *ten* years, or *sixpence per cent per annum*, only! On half-sovereigns the trials at the mint make the loss to be *five shillings and seven pence* per cent in ten years; a little more than on sovereigns. On shillings the loss is also found to be *five per cent* in ten years; on half-crowns and crowns it is less than on shillings: and with these facts staring them in the face, we have people absurd enough to call a metallic currency "expensive," and imagine a paper currency costs a country nothing; though they must be aware that no bank will issue paper at all, unless it first is *paid interest* upon the issue; and that the whole of the *profits* of bankers, amounting, according to their own statements, to sometimes *seventeen per cent per annum* upon their capital, *clear* of *all the expenses of salaries, rents, stamps, licenses, and bad debts*, is really got from the public who use the money!

To such an outcry, mixed up as it was with the arrant nonsense about "cheap currency," the minister-duke, without knowing much of the matter, was naturally deaf, whilst his colleague Peel, who perhaps knew somewhat more, was pledged doubly deep against the small-note circulation. The extinction act of 1826, was, therefore, doggedly persevered in; but the military minister soon felt the weakness of his government, amidst the universal discontent which began to rage. Unawed by his renown as a general, the Catholic Association in Ireland, with O'Connell at its head, bearded him in his loftiness, and braved his anger. Well it might, when half the regiments in Ireland were paying "Catholic Rent." This was enough for the duke. He felt the die was cast: and the first act of this iron soldier and his super-supple colleague, albeit both of them had been through life the greatest enemies of the Catholics and their religion, was to pass the emancipation bill of 1829.

This was a severe blow to the system, which had been so many years successfully carried on; but the extinction of the small paper-money in 1829, was, really, a much more fatal blow; inasmuch as it unquestionably was the grand cause of the accession to power of the Whigs and the passing of the miserably imperfect, but still, in its ultimate consequences, important reform-bill.

In May, 1829, the one and two-pound country bank-notes ceased to be circulated, and the diminished quantity, floating out, was, in no long time, returned to the various banks, never to be re-issued. The places of these notes were not, however, filled with gold and silver coins: because of these, bankers issue as few as they can, whilst of the other they issue as many as they can. Hence, there being less of the coins of smaller denominations to support prices in retail, wholesale prices fell still further, and the whole currency was reduced to a narrower compass. The effect of this narrowing of the circulation was, as is ever the case, most severely felt by the landed interest in the reduced prices of grain. The seasons of 1829, 1830 and 1831, were by no means favorable; yet in January 1830, the average price of wheat was only *fifty-one shillings*; and in July, 1831, after the deficient crop was apparent, only *sixty-four shillings*, from which it quickly went down nearly to fifty again.

This state of affairs forced the farmers, in 1830, to make the most violent efforts to reduce the wages of the labourers, who, in their turn, driven to desperation by the view of famine, resisted the farmers in every way, until the whole country presented a scene to be matched no where, save in Ireland. They did not in England, certainly, resort to "agrarian murders," as is done by the miserable cottagers of Ireland, when their holdings are taken from them, and certain starvation ensues, there being no POOR-LAW to present a resource: *this* they certainly did not resort to in England; but the labourers were, at last, driven to a step only one degree less terrible; and that was incendiarism, which now became general in most of the Southern counties, as far north as Lincolnshire. In point of fact the nation was on the verge of confusion, which was only averted by the election of 1830, on the death of George IV, which broke up the Wellington administration, and brought the Whigs into power, with a promise of reform and retrenchment, which allayed, joined with other causes, for a time, the exasperation of the people.

In order to afford the reader a compendious and bird's-eye view of the effects of the alternate drawings-in and puttings-out of the paper, from 1819 until the extinction of the small notes in 1829, I insert the following statement of the receipts of a tradesman in those years. I take it from "The Emigrant's Guide" of Mr. Cobbett, where it is quoted by that great writer. This statement shows, better than words can do, the instant effect upon prices caused by changes in the quantity and value of the money in circulation; and the rapidity with which prices and expenditure, and with them, profits ultimately fell, as soon as "Peel's bill" came near to its fullest operation, in the last year of the series.

In our next, we shall examine the financial doings of the Whigs and of their reformed parliaments, and see them in a few years ruined by causes, *as nearly as may be similar to those* which, in 1830, destroyed the power of Wellington, Peel, and the Tories! The Tories fell after the failure of the *palliatives* applied to avert the effects of Peel's bill; because they refused to take *direct measures* to remove these consequences. We shall see the Whigs, after a time, perish in much the same manner.

	1819.			1820.			1821.			1822.			1823.			1824.			1825.			1826.			1827.			1828.		
	£	s.	d.	£	s.	d.	£	s.	d.	£	s.	d.	£	s.	d.	£	s.	d.	£	s.	d.	£	s.	d.	£	s.	d.	£	s.	d.
January	110	15	9	106	4	1	104	9	6	85	7	8	92	17	6	101	4	8	125	10	1	165	18	8	56	6	1	49	10	5
February	82	12	11	101	1	5	91	16	0	85	0	5	72	4	1	56	0	8	168	15	5	103	6	3	79	0	1	44	1	5
March	108	18	8	137	7	11	94	14	7	40	13	6	108	8	6	68	18	3	254	15	8	133	19	11	63	10	9	75	0	2
April	180	5	9	166	12	9	134	8	8	141	1	2	135	3	11	115	3	4	315	0	9	193	0	8	118	16	9	72	10	9
May	186	13	4	168	13	6	141	8	4	159	8	5	168	7	5	169	13	10	283	19	6	133	4	3	113	5	11	119	10	2
June	165	8	4	210	0	7	182	4	0	154	10	10	167	8	9	111	5	5	209	19	0	84	15	6	122	16	11	84	15	6
July	153	9	6	181	4	5	95	0	5	125	0	9	111	7	10	142	14	11	183	13	4	102	11	9	112	16	10	81	1	5
August	134	18	8	144	3	2	68	4	5	75	12	10	111	6	6	135	14	7	159	15	7	64	15	3	86	1	2	70	18	10
September	134	3	7	108	15	1	54	8	5	71	16	10	94	19	11	125	17	9	133	14	3	87	8	9	72	16	4	45	3	9
October	144	16	2	142	8	0	88	10	3	80	16	10	96	5	3	223	7	6	183	19	0	50	4	3	94	4	9	65	12	11
November	131	5	2	130	16	9	71	12	5	93	18	7	144	18	7	226	10	7	169	0	5	83	1	0	55	2	4	35	14	8
December	129	19	11	92	9	0	61	18	2	90	8	6	81	3	11	163	11	3	117	16	7	48	4	10	63	9	8	30	14	4
Total	1663	7	10	1689	16	8	1188	15	2	1183	16	5	1384	12	2	1640	2	9	2304	19	7	1250	11	1	1040	7	7	774	14	4

The above is an Account of Money taken over "the Counter," and is exclusive of any dealings or credit, during these years.

LETTER XIV.

THE WHIG PARTY IN POWER.—STRUGGLE FOR THE REFORM BILL.—MINISTERS RESIGN MAY 1832.—WELLINGTON BECOMES DICTATOR.—A RUN UPON THE BANK OF ENGLAND.—THE WHIGS BROUGHT BACK IN NINE DAYS.—BANK OF ENGLAND NOTES MADE A LEGAL TENDER.—THE EFFECTS OF THIS EXHIBITION ON FOREIGN NATIONS.—TREATY OF VIENNA VIOLATED.—CRACOW OCCUPIED.—THE UNITED STATES REFUSE TO ACCEPT THE DUTCH KING'S AWARD ON THE CANADIAN BOUNDARY.—THE VIXEN CAPTURED BY A RUSSIAN CRUISER, AND CONFISCATED.—FALL OF PRICES OF GRAIN.—POOR-LAW-AMENDMENT-BILL.—SPREAD OF JOINT-STOCK BANKS.—EFFECTS OF THEIR ISSUES.—GRAND COTTON AND RAILWAY SPECULATIONS.—PRESIDENT JACKSON'S MEASURES.—AMERICAN TRADE BREAKS DOWN.—GREAT DEFICIT IN THE REVENUE.—FALL OF THE WHIGS.—PEEL'S MEASURES.

We have seen that the one and two-pound notes were destroyed in England and Ireland, though left to circulate as they might in Scotland, in the year 1829. We have seen that the pressure and growing distress caused by this destruction of the small paper (aided, no doubt, somewhat, by the abortive and ill-managed revolution which took place in France in the following year), produced a reaction in England, which destroyed the tottering *régime* of Wellington and Peel. The Whig *régime* which followed, under the auspices of the new king, William IV., was not, however, by any means secure until the success of the Reform-bill in the summer of 1832, which certainly, to all appearance, and in the eyes of ordinary men, gave them an unlimited lease of almost irresponsible power.

Their conduct, after this period, unquestionably proved that this was their own opinion; but they did not attain to this apparent triumph, without causing that to take place, which, at all events, opened such eyes in Europe as remained still shut to the real situation of this country, and the real tenure upon which such precarious power as now can alone exist, is actually held.

This event was the resignation of Earl Grey, in May, 1832; the Duke of Wellington's acceptance of a dictatorial power; and the demolition of that military dictatorship; and the restoration of Earl Grey to power, in nine summer's days, after he had tossed it down at the feet of the weak and vacillating king. This, to those who have sense and knowledge enough to understand all its bearings, is perhaps the most extraordinary event, and certainly is one of the most instructive, that have happened in modern times. There can be no doubt that the Duke of Wellington, together with the whole army, and the great body of the aristocracy, by whom he was supported, were, at this crisis, determined to go all lengths to preserve that system of rule, which in their apprehension was about to be immediately subverted. They believed the Whigs to have raised up a popular power which they could not manage. It is by no means clear that the Whigs themselves did not, in some degree, share this opinion. This dreaded power, the dictator (for at this moment he was nothing short of this) was determined to crush, at all hazards, by main force, stripped of all disguise, and all remnant of pretended regard for the name of constitutional liberty. This was apparent in the few steps which he had time to take amidst the storm that followed. The petitions of the people were insolently sent back from the Home-office. Those public meetings which he had before termed "a farce," he was now prepared to change into tragedies. In the Home-office, after his defeat, were found twenty-seven warrants filled up, but unsigned, for the apprehension of the leaders of the great Political Unions. The troops were begun to be moved towards every spot, where popular remonstrance might venture to show its head. The morning had actually dawned upon a military tyranny. The people, though full of spirit, were mostly without arms, or any means of successful physical resistance; and yet this grand conspiracy which appeared ready to plunge England in blood and tyranny, was blown to the winds in the space of nine summer's days, and by the "so potent breath" of seven cabalistical words, "To stop the duke, go for gold!"

I have had mentioned to me, on good authority, the names of the four men who had the merit of issuing the placards with these words, so wondrous in their effects; but as they themselves have not assumed the credit certainly due to them, it would be wrong in me to thrust upon them honour which is unsought. Suffice it to say, that these seven words effectually turned back the "Hero of Waterloo" and the military revolution. It is probable that the Bank, at this precise moment, had in her vaults very nearly eight millions of gold and silver. In the preceding February she had more than eight millions; and in the following July rather more than seven. Be that as it may, it is certain (for it came out in evidence, soon after, before the secret committee), that in these nine days of May, which comprise the dictatorship of Wellington, TWO MILLIONS were drawn out, by the run which took place in London alone! The abstraction of these two millions blew up "the dictatorship." In nine days more, the run would have spread over the entire country. Every bank in it, including the Bank of England, would have been stopped; paper credit completely destroyed; and "the dictator," left without the means even of paying a hangman to tuck up the leaders of the political unions, against whom he had sworn vengeance. Against such a state of things as this, the possession of cannons and bayonets, and powder and grape shot, is of no avail. The men who are to use them, will neither slaughter their fellow-countrymen *gratis*, nor can they live any better than other people without subsistence; and, without money, how is subsistence to be got? The end was the hasty recall of Earl Grey to power, just in time to save the paper-money, and the whole system built upon it, from utter annihilation; this being the fourth hair-breadth escape which an inscrutable Providence had thought fit to suffer it to have!

Such was the advent of Whig supremacy in 1832. The ministers were re-seated in almost absolute power; the gates were once more shut upon the Tories: but the eyes of all Europe, Asia, and America, were opened by the circumstances of that re-seating. It was now evident, that the paper-system had arrived at that degree of rottenness, which rendered it incapable of bearing a serious shock; and that, consequently, a war with any great power, or any other event which should be calculated to excite general alarm, must be fatal to it. It is a known fact, that persons of excessively depraved habits, sometimes are found with livers so completely diseased, as to make any unusual exertions perilous in the extreme, and, if forced upon them, to be certain destruction. To a state very similar to this, foreign nations began to perceive the system had now come: and in this they immediately saw their own "vantage ground." The best illustration of the position in which the system now stands with relation to foreign powers, is to be found, perhaps, in a singular case of hypochondriacism, which afflicted an unhappy person, of whose family I myself had some knowledge, and which is, I believe, perfectly true as to the details. The unhappy patient, to whose case I now allude, was a female, whose general health and strength were to all appearance good and perfect, but who laboured under the strange delusion, that her head was made of thin glass, and liable to be shivered by the slightest violence. She was the wife of a banker, and man of good fortune, in the town of Alnwick, in Northumberland, the mother of two healthy sons; but who, yet under the influence of this cruel delusion, sat for many years, propped up, amidst the softest pillows that could be procured, and trembling at the opening or shutting of a door! In all other respects, she was a sensible and spirited woman; but during her latter time, was entirely paralysed by this singular hallucination, which did not suffer her to move for some years. Nothing could rouse her. If one had come to rob her house, or to set it on fire, she dared not stir to prevent it; for, in her diseased fancy, the act of resistance carried destruction to herself in its very first step. There she sat; a woman in full apparent health and strength, but paralysed by a "glass head"!

Now, if we suppose for a moment, that her fancy could have been fact, she would actually have been in the situation in which the run of 1832 proved the system now to be. The paper currency and the funds are the system's "glass head." In other respects, all seems sound and strong. There are an army and a navy, and all the elements of physical power; but whilst the "glass head" remains, they cannot be used against any really powerful aggressor. This, foreign nations now see; and, hence, the period since 1832, has exhibited a scene of constant, but quiet, aggression by foreign powers, carried on as silently, but as deliberately as possible, under the conviction, that nothing short of some intolerable national outrage, openly perpetrated, can by possibility rouse in England any efficient resistance. They now know, that the operation of the currency-bill has put the landed interest, once all-powerful, completely into the clutches of the Jew or moneyed interest. Consequently, they know that the period foretold by the celebrated Hume has now arrived, when public credit will be preferred even with the certainty of national disgrace, and when it will be preserved even at the price of national degradation, national loss, and, perhaps, ultimate national ruin. In this sense, are interpreted all the professions of "*love of peace*," that have, of late, become so fashionable in once high-spirited England. These professions, they perceive, are meant only for the really great powers; whilst against the weak and distant ones, such as Affghanistan, China, Brazil, or Syria, wars or threats of war are resorted to without ceremony.

It would be quite inconsistent with the plan of this work, for me to do more than barely refer to the instances of insolent aggression on the part of foreign powers, and especially on the part of Russia, which have been exhibited since the period to which I refer, but some of them it would be unpardonable not to quote. In 1832, Russia, after a revolt which her own violations of the stipulations of the treaty of Vienna had provoked in Poland, incorporated all that remained of Poland into her empire, against the wish of all the Great Powers, and in defiance of the treaty of Vienna, as agreed to in 1815. There can be no doubt, that the fears of the fund-holders, lest a general war should ensue, compelled the ministry to stop a movement, in which, strange to say, France, Austria, Sweden, Turkey, and Persia, would have combined, and as to which Prussia alone stood neuter. It is in vain to attempt to explain the conduct of the English rulers as to Poland, by a reference to Lord Palmerston's supposed treacheries or prepossessions, because Sir Robert Peel plainly assisted him to throw cold water upon the rising spirit in behalf of Poland, and to crush in the womb the embryo coalition then forming against the tyranny and ambition of the Muscovite. But if this were not plain enough, the language held on the violation of the little independent commercial depôt of Cracow cannot be mistaken. On that topic, when before the House of Commons in 1840, Lord Palmerston openly said, that "it was one thing to state an *opinion*, and another to *compel* powers to undo acts which they had done, whilst from geographical circumstances, there were no means to *enforce* the opinion of England, SAVE BY AN APPEAL TO ARMS"! And into this bottomless degradation the House of Commons silently suffered itself to be thrust. Well might the eloquent author of "England under Lord Palmerston" say, that "Lord Nelson, Lord Chatham, and William IV., must have turned in their graves at so fearful a moment as this"! Equally insulting was the conduct of the United States, and equally disgraceful that of England, with regard to the much-disputed question of "the Maine Boundary." This matter had remained in a state of incurable doubt from the period between the years 1783 and 1814, in consequence of an imperfect description, designedly put into the treaty of 1783 (as it is thought) by the American negotiators of that time, and undiscovered, until too late, by England. In 1814, however, it was agreed on the part of the United States, at the instance of the British Government, to leave the settlement of the whole matter to the king of the Netherlands. In 1831, the king gave his award; an award highly favourable to the State of Maine, who would have obtained by it two-thirds of the territory in dispute. To the astonishment of most men, however, the State of Maine immediately, but on grounds the most frivolous, protested against this solemn decision, and the Federal Senate ultimately refused to ratify it! No insult could well be more gross than this; nor could any words convey more completely than did this disregard of an obligation the most solemn, the determination of the Republic never to settle this question, until they could push their pretensions to a claim to the navigation of the St. Lawrence. This conduct, at any other period, must have led to a war between the two countries. It was, however, tamely acquiesced in; and if the question be really, as asserted, now *set at rest*, it must have been at the expense of sacrifices which will, in the end, give to Republican America all that she seeks on her northern boundary. To the monstrosities of the French blockade of Monte Video, and of the behaviour of the Dutch as to the Java duties, I shall not do more than refer; but the outrage of Russia in the Black Sea, as late as 1837, deserves a more particular mention.

It may be known to many of the readers of these letters, that, for many years past, Russia has been making incessant, but hitherto fruitless efforts, to subjugate Circassia; a strong mountainous country on the north shores of the Euxine. So fruitless have been her efforts, that she has never, in fact, been able to keep possession of a single fortress, port, or tower, belonging to these warlike mountaineers. Yet, such is the importance of this acquisition, as one great step in her designs upon Turkey on one hand, and British India on the other, that these exertions have never slackened, and are continued to this hour. To the coast of Circassia sailed in the year 1837, the British trader, Vixen, with a cargo of salt chiefly, having her owner, a Mr. Bell, and a crew of thirteen persons on board. When off the port of Soudjouk Kalé, she was pursued, fired at, and stopped, by a Russian cruiser. The owner and crew escaped *on shore* in their boats, and were hospitably entertained by the Circassians. The ship and cargo were confiscated by the Muscovites. When this most monstrous outrage was brought before the House of Commons, it was distinctly shown that the Russians were destitute even of a colourable excuse for this act of open piracy; that no blockade had ever been pretended; that their assertions that they had possession of the port and a custom house, was falsified by the very circumstances of the seizure, and the escape of the crew; that, in short, this was a case of undisguised and most insolent atrocity; and yet, after a few unmeaning subterfuges from the Foreign Secretary, and a *refusal to divulge the opinions of the law officers of the crown*, this monstrous outrage on all international law and open robbery of a British subject were passed over, without an attempt even to vindicate either British honour, or British interests! It is in vain to attempt to rest the *onus* of this open shame upon a supposed treachery of the Foreign Secretary. Lord Palmerston's conduct on various points is no doubt highly suspicious, and demands the most searching investigation. But the whole House of Commons was party to this dreadful degradation. In the deep disgrace of it, the whole legislature is involved. Individual treachery then is out of the question; and some other solution must be sought of a fact so damning. In the fears of the fundholder and moneyed aristocracy is that solution alone to be found. They knew a war with Russia, however popular, would, as its first effect, bring down public credit, and the paper money;—and hence, even under such circumstances of deep and dangerous disgrace, they forced the miserable government to repeat the memorable declaration of 1823, when the Bourbon armies dispersed the Spanish Cortes, that "let other countries act as they would—England was determined upon peace"! A declaration of which it is difficult to decide, whether the disgrace or the danger be deepest.

The exhibition of weakness, which, in 1832, seems to have opened the eyes of the world as to the real position of Great Britain, was not without having its effect upon her ministers. They now saw how short an alarm might discredit and send down to utter destruction the whole fabric of their paper currency, now demandable in gold—but to pay which in gold, "on demand," the bank never possessed one-sixth of the metal requisite! If we take the bank circulation, the probable country circulation, and the amounts due from the savings' banks, we shall, without including the amount floating in exchequer bills, obtain a total amount, which can hardly be much beneath *seventy millions of pounds;* yet if we look at the returns of bullion by the bank we shall find *twelve to fifteen millions* as high an amount as she is ever capable of realising in gold and silver. A run upon the savings' banks alone might in a month, of itself, stop the wheels of government; and to this peril, some of the questions asked in the secret committee of 1832, show the Chancellor of the Exchequer of that period, Lord Althorp, to have been keenly alive. These dangers could not be cured nor averted; but the ministers appear to have hoped they might be diminished, by means of a measure passed during the ensuing session of parliament; that is to say, by making the bank paper, in nine cases out of ten, a "legal tender." This was, to be sure, a direct violation of the currency bill of 1819; upon which so many reputations were pledged. It was a step which the all-omnipotent Pitt, in the plenitude of his financial sway, had never brought himself to propose. In this move alone, however, was there to be found the slightest chance of even diminishing the risks of another general alarm, whensoever it should occur; and to this the minister therefore resorted. Yet in doing this, he did not dare to go the whole length of absolutely compelling the people to take as money, even for wages, little bits of paper, the genuineness or falsification of which they had no means to distinguish. Of a universal legal-tender-bank-note, Lord Althorp stopped short; but he barely stopped short of it. His bill enacted that the bank-paper should be legal tender for payment of all sums *above* five pounds; thus leaving to the poor man, who had only one note, the power to demand gold or silver for it. It also left it in the power of any person to get money for notes, by taking it in sums of five pounds at a time; but not otherwise: and this miserable obstacle would, he hoped, diminish the force of any future run upon the banks whenever it may chance to occur. That it could have any such effect, I do not believe. Country banks can only hold reserves of these notes as they do reserves of gold; that is to say, by locking up so much of their capital. They will not, therefore, keep Bank of England paper, rather than gold, when not only no advantage accrues, but a disadvantage may be felt. As for the Bank of England herself, she is as liable as ever to be drained of the metals, when a necessity occurs, as we shall shortly see. This legal tender measure, or rather half measure, appears to me, therefore, I must own, nearly to be a dead letter; but the motive for resorting to it was sufficiently palpable.

Whilst these things were going on, the extinction of the one-pound notes, and consequent reduction of the entire of the circulation, backed by some seasons of more than average fineness, was producing its inevitable effects. The price of grain went on slowly and progressively falling, until in the years 1833, 1834, and 1835, wheat of average goodness was selling currently, in many parts of the kingdom, as low as *four shillings and sixpence* or even *four shillings* the bushel, and the average prices were not *forty shillings the quarter*. The prices of live stock, owing to a scarcity both of sheep and oxen, did not go down quite in the same proportion. Nevertheless, prices were, upon the whole, lower than they had been for half a century before, and agricultural distress pervaded the land from one end to the other. The labourers in some parts of the kingdom preserved the rate of wages by the desperate resort of rural incendiarism; but farms were soon standing unlet, and rents unpaid; whilst the landlords, who had a committee sitting in London, besieged the houses of parliament and ministers with petitions, the burthen of which was, that, by some device or other, wheat should be made dearer, or the expenses of growing it less. The first was beyond the powers of Parliament to do, unless by letting out the small notes again, the seasons being beyond their power. To bring about the second seemed an attempt somewhat more feasible; and in pursuance of this object, they ventured upon and matured a scheme, the most atrocious, probably, ever entertained by any legislators calling themselves civilised; and not less opposed to every humane and Christian feeling and dictate, than to the constitutional law of the country, whose poorer inhabitants they were especially bound to protect.

In their search for something to sacrifice to the clamorous race who now afflicted them with increasing complaints; the ministers, in sheer desperation, cast their eyes upon the *poor's-rate.* This rate had now, as misery became every year more and more prevalent, and as the population grew more rapidly, as nature's law provides, the more it was scourged and pressed down, become an enormously heavy tax upon the country. During the war, and the circulation of the inconvertible paper, it had reached the nominal sum of about *eight millions of pounds per annum.* After the revulsion of 1816, the reduction of the paper-issues, and the ultimate enactment of the Currency-bill of 1819, it fell very considerably; but, as the effects of the bill of Peel began to shew themselves in the reduced means of the working people, and a population rapidly increasing, step for step, with destitution and diminished employment, these rates naturally began again to increase, and at a fearful rate; so much so, that in 1832 they stood again as high as *seven millions of pounds sterling!* This was, to be sure, a terrible amount; far exceeding, not only the revenue of the Stuarts, or the Long Parliament, but of the stock-jobbing governments of the Dutch king William, and his successor Queen Anne. Of this huge sum, the poor never really received more than about two-thirds; the whole, however, to the eye of the avaricious and unprincipled, seemed huge and disproportioned; and such an eye did the ministry of the year 1833, cast upon it.

The end was, that, at last, the political economists and disciples of the mischievous and mistaken Malthus triumphed, and an attempt was made, not only to reduce these rates, but to drive the whole labouring population to exist upon the meanest, poorest, and coarsest aliment that will support nature, by a virtual denial of all relief; inasmuch as, under the new law, relief was to be offered in such a manner only, as was sure to cause it to be refused by all not in the very last extremity of starvation. To reason with the description of reasoners that stood forth as the promoters of this most atrocious of all deliberate examples of "civilised legislation," was to talk to the deaf adder. It was in vain to point out to these men, that, to throw our destitute brethren "on their own resources," (as it was termed) was not only an act in the very teeth of ordinary humanity, and of all Christian principle, but was actually to *out-law them*, for no fault of their own, as if poverty were "a high crime and misdemeanour." For, upon *protection* for person and property in all cases of need, resides the *ligamen* which binds the subject in allegiance, which forms the sole foundation of regal or national dominion, and gives either a king or a nation a right to call upon individuals for the performance of the duties of citizens, which are only a return for the preservation of this great right of protection in all times of real need. Hence, to all men willing to work, but who cannot obtain it, and to all poor, aged, or crippled persons, the "right to relief" is the practical re-payment for their duties of citizenship, and for their allegiance to the constituted authorities and laws. Were this otherwise, NATIONAL DOMINION would be gone, and power the most dreadful vested in the rich; inasmuch as they, then, could starve all those who had not house and land of their own, or else immediate means to procure shelter, raiment, and food. These things it was in vain to press upon the men who had brought themselves into a state of mind to support such a law as this now proposed. They had, in truth, ceased to be legislators. They were in "a crusade" against the poor, burning with all the zeal of theorists, absorbed in one grand mistake, and having the same feelings as those with which inquisitors, under another form of bigotry, used to send their victims to the rack or stake. Yet there was *one* argument adduced, to which, it might have been supposed, even they would have listened; and this was the suicidal effect upon the *revenue* which this horrid measure was, in the end, sure to bring along with it. It was represented, and most truly, to the advocates of this monstrous measure, that no money went so immediately and surely to *the Exchequer*, as the greater part of the wages paid to those who do the work of the country. This is, one would imagine, clear enough, when it is called to mind that wages are totally spent on heavily taxed commodities of daily consumption: on tea, on sugar, on coffee, on beer, on tobacco, and on spirits. It was proved, a few years ago, that a man who earned *twenty-two pounds* in wages, paid *eleven pounds ten shillings* of the whole in taxes, on necessary articles of consumption for the most part. If these wages be taken away, and given to a landlord, or a merchant, and the people reduced to destitution, the treasury may lose the whole; as is the case in Ireland, which pays little tax, because the landlords have deprived the government of their share, by making beggars of the people. The money which, if paid in wages, would have gone to the Exchequer, goes into the lap of a Parisian opera-dancer, or the till of a restaurateur, or to the jeweller, the picture-dealer, or the virtuoso, whose commodity is untaxed, or nearly so. This was an argument which political economists might, at all events, have appreciated; for that they could not take away the wages, and, yet, at the same time, keep the taxes, was as plain as that "twice two are four." Nothing, however, would stay the zeal of these preachers of a "Crusade" against the unfortunate poor. The measure, after being opposed and reprobated by every sensible man in the kingdom, was passed by large majorities of *both* Houses; and thus the working men of once rich and merry England, after being robbed of their share of the tithes and abbey-lands — after being robbed of the common-lands, all of which they had enjoyed for many centuries — were robbed of that "right of relief" which was given as a compensation for the first, — and left to starve, or be imprisoned for life, in a country naturally one of the richest in the world! It is impossible for words to do justice to this deed. Future annalists may try, but I shall not try. Those whom *the facts* do not stir, will not be stirred by pen of mine.

The certain consequences of this suicidal outrage, bitter as they were seen to be, were not long in beginning to be felt by the authors of the atrocious enactment. They would, however, have been felt much sooner, had it not been for the occurrence of one of those respites, which Providence, in its inscrutable wisdom, has deemed it fit to give this enormous system of iniquity, from time to time; probably to render its final fall the more signal, and the ultimate retribution more clearly and palpably just. It will be remembered, that, after the crisis of 1825–6, and the preservation of the entire thing from utter ruin, by the finding of a box of one-pound notes, which had been tossed, as of no value, into some corner, thence to be snatched to preserve for a time the whole Funding System, and its adjuncts—dividends, civil list, dead-weight, half-pay, salaries, Exchequer bills, deficiency bills, and the rest of it—it will be remembered, that, after this famous panic, Lord Goderich, then about to become prime minister, from the sudden deaths of Liverpool and Canning, brought forward a scheme for putting down the existing country banks, and hatching, in their stead, a brood of things, to be denominated "Joint-Stock Banks," in imitation of some banks, upon this principle, already existing in Scotland. For this purpose, an act was passed in 1827, to authorise the setting up, under certain regulations, of "Joint-Stock Banks," the money-stock of which was to be subscribed by shareholders, and the management of which money-stock, in the trade of banking, was to be committed to directors chosen by the shareholders. It was not easy to see why these banks were to be, in reality, safer than those on the old system; or why directors having only a modified interest in the success of the establishment, or having, perhaps, sinister interests of their own opposed to that success, should be safer agents than were persons whose all was bound up in the undertaking. Neither did it follow, that these centipede banks, standing upon many legs, were really stronger than those supported by fewer; because, in case of danger, it was not difficult for the wealthy shareholders to sell out, and replace themselves by mere speculating adventurers, or men of straw. It, however, pleased Lord Goderich to imagine that there was some charm in these "joint-stock" establishments, which was to render them invulnerable by runs or panics; and the act under his guidance was accordingly passed, and sent forth to save the country from all future paper-money catastrophes. For a few years the scheme was only languidly taken up. Men waited to see the event of the final destruction of the one and two-pound notes, and its consequences. After the fall of Wellington and the success of the Reform bill, however, Speculation began again to breathe freely, and to look briskly about her; and she quickly had her eye upon the joint-stock banks, and upon the game they were capable of playing, if under her management.

In the year 1834, this new machinery for grinding a two or three years' batch of paper prosperity, had got into tolerably full operation; and it was assisted, during the following year of 1835, by a change in the seasons, which quickly raised the prices of grain, brought corn speculators and their artificial averages into energetic action; and by a lucky blast of wet, cold, and mildew, dispersed, joyfully, to their homes that "agricultural committee" which had sat, for three long years, in a house at Charing-cross, to direct the landlords' siege of the Whig ministers. The whole country, but most especially the districts in which the cotton and woollen manufactures are carried on, were, about this time, covered with these joint-stock banking establishments, which quickly began to issue their paper in plenteous exuberance. The effect was, in many points, unlike that of the issue of 1823, 1824, and 1825. The small notes were wanting; and hence prices, *universally*, could not be propped *in retail*, as during those years. As speculation drove on, however, a tolerably general improvement in prices was induced by the increased issues of gold and silver, in the shape of wages, which came to the aid of the five-pound notes, and assisted, by their action on prices, to keep them out. The current of speculation, at this period, ran in two main channels, each forming a mighty stream. It first took the shape of an enormous addition to the mills and machinery employed in the cotton and woollen trades, in all their branches; and then dividing itself, another enormous stream of speculation ran upon railways, which at this time over-spread the land, and seemed to turn some brains that were unturned before. These two grand torrents of speculating mania, of course, caused some minor streams to be set in motion. The rage for railways begot a rage for iron-works, naturally enough; and this, again, begat a rage for coal-mines. The setting up of the new mills and their machinery, in its turn helped all this again; whilst the increased demand for raw-cotton, in its turn, also gave a stimulus to the many minor markets which are governed by it. Putting all this together, a very pretty fabric of factitious prosperity was again formed; and the millions, who look no deeper than the surface, were in a fools' paradise, nearly as complete as that of 1824-5! The ministers again began to sound notes of triumph about "national resources," through the old brazen trumpet of a speech from the throne; and those who had been disappointed by the Tory paper-plethora of Lord Goderich, and the flashy Canning, now began to deem that the Whigs had really brought in "the millennium" along with them. It was in vain that this folly was combated by the few persons who understood the whole delusion. In vain was it shown, that the duplication of cotton and woollen machines must end in an overtrading, that, looking at what the continent was doing, must shortly finish in a crisis. It was in vain to tell the railroad-speculators, that, after buying the fee-simple of the land, paying the interest of the money sunk, laying down the line, and paying "wear and tear and expenses," no great general profit could accrue to them, however great might be the benefit to the world at large. These things it was in vain to urge. The spell was again upon the community; and on they went. The height of the joint-stock-bank mania was from 1834 to 1836; when the bubble was made to burst, a little before its natural time, by external circumstances.

The enormous additions made to the weaving machinery, after the period of 1834, caused an unusual necessity for the export of certain fabrics, which could not by possibility be consumed either at home or in our extensive colonies. The continent of Europe, seeing our weakness, had been now for some years gradually closing their markets against our goods. The stream of forced export ran, therefore, of necessity, across the Atlantic, and, most of all, to the United States. The trade was altogether an unnatural one. The real exporters of the goods were too thankful, if they got accounts of sales free from loss; but the intermediate houses who fostered this trade profited largely; and the more bloated and artificial it grew, the more grew their profits. Advances on goods, discounts, and brokerage, brought in pelf on all sides; and by means of these middle men, it was at last swelled to such a pitch, that the goods sent to the States, beyond any raw produce shipped in exchange, were in money-amount *twelve millions of dollars*, or *three millions sterling*. This strange position had been attained through the medium, chiefly, of "the United States Bank;" a gigantic establishment, supported mostly by the English speculators, and which, for a time, seemed as if it were about to domineer over the Republic itself!

To this portentous state of affairs, the measures of the illustrious President Jackson at last put an end. He refused, during the first four years of his Presidency, to sign a renewal of the charter of the bank; and, on being re-elected, his cabinet, under his auspices, carried a series of measures, one of which was a return to those cash payments which had been suspended from and after the war of 1814, to the great injury both of the morals, credit, and prosperity of the union. The first effect of President Jackson's measures, was to cause a drain of the precious metals from the vaults of the bank of England, in order to send them to the States, where President Jackson took care that they should bear a handsome premium. This went on through the years 1835 and 1836, and was in preparation for the return to cash payments by the American banks. When the dreaded hour, however, arrived, it was found that the major part of these ill-managed, reckless, and, in point of fact, swindling establishments, could not bear the ordeal of paying real money, though only in part; and a scene of bankruptcy ensued that beggars all description. The great leviathan bank of Pennsylvania, formerly the United States Bank, having speculated to the amount of many millions of dollars in cotton alone, was one of the first to fall. The minor banks followed by scores; and, with them, carried down the merchants and traders by hundreds. The end was, that the dividends of many of the States debts ceased to be paid; and the whole of the money which America was indebted to England was lost, together with about *ten millions* of dollars of *surplus revenue*, which the president had been compelled to deposit in the banks of several of the States.

The effects of this paper catastrophe could not but be felt in England, connected as she was with America, and having over-traded to the preposterous extent before described. A panic took place in England; in the course of which nearly all the houses engaged in the United-States trade were swept away, despite the efforts of the Bank of England to support them; efforts by which the Bank itself was, at length, in conjunction with other causes, brought to extreme jeopardy. The panic and drain of the metals began to be excessive in 1837, and was felt not only in England, but more or less over the whole of commercial Europe, wherever the States had dealings. Immense bales of American paper securities; state-stocks; canal shares, bank shares, railroad shares, etc., were sent to Europe, pledged for what they would bring, and the proceeds remitted in silver and gold across the Atlantic, to prop the tottering paper-issuing establishments of the various states. Throughout the years 1838 and 1839, this drain was aggravated in England by short harvests, bad weather, and a consequent large import of grain. Such, at last, was the condition of the coffers of the Bank of England, that she was *(proh pudor!)* reduced to beg assistance from the *bank of France;* and the indirect aid of that establishment alone saved her from ruin. I say *indirect*, because direct aid was refused, as contrary to rule, though aid was obtained by an indirect medium. That, but for the aid of France, the Bank must have stopped payment, was fully proved by Mr. Samuel Lloyd, the banker, in a pamphlet published in December 1839. The bank averages of bullion for the last four months of the year 1839, standing thus:

September - - - -	£2,816,000
October - - - - - - -	2,522,000
November - - - - - -	2,545,000
December - - - - - -	2,887,000

These averages being each upon three months stock; and the credit on the bank of France, for the amount of two millions and a half sterling, having been all used, it seems to follow, as a matter of calculation, that, had it not been for the application of these two and a half millions, one of these must have been "*nil;*" otherwise some one of the four must have shewn a higher amount than it does: and hence Mr. Lloyd is correct in asserting, upon these returns (as he most unreservedly did), that "we are justified in saying, that, *without the protection of this peculiar operation*, the bullion of the bank would have been COMPLETELY EXHAUSTED!" To such a complexion as this must all systems, like that of England, come at last;—and here the cup of bitterness was surely filled to running over. Yet strange and sad to say, so accustomed to difficulty and disgrace has this once high-spirited nation become, that even this lesson seemed scarcely to be felt whilst passing, and to be forgotten as soon as past.

With these scenes of dismay and confusion, began the downfall of the Whigs. As the American trade was convulsed, the Bank of England withdrew her discounts from the American houses; and as these began to fall, the Yorkshire and Lancashire cotton and wool spinners fell with them, and, in their fall, dragged down the joint-stock-banks. The joint-stock fit of prosperity was now at an end; and from that hour, the effects of the poor-law-amendment-bill upon the revenue began to be felt. By the denial of relief the destitution of the population was made much greater and more extended than it had hitherto ever been, on any occasion, or during any crisis. A cessation and growing diminution in the consumption of taxed articles immediately commenced; and from 1837 to the present time, the revenue has been in a rapid decline:—and this, although in the Northern English counties, owing to the strenuous resistance that was set on foot, under the auspices of the late Mr. Cobbett, and his excellent colleague Mr. John Fielden, M.P. for Oldham, this horrid law could never be carried into full effect.

In 1839, the ministers attempted to prop the falling revenue by an addition of *five per cent* upon the whole of the taxes. This ought to have raised *two and a half millions* sterling; but, instead of this result, a greater defalcation appeared. In the mean time, the forced and artificial American trade wholly broke down; and the European continent increased the existing prohibitory laws against British manufactured goods. Stagnation universal, and distress in its most awful form, now overspread the land; and it became evident that something must give way. At length, in 1841, in utter despair of extrication by any other means, the Whig government proposed a repeal of the existing corn-laws, and the substitution of a small fixed duty, by which it was thought a revenue might at once be raised, and the export-trade of the country revived. This step of desperation, however, the existing House of Commons would not sanction; and the people, universally and in disgust, joining the Tories, in the elections of the members of the new parliament, the end was a triumph for Sir Robert Peel, and the reinstatement in office of the Tories, within eleven short years after the Whigs had succeeded to their places, clothed with a power that, in the eyes of the ignorant, seemed all but absolute and endless.

In our fifteenth letter, we shall trace the financial

and economical deeds of Sir Robert Peel. Before turning to that letter, I shall, however, insert a table drawn up, in the year 1832, by the excellent Mr. John Fielden, M.P. for Oldham. It illustrates most completely the effects of the financial mistake of 1819, as displayed upon all connected with the cotton trade, at whose expense it is cramming the pockets of the fundholders, and all other fixed annuitants. All other trades and manufactures are feeling similar effects; but they do not admit of the same rigorous analysis; and in many, the wages of labour do not form so large or important a constituent part of the price:—

Years.	Bags of Cotton consumed, of 300 lbs. each Bag.	Prices of Cotton per lb., Duty paid.	Prices per Bag.			Total Cost of Cotton.	Pieces of $3^d\ 74^s$ Calico the Cotton would make, at 70 Pieces per Bag.	Value of $3^d\ 74^s$ per Piece.		Total Value of $3^d\ 74^s$.	Total Sum for Manufacturing.
		d.	£	s.	d.	£		s.	d.	£	£
1815	338,400	19½	24	7	6	8,248,500	23,688,000	18	0	21,319,200	13,070,700
1824	598,000	8½	10	12	6	6,353,750	41,860,000	9	6	18,837,000	12,483,250
1831	847,600	5½	7	0	7½	5,959,687	59,332,000	5	9	17,057,950	11,098,262

Years.	Prices of Cotton per lb., exclusive of Duty.	Total Value of Cotton, exclusive of Duty.	Pieces of $3^d\ 74^s$, the value of one Bag of Cotton, exclusive of Duty, would purchase		Pieces of $3^d\ 74^s$, *Three Pounds* (Consols), would buy the Fundholder		Wages per Piece to the Hand Loom Weaver.		Total Sum to the Hand Loom Weaver.	Proportion of a Piece to the Hand-Loom Weaver, if paid in kind.	Proportion of a Quarter of Wheat to Weaver, for weaving one Piece.
	d.	£					s.	d.	£		
1815	17½	7,402,500	24	33	3	30	4	6	5,329,800	¼ nearly	1-20th part
1824	8	5,980,000	22	22	6	66	2	3	4,709,250	¼ ,,	,, ,,
1831	5¼	5,562,375	22	82	10	43	1	4½	4,079,075	¼ ,,	1-42d part

"No one (says Mr. Fielden) seeing this Table, need be at a loss to account for the weaver's distressed condition; nor for the reason why the manufacturer cannot give the weaver more than he does for weaving; seeing that he receives nearly the same proportion of the cloth he has woven at any period for his labour, and that the employer is, together with his poor weaver (whose condition he deplores, but cannot alter), progressively sinking." This was in 1831. The progress downward in this and all other trades, has gone on ever since, with only one period of palliation, from 1834 to 1838; and thus we see, how even with the shield of the poor-law of Elizabeth, a nation may, by this system, be ground down to general pauperism and destitution. Since the wicked and suicidal abrogation of the old poor-law, the nation has gone down still more rapidly to general distress and starvation; and, if it were possible the system could last so long, would, in the end, reach a state like that of wretched Ireland, where *one-third of the whole people* know not the meaning of a settled home, a decent garment, or a wholesome meal!

In the next and in the last letter, we will "sum up" the great results of this "eventful history."

LETTER XV.

SIR ROBERT PEEL'S ADMINISTRATION.—DEFICIENCY IN THE REVENUE AS STATED BY HIM.—INCOME-TAX RENEWED.—ITS INJUSTICE.—TARIFF RELAXED.—CORN-LAWS RELAXED.—MISGIVINGS OF THE HIGH TORY PARTY.—BANKING COMMITTEE.—MR. GILBART'S EVIDENCE.—BANKING ACT.—DESTRUCTION OF THE POTATO PLANT.—FAMINE IN IRELAND.—REPEAL OF THE CORN-LAWS.—RESIGNATION OF SIR R. PEEL.

I ORIGINALLY concluded this treatise at the period of the date of the last Letter. Circumstances, however, at that time, delayed its publication, and of the eventful years that have passed since then, I am now to give the history. I, at that period, anticipated the coming destruction of the corn-laws, as they then existed, and predicted it accordingly. That destruction, and the steps that led to it, are now to form part of the following narrative. Of the effects of that repeal we shall also have to consider; and they can be anticipated as surely and as confidently as was the repeal itself. Such vaticinations will not be without their use. Next to the passing of the Reform-bill itself, and the destruction of the rotten boroughs to a considerable extent; and to the passing of the currency-bill of 1819, which has really been the root of all the changes that have since distracted this country; this pulling away of all protection from the land is the most important event that has happened for half a century, not only in its present, but in its future consequences. When we come to treat of it, we shall treat of these probable consequences. In the meantime, we must describe the many strange events of the strange administration of Sir Robert Peel, in the order in which they occurred.

We have already seen what was the nature of the causes, that, at length, and after no long time, produced the decline, and downfall of the power of the Whig-party. In the year 1832, after the first general election under the reform-bill, the influence and popularity of this party seemed to be so immense, as to amount almost to an interminable lease of power. They, past all doubt, thought so, and did not refrain from saying what they thought. Men more profound thought otherwise. They turned out to be the true thinkers. Nine years sufficed to bring the sway of the Whig-party to a final close; and during the greater part of these years, they were kept in power only by a small majority, which depended for its existence upon Mr. O'Connell and his adherents. The popularity of the party was, however, diminishing with all classes of its supporters every day. A state of things like that could not last; and in 1841, the Whigs quitted office, expelled from it by the House of Commons which they had then caused to be chosen. The true causes of this catastrophe may be briefly indicated. They fell, because they pertinaciously resisted every wish of the people for those beneficial changes which ought to have been the fruits of the reform which they made; and because the changes which they did make were so bad in themselves, and so abhorrent to the better portion of the country, that "the Liberal Administion," as it affected to call itself, became almost as deeply hated and distrusted by a large majority of the three kingdoms, as the old Tory *régime* had formerly been. The enmity of the working millions, who have no votes for members of parliament, they could set at defiance for six years. The hatred of the great landed aristocracy, and of the church, they resisted. But the coldness of the trading community, where alone their real strength lay, was speedily fatal to them.

> "Sed periit postquam cerdonibus esse timendus
> "Cœperat ———."

Their resistance to a repeal of the corn-laws was at last fatal to them. It filled up the measure of their deficiencies. The efforts of the energetic and able founders of the Anti-Corn-Law League were at last successful. They persuaded almost the whole of the trading classes, that a total repeal of these oppressive and obnoxious laws would alone cure the enormous pressure under which they continued, with short accidental intervals of feverish ease, to labour and despond. Never was delusion greater than this: but, as delusion often does, it succeeded as far as the immediate object, the repeal of the grain protection, was concerned. Those who saw through the delusion did not care to expose it, because they, too, though for reasons and with views very different from those of the Anti-Corn-Law League, wished also to carry the repeal of all protection for the landlords. The determination, therefore, to destroy the protective code at last became universal, not only amongst manufacturers and shopkeepers, but amongst the working classes, who hoped to derive at last some advantage from it. Unable to resist this feeling, the cabinet of Lord Melbourne at last yielded so far as to propose a fixed duty on wheat of eight shillings per quarter. This concession was, however, too late. Their supporters were alienated, and a large majority of the House of Commons, elected in 1841, were, as we have seen, adherents of Sir Robert Peel. The absurd doctrine of "finality," which was that of Lord Eldon also, was, therefore, really the cause of the failure of a party composed of persons calling themselves "reformers." This was seen by all sensible men, at the period when it occurred. Events have since amply demonstrated it. When Sir Robert Peel came into power in the memorable year 1841, he seated himself upon an eminence amid a rising sea of dangers and difficulties of every conceivable sort. At home and abroad, all was confusion and peril. Against the unoffending Chinese, a murderous war was not yet brought to a bloody close. In India, the ill-concerted and worse-conducted occupation of Cabul had put our very empire into jeopardy. In Syria, by the adroitly-conducted operations there, the nominal rule of the Porte was restored; but France was totally alienated without any conceivable advantage to England being gained; and between the United States and this country, the insidious dispute as to the boundary of the state of Maine was every day adding fresh bitterness. All this was alarming in the extreme, to any statesman who had really brains enough to enable him to feel and see the real position of his country. But, if our foreign relations were unsound, still more so was the internal state of the country. The toiling millions were universally disaffected to the Government. Of the promised fruits of the reform-bill, not one had fallen to their share. The middle classes, whom the act of 1832 had admitted within the pale of free men, at once turned round upon their poorer brethren, and refused them any participation in those advantages which they had only obtained by their assistance during the struggle. To this ingratitude, had been added the monstrous insult and injury of the atrocious code, wrongly intituled, "the Poor-Law Amendment Act;" an act universally patronised and advocated by the middle ranks of society: and to this, again, were added, the privations caused by that dreadful stagnation of all commerce and trade, which was the legitimate re-action of the bloated American trade, the reckless conduct of Lord Ripon's much-lauded joint-stock banks, and the difficulties of the Bank of England, which came to their climax, and narrowly escaped ending in bank restriction, or total stoppage, in the winter of 1839 and 1840. To all the bitter feelings of animosity and disappointment engendered during these dark and disastrous years, during which the working population of these realms, whether agricultural or trading, suffered more privations, injuries, and insults, than perhaps at any former period of our annals, Sir Robert Peel succeeded. He was placed in power more as a negative, than as a positive element in politics. Hatred to his opponents, and the bitter revenge of long-cherished hope finally dashed down and disappointed, mostly seated him there; and he was made prime minister without possessing one jot more of the actual affections or confidence of the people at large, than did his predecessors. No man, in short, ever undertook the government of a powerful people, under circumstances more embarrassing and strange than those that attended the accession of Sir Robert Peel By his active friends and coadjutors, he was carried into power avowedly to do that, the attempt to do which had ruined his political rivals—that is to say, to refuse all further concessions to the demands of the British and Irish people. By his passive supporters, he was installed to get rid of the other party at any rate, at any price, and at any sacrifice. The people had got a notion, and a perfectly well-founded and just persuasion it was, as events have proved, that *any* change must be for their eventual benefit. They therefore assisted the Tories, or stood neuter and let them win. Such was the brief history of the accession to power of Sir Robert Peel—a history passing strange. The Tories put him in as a saviour; the people, as a *pis aller*. Both have been disappointed somewhat. The Tories disagreeably, the people rather agreeably.

It was manifest enough to all clear-headed men, that Sir Robert Peel, from the very first, could not keep the position he appeared to assume. He had been suffered indeed to acquire a majority in the Commons' House; but out of doors he was actively aided only by a small minority; and the press was for the most part against him. Stagnant trade, and the atrocities of the poor-law, had raised the popular mind to so high a pitch of exasperation, that some concession to it was unavoidable. Against the latter measure, the pertinacity of an unconquerable resistance had never ceased to agitate. At first, Lord John Russell and his colleagues treated the agitation with contempt. The whole noise was, as they said, caused by not more than "a dozen" of wrong-headed persons, scattered over the country. Truth, however, is invincible. The atrocities hourly enacted under the law, had made hourly converts. Some men of great talent, amongst those who cultivate our lighter literature, also took up the cause of the poor; and what the battery of more solid argument would not do, the more manageable artillery of the novel and the tale effected. The atrocious enactment was rendered thoroughly unpopular. All ranks were staggered; and as the stagnation of trade, and the consequent privations of those who toil, brought the full hideousness of the principle into view, the law became more and more revolting to the feelings of the public. In this position, it was found by the new premier; but, beyond all this, he succeeded to another difficulty, more immediately pressing than all the rest. This was the appalling state of the finances. We have seen, that, in 1830, the Whigs came into office with colours, on which were inscribed the words "Economy, Retrenchment, and Reform." We have seen the measures of reform accorded, and its immediate fruits. We have seen also, that by means of distant wars, by the emancipation of the black slaves at a huge cost and sacrifice, and by expensive commissions, etc., the ministries of Lord Grey, and of Lord Melbourne, had gradually increased the national expenses from under *forty-eight millions a year*, where they were under the Duke of Wellington, to *fifty millions per annum*, their amount in round numbers in 1841. This enormous outlay no ordinary taxation would meet. After the disasters of 1836, 1837, 1838 and 1839, caused by the commercial pressure in all these years to a greater or less extent, a defalcation of the revenue became apparent. Neither shifts nor evasions could prevent this. *Five per cent* was added to all the taxes in the lump. They yielded no more. The moneys lodged in the savings banks were taken; and the debt, under an insidious clause in the last act for savings banks, thus privately augmented: but all would not do. Sales of crown property were made and the proceeds added to the revenue; but it was still deficient. The result was, that when Sir Robert Peel, in 1841, entered the treasury, he found a probable deficiency, as he himself stated, of *ten millions sterling* in round numbers! This defalcation occurred during the four concluding years of the Melbourne administration, after the break-down of the bloated American trade, the panic of the joint-stock-banks and their failure, and the cessation of the railway speculation, which followed the difficulties of the banks, and that series of disasters which the bad harvest of 1839 brought at length to a perilous climax. Such was the position of the new minister of 1841; and such the varied expectations of the people whom he then undertook to govern.

In the exigence in which he was placed, the measures of the *soi-disant* Tory premier, were, as all acute men had foreseen, necessarily adapted, and most cunningly adapted, to the absolute requirements of a position so strange. They were at once artfully fashioned to relieve the alarms of the fundholders, by giving them a direct hold on the pockets of the nation, and laying all property, whether in land, houses, trade, or manufactures, open to their remorseless grasp; to flatter the free-traders by some concessions to their opinions; and to soothe the landlords by seeming to settle, on a modified and permanent foundation, the now fiercely debated question of the corn-laws. Sir Robert Peel's measure of relief was contained in three distinct propositions. The *first* was the immediate imposition of an income tax. The *second* a modification of the sliding-scale of the existing corn-law. The *third*, a relaxation of the tariff, or list of duties levied on imports generally. It was clear to all thinking men from the first, and the premier soon made it clearer, that the income-tax was the thing he really relied upon for getting the fundholders out of their present alarming predicament. The other two proposals were thus thrown out to amuse the whale of the League, whose energy and increasing influence Sir Robert evidently dreaded, and whose statements as to the critical position of the export cotton trade evidently had great effect upon his mind. This was from the first visible, not only to such members of the house as were members also of the Anti-Corn-law League, but to all others; and the astute leaders of that just-named powerful body profited by it, in the sequel. The free-traders, as they now styled themselves, were not mollified, but encouraged by the concessions to their opinions thus made; whilst the confidence of the landed interest was shaken to its centre, both by the acts and language of their own chosen leader.

Even in these, his first steps, Sir Robert had no little difficulty to encounter. As in the Catholic question, he was again deeply committed against the very point on which he was soon to lay most stress. Against the principle of an income-tax he had spoken in language the most bitter. On a former occasion, when the Duke of Buckingham, then Marquis of

Chandos, Mr. Handley, and other "farmer's friends," had assailed the heavy oppression of the excise on malt, and most justly assailed it, Sir Robert stopped them by the bug-bear of the very impost he was now to propose. "If you repeal this tax (said Sir Robert Peel), to a PROPERTY TAX we must come; and I congratulate you on finding yourselves relieved from the pressure of the malt-tax, and falling back on a good comfortable Property-Tax, with a proposal, probably, for a GRADUATED SCALE! If (he went on), you believe this substitute an advantageous one, be it so; but do not blame those who warned you, in time, against exchanging the light pressure of the malt-duties, for the HEAVY SCOURGE of a Property-Tax." This was pretty strong; and this expression was, we may be sure, not forgotten at this time. It was, in fact, remorselessly thrown in the premier's teeth by those who naturally shrunk from the ill-assorted union of a relaxation of protection for those who live by the soil, with the imposition of a heavy tax on the profits arising from tillage. The plea of necessity was however all-powerful; and the exhibition by the premier of two nice, short, pithy, but most plain-spoken of little documents silenced all opposition. They exhibited the success of the attempt made by Mr. Francis Baring, the Whig Chancellor of the Exchequer, to cure the financial *deficit*, by the imposition of five per cent more of indirect taxation. They are to the point certainly.

AN ACCOUNT OF THE DEFICIENCY OF THE INCOME OF THE UNITED KINGDOM FOR SIX YEARS, ENDING APRIL 5, 1843.

Years.	Ending January 5.	Ending April 5.
	£	£
1838, estimate	655,760	1,428,534
1839 ,,	345,228	430,325
1840 ,,	1,512,792	1,457,223
1841 ,,	1,593,970	1,851,997
1842 ,,	2,101,369	2,354,559
	£6,209,119	£7,502,638
1843, *Ascertained Deficit* -		2,570,000
DEFICIT *in Six Years* -		£10,072,638

MR. F. BARING'S ANTICIPATION OF INCREASED REVENUE TO BE DERIVED FROM TAXES IMPOSED ON CUSTOMS AND EXCISE, IN 1840.

Net produce of Customs and Excise for the year ending January 5, 1840, was - -	£37,911,506
Estimated increase at 5 per cent additional - -	1,895,575
Total *ought to have been*, January 5, 1842, - - -	£39,807,081
Actual produce *was* -	38,118,221
Deduct - - - -	37,911,506
ACTUAL INCREASE -	£206,715

Thus, then, the actual deficiency in the finances, had nothing been done, must have been upwards of ten millions, as the first of these documents goes far to prove; although it does not quite prove it, inasmuch as but for the income-tax, the people might have consumed more taxed articles. That this, however, could not have been much, is evident in the fact, that the loss to the revenue has never been made up upon any of the articles on which the duty has been reduced, with the sole exception, I believe, of coffee. On tobacco and wine, the reduced duty was never made up by increased consumption; and yet these are desirable articles of luxury. On hemp the failure was equally decisive; and there is reason to suppose, that the increase of the consumption of the article coffee was partly obtained by a somewhat diminished use of beer, tea, and spirits. As Sir Robert Peel was aware of all these facts, we may deduce from his conduct two conclusions. One, that in altering the tariff and reducing the scale of the duties on grain, he was acting with a view to conciliate the free-traders, rather than on his own convictions; the other, that though he proposed the income-tax only for three years, he must have intended it really as a permanent resource. He had proved to the House, that indirect taxation had, in his own phrase, "reached its limits." He had seen, that the reduction of the duty on wine, tobacco, and hemp, had injured the revenue; and yet he reduced, or struck out so many articles in the tariff, that, had not the income-tax produced an amount beyond all expectation, he would not, at the end of his administration, had much of a surplus of which to boast.

The income-tax proposed by the Premier, though not apparently heavy as an impost, was of an unjust and sweeping character. To tax the income of those who derive it from real property, in house, or land, or money, is one of the most just modes of taxation. It is to make property pay for its own protection, and to take from those who have: to tax the income derived merely from the labour and talent of the individual, and in the same degree, is flagrantly unjust. By preventing accumulation, and discouraging prudence, it is at once an injury to the state, and to the family of the individual thus circumstanced: and it falsely puts the frail tenure of life and health in the same position as actual wealth, which is a permanent thing, and not subjected to the casualty of the individual's lot. These manifest distinctions were, however, unheeded by the Premier, whose sole attention seemed to be fixed upon making his new tax productive, no matter how. The answer to all objections was, Take your choice; income-tax or national bankruptcy: and to this no man had the courage to make any reply. The assessment was fixed at *sevenpence* in the pound upon all incomes of £150 per annum, and upwards. As a direct attack upon the pockets of those who are rich, and those who would wish to appear to be so, even at a sacrifice, it has succeeded beyond even Sir Robert Peel's most sanguine expectations, and probably beyond the anticipations of all parties in and out of Parliament. When Sir Robert calculated the landed rental at thirty-nine millions sterling, the amount in 1814, most men believed him in error. It was notorious, that the scale of rents had been heavily reduced by the immense increase given to the value of money, and by the fall of prices created by the bill of 1819. This no corn-law could prevent; though unquestionably those laws prevented the fall in the prices of grain, on the average, going, for wheat, below *fifty-six* or *fifty-seven* shillings the quarter. But with wheat at 57*s.* the quarter, the war-scale of rents could not be maintained, nor anything like it. The only way, therefore, to account for the result which has realised this calculation, is to refer it partly to the vast inclosures of common lands made since 1814; and partly to the enhanced rentals of all those lands adjoining the great manufacturing towns which have sprung up during the last thirty-three years. Nothing but these causes can account for the total rent of land in England being nominally the equal, but in reality about the double of that of 1814, if the alteration of the value of money be taken into account; to which, of course, must be added the improved cultivation of land since that period, and the much higher comparative rents paid by farmers at present, arising out of a morbidly growing population, and an increased competition for land. There need be no doubt, that this enormous rental has been swelled by the impoverishment of the farmer, and the sad degradation of the labourer. All the evidence on the state of the agricultural districts proves this dreadful truth. The result, as it stands, however, surprised most men, the Premier himself probably not excepted. It gave him new courage for those further relaxations of the tariff, which he has conceded to the clamours of the manufacturers; and to which we shall have to advert at the proper time and place.

If the proposition of the income-tax excited alarm,

that alarm was nothing, when compared with the misgivings produced by the proposition coupled with it of tampering with the corn-laws. It gave the landed supporters of the new prime minister the first hint of his deficient firmness, when assailed by the arguments, clamours, and threats, of a manufacturing community, which seemed to be verging fast to a state of desperation. When he succeeded to the helm of the state, it cannot be denied, that the seats of our great manufactures, were steeped in misery extreme. Foreign markets were overloaded to a ruinous extent with their goods; for what could not be sold at home, was forced abroad at any risk or cost. Added to this, the catastrophes in the United States had crippled the demand from that quarter; and the high prices of food produced by consecutive bad harvests, had also miserably curtailed the only very profitable trade, that at home. The representations and clamours arising out of this appalling posture of trading matters, Sir Robert could neither evade nor resist. Nor was it to be expected. The distress at Glasgow, Paisley, Leeds, Manchester, and various other seats of manufactures was extreme. It could hardly be exaggerated, and it could not be denied. Where masses of misery are brought together, the peril is enormous. The agricultural labourers were also suffering; but it was less seen. The consequence was, that congregated distress was more powerfully voiced than misery in a more scattered position. Lancashire was heard, whilst Wiltshire and Dorsetshire were neglected; and a relaxation of the restrictions on the importation of food was wrung from the very man, who had been avowedly raised to power, in order to put an effectual stop to all such innovation. Thus, at the end of a peace of nearly thirty years' duration, England was reduced by manifest necessity to have recourse to a tax, which was always held to be her surest card in case of a war; and a relaxation of a system upon which the wealth of the landed aristocracy seems to rest, was compelled to be yielded to the groans and menaces of a population, absolutely threatened with death by starvation.

It may be easily supposed, that even this first step towards the relaxation of a code upon which interests so powerful depended, was not to be made without subjecting its author to strong suspicions and stronger remonstrances. Invectives of every kind, and accusations of double dealing, were not spared; and the language of the prime minister, who, while he still denied them by his acts, strangely enough admitted in his speeches the abstract truth of the doctrines of the economists and free-traders, struck more dismay into the minds of his former friends than did even his measures. In point of fact, whilst Sir Robert appeared strongly to advocate the necessity of protection for British agriculture, and whilst he condemned a fixed duty of 8s. as inadequate, he really deserted the only ground on which a corn-law can be defended. Instead of resting it upon the broad basis of the truth, that the *general* taxation of the country has so enormously enhanced the expenses of a tillage farm, that the English farmer cannot stand competition with the corn of lightly taxed countries, he put the defence upon the usual ground of *peculiar* burthens resting on land, which is not the case to any extent. This was in reality to give up all corn-laws, because if this be all that can be said, it really amounts to nothing. What is the use of talking of land-tax, and highway-rate as a reason for protection? In spite, however, of the misgivings of his landed supporters, the minister persevered. He worked upon the hopes of the landlords, that this modification might be a final settlement of this dreaded question. The former scale was intended to preserve the average price of wheat, at about sixty shillings the quarter—which, however, it failed to do. The sliding scale of 1842, was an attempt to keep it at about fifty-six shillings per quarter on the average, which was the actual result of three years' trial. The highest duty was 20*s.* per quarter. This took place when wheat fell to 50*s.* the quarter. When the price rose to 73*s.* the quarter, the duty fell to 1*s.* After long debate, this scale was finally carried; and the rest of the tariff measure passed with little opposition. Most of the duties removed were on trifling articles. Some few of the modifications subjected the English handicrafts to foreign competition, which they before escaped; but for this the landlords cared nothing! This competition was not in corn. The admission of cattle at a moderate duty provoked violent rage, and so did that of salted provisions; but the import of French shoes was disregarded. Such was the great measure of the session of 1842. The whole tone of the debate, although great disappointment was asserted to be felt by them, manifestly raised the hopes of Mr. Cobden, the champion of the League, and his coadjutors hither than ever. The exertions of that powerful and well-managed association, were from that hour redoubled. Mr. Villiers, the able spokesman for freedom of trade in grain, renewed his notices of motion for a total repeal of all restrictions on the import of grain. Mr. Cobden harangued. The lecturers and agents of the Anti-corn-Law Association threaded the country. A newspaper called "The League" was started, and the whole country agitated to its very core on this all pervading question. The success of this most ably constructed and ably-worked machinery we shall soon see. It was not long doubtful: but another measure equally important was also now contemplated by the prime minister, and to that measure we shall now turn our attention.

We have seen the critical position to which the events that preceded the close of the disastrous year 1839, reduced the Bank of England, which was only saved from stoppage by the indirect aid of the Bank of France. That these events had deeply affected the mind of Sir Robert Peel is very certain; and he now set himself to work, to find some method, if possible, of preventing the occurrence of similar perils in future. With this view, he, in 1843, had procured a committee to sit and examine the question of banking, with a view to improve, if possible, the management of that two-edged tool, a paper-money payable in gold on demand at the mint-price of *three pounds, seventeen shillings, and ten pence half-penny, the ounce.* By that committee, the opinions of many bankers and others, concerned in money affairs, were asked, and their evidence taken on every point connected with banking, and the regulation of paper currency. It is needless to say, that much of that evidence went to prove the extreme difficulty of managing such a circulation, and the multiform casualties and dangers by which it must ever be surrounded. This was to be expected: but one piece of evidence as to its possible effects on the foreign relations of the country is so important, that I must give it entire. We here see the reason why England, once so haughty and high-spirited, has of late succumbed under so many injuries, insults, and encroachments from foreigners. We here see why one of her secretaries for Foreign affairs has been openly accused of being the tool of Foreign courts, and stigmatised as a traitor. We here perceive the real and first cause of the weakness and apparent cowardice, treachery, or imbecility of British diplomacy, ever since the year 1819. Here we see exposed the tap-root of all this degradation. When diplomatists dare not do their duty, they must sometimes seem to be traitors without being so. What wonder, if in such circumstances they sometimes become so? The plain truth is, without the power of a final appeal to the sword, diplomacy is in vain, and a minister may as well make money as not, of surrenders and submissions that are inevitable. The necessity three parts excuses the crime. The evidence I am about to quote, is that of J. W. Gilbart, Esq., a man of talent, and known in the literary as well as the commercial world, as the author of a "History of Banking," and as manager of the London and Westminster bank.

"1064.—Your answer assumes that the exchanges are never likely to be adverse during a war * * * How do you reconcile that with the circumstances of the war in 1797, when the bank was reduced to a state of exhaustion of its treasure? I do not know that my answer assumes that; but as a political question rather than a banking one, I confess, if I were prime minister, I would, immediately on commencement of a war, issue an order in council for the bank to *stop payment.*

"1065.—Then you are of opinion that suspension of payment is necessarily the consequence of war?—'Necessarily' is a strong term; but I should think it the best measure, and I should decidedly adopt it."—*Second Report on Banks of Issue*, p. 112.

In another place Mr. Gilbart thus answers Sir Thomas Freemantle.

"1144.—*Sir Thomas Freemantle.*—Do you mean to say, the bank could secure the convertibility of its notes in a time of war?—In a time of war I should *stop payment at once.* It would be better to stop *before the gold was gone* than afterwards.

"1145.—*Mr. Warburton.*—You would recommend that as a desirable thing in itself?—Yes; as an expedient thing."—*Second Report on Banks of Issue*, p. 118.

Again, on Sir Robert Peel taking up the question, Mr. Gilbart gives an answer in a tone equally manly.

"1148.—*Sir Robert Peel.*—You would advise then, under certain circumstances, a 'bank restriction' as an immediate measure?—If you had a war, a 'bank restriction,' *immediately, I should recommend.*"—*Second Report on Banks of Issue*, p. 118.

Being further cross-questioned on this ticklish topic, Mr. Gilbart gave the following very veritable and manly explanation.

"1272. * * * * * I stated that if I were prime minister, I would immediately, on the commencement of war, issue an order in council for the bank to stop payment. I stated also, that I spoke as a politician, not as a banker. The only war that has occurred in my memory is the war of twenty years with France; that is the war to which I referred. * * * * Now, under such a war as that, it appeared to me that a suspension of payments would be advisable. I recollect some time ago investigating the circumstances attending the suspension of 1797; I came to the conclusion, that, under the circumstances, a suspension of cash payments was not a matter of *choice*, but *necessity*. * * * * That is the opinion at which I arrived, after a careful investigation of the circumstances: it has since been confirmed by the writings of Mr. Maculloch; and when I referred to a war, it was to a war similar to that." —*Second Report on Banks of Issue*, p. 131.

It is impossible enough to admire the boldness and candour of these replies. Beyond all doubt or question, through the mouth of Mr. Gilbart, we got the real opinion, as to this ticklish matter, of all bankers and most commercial men of note and experience. The grand question is what effect must these opinions have upon the minds of the ministers of Foreign powers? To all governments abroad, these answers are known. They have, doubtless, been read and commented upon by President Polk, by Baron Bulow, by Prince Metternich, and by MM. Guizot and Thiers. They here see, that it is the opinion of all who deal in money, that a war by England would cause an act, the sure result of which would be to reduce the English money in circulation to at least half its present value – probably worse than that. At the same time they see this, they know that the question of peace or war depends upon that very moneyed interest, which gains so largely by cash payments in gold and silver. What must be their conclusion? Why surely this—that the British government must, and will submit to any degradation or sacrifice, rather than resort to hostilities. To this conclusion they must come; and surely the consequences are not difficult to be imagined. We find them in the submission of Wellington to the blockade of Enos by the Russians, in 1829; in the capture of the Vixen; and the extirpation of Poland as a nation; in the annexation of the Texas, without reference to our treaties with that country, which we had guaranteed as an independent state; in the overthrow of Espartero and of British influence in Spain, by the king of the French, together with the alliance of his son to Donna Luisa, the queen's sister and probable successor; in the Russian agressions on the Turkish empire, whose existence as an independent power is so essential to British interests; and, lastly, in the destruction by the Muscovite of all the influence of England in Persia, and the continual intrigues in central Asia, carried on by Russia, with the avowed purpose of shaking our empire in Hindostan; in all these things, we clearly perceive the total loss of domination by a country, which once boasted in the words of Lord Chatham, that "not a cannon should be fired in Europe, without her knowing the reason why." The cause of that disregard and contempt which she now experiences in all parts of the world, is to be sought in the fact detailed by Mr. Gilbart. A nation that dares not fight (for whatever cause) loses all diplomatic influence, and in this predicament England now stands. Foreign governments, one and all, know that those who really rule the councils of the realm, prefer national degradation to a blowing-up of the present unstable currency, which the first blast of the war-trumpet would assuredly ruin; and knowing and seeing this, they do what they please, keeping up a mere hollow appearance of amicable intercourse.

This was by far the most important piece of evidence elicted by Peel's committee on banks of issue. It was no doubt shown, in evidence before that committee, that much of the enormous over-trading and consequent mischief during the years 1836, 1837, 1838, and 1839, had been caused by the reckless conduct of some of the great joint-stock banks; but, in my humble opinion, the manly revelations of Mr. Gilbart far out-do all the rest in real and vital importance, and so ought to be deemed. The evidence as to the insane conduct of the joint-stock-banks seems, however, to have produced a mighty effect upon the mind of Sir Robert Peel, the fruits of which were not ripened until the year following. These fruits were the enactments of the famous banking act of 1844, which put a bar of adamant in the way of all future issues of paper money; and which took at once out of the hands of the directors of the Bank of England, all future power over the circulation of the country beyond very narrow limits. In fact, by this act, Peel said to the Bank of England and its managers, what Dean Swift once said to an old toothless couple who came to be married "rather than do worse"—"Get you home, you silly old fools, and *do your worst!*" The Bank was, in truth, by this enactment really deprived of its virility, and reduced once more to the state of the child, creeping about in leading-strings or tottering in a go-cart!

The year 1844, and its Session of Parliament, produced before the astonished world the Banking Act of the Premier. Its enactments were of the most extraordinary character; and the speech by which they were prefaced was not much less so. The real intent, nature, and character of the bill now brought in, may be described by a very apt illustration. If a man wanted to prevent the mischiefs that often arise from *high spring tides* by act of Parliament, and were to bring in a bill for perpetual *low water*, this would be the counterpart of the currency act of 1844. This act, in fact, tied down henceforward the paper-money issues of all bankers to the narrowest limitations possible, and thus prevented over-issue. It caused all banks that issued their own promissory-notes, to give in an average of their circulation for the three preceding years. To this amount it tied them down. It compelled them to publish in the Gazette, at short periods, a return of the circulation of each Bank, and if any exceeded the average allowance, the bankers were compelled to hold coin or bullion to the amount of the excess. The Bank of England was treated just as cavalierly. She was allowed to issue notes to the amount of the debt owing her by the Government, etc. etc., to the extent in all of *fourteen millions*. In addition to this, she was also permitted to issue two millions' worth of bank post-bills, for the convenience of remitters. All her issues of paper, beyond this, were to be based on bullion and specie; meaning thereby, that for every five-pound note issued beyond the £16,000,000, she was to have five pounds in coin or bullion in her coffers. Thus were the Bank of England, and the Country Banks that issue their own notes, put into one category. For every note issued beyond these narrow limits, a security in gold was required to be producible; and should any untoward event draw the reserves and deposits of the precious metals out of the hands of the Bank of England, she must, no matter at what risk to the trade of the country, reduce her circulation down to sixteen millions in all, and keep it there until gold and silver come back to her, or else buy them, if she can, where they are to be had.

This stringent enactment seems to prove, that all the mischief, misery, and national torture produced by the monstrous injustice of the act of 1819, have not produced the slightest effect on the singularly constituted soul of this singular man. That mischief, that misery, and that torture still rage on. They must go on, and continue to be felt, as long as the provisions of that act continue in force, unmitigated by other measures. These terrible results of his deed in 1819, have been over, and over, and over again, and yet again, held up before its author; yet, as if totally unconscious of these effects, and blind to their continuance, he proposes and carries another act, to render the enactments of the first still more stringent and galling, and to shut out even the possibility of those expansions of the currency that were the only temporary mitigations of the evil. This act is, in reality, an act to *stereotype* low prices and diminished profits; and to squeeze and crush down the producers, whilst it improves the position of the fund-holder, the pensioner, the half-pay officer, the government official, and every description of national leech or state annuitant. It is probable, that Sir Robert Peel, when he proposed this act, imagined that, by its means, he should take away the possibility of the future recurrence of those turns in the Exchanges, by over-trading, that send the gold abroad, and are the causes of such money panics as we have described; but he forgot that the seasons will do this as well as over-issues of paper; and that a scarcity of grain, and a large import, may send away the metals, without false or unsound trade being in the case. Putting this aside, the act is, no doubt, a very successful expedient to keep a country "at low water," and so it will be felt, and has already been felt. On proposing it, his introductory speech was remarkable. To all the multiplied evils which the bill of 1819 has occasioned; to the enormous increase of the poor-rate and the bankrupt lists; to the fall of rents, and yet more of profits; and to the deteriorated condition of whole masses of the toiling millions, both manufacturing and agricultural, he never once alluded. The over-trading caused by extended issues of paper-money, and the revulsions and panics, and the evils of these, were the topics on which he harped; and whilst he harped upon them, he seemed to be quite unaware, that even those issues which he deprecated, and not unjustly, were still, whilst they lasted and before revulsion came, the only mitigations of that deep stagnation in the general commerce of the country, which invariably must, and does fill up the intervals, between the apparent brief fits of a transient prosperity, which the recklessness of bankers and the wildness of speculators from time to time occasion. One expression, the Premier made use of, which seemed to betray a half-consciousness of the truth, and a wish to shift the blame from his own shoulders—if blame there should be—to those of others. Alluding to the bill of 1819, Sir Robert used the following remarkable words:—"I am free to confess, that the Houses *might*, at that time, have taken into consideration *the consequences arising out of the alteration of the value* of money—BUT THEY DID NOT DO IT"! "But they did not do it"! No! sure enough, they '*did not*'—but WHY, Sir Robert Peel, WHY did they 'NOT DO IT'? They did not do it, *because* they, understanding nothing themselves of the question, and pinning their faith upon the sleeve of two or three oracles not more infallible than themselves, were told by yourself, and more especially by the late Mr. Ricardo, that the whole difference involved was only a matter of *four per cent!* Upon this assurance, having already, in case of the worst, secured a corn-law which they thought would protect themselves, the Houses voted. The readers of this volume are already aware of the enormous folly of this assurance, and of the causes of the error; but what are we to think of Sir Robert Peel? He must, now, either be aware or not aware of the injustice of his own bill. If he is not now convinced of its injustice, what are we to deem of his intellect? If he is aware of it, what are we to deem of his honesty? There is no escape here. It will not avail, to urge that Peel might be sensible of the dreadful error of the deeds of 1819, but deem the mischief once done incapable of reparation. This excuse it is of no avail to urge, because every year that passes is adding to that injustice. Every year that passes takes from the injured people of England at least *twenty millions sterling* which they ought not to pay, and hands this prodigious plunder over to the fund-holders, pensioners, half-pay officers, and other public annuitants. The injustice is therefore perennial, and every year that slips away without an equitable adjustment being made, adds to the amount of spoliation and consequent misery. Whatever might be the motives of Sir Robert Peel in uttering the words quoted, neither words nor motives were understood by his auditory. They passed unheeded and uncommented on; and after a feeble resistance on the part of the few members who have any knowledge of this momentous matter, the bill passed both Houses. The only concession made was to the Scottish Bankers, who again preserved their darling one-pound notes for their own benefit; for to the public it can now make no difference as to results, whether a banker issues a one-pound note or a sovereign of gold, whilst the quantity of the notes is limited. Such is the history of this bill, which has been well called "Peel's Bill the Second." It proves, that this strange man is determined to persevere longest in his greatest error, and that if atonement is to be made by him, it shall be deferred to the latest possible moment.

Few readers of this book can fail to see, that the assured tendency of this "Peel's bill the second," is to press and crush down still lower the prices of commodities, and the profits and wages of those who produce them. Indeed, to those who have looked narrowly at the course of trade since that time, as well as at the finances, this is really manifest. Circumstances have, however, since its passing, tended greatly to counteract the effects of this bill both on commerce and the revenue. These circumstances are, the enormous extent of speculations in railways, that have characterised every year, save that of the enactment of this bill. The enormous sums embarked in these schemes, are for the most part paid away in wages of labour. These wages are spent in articles of consumption highly taxed; in coffee, tea, soap, beer, spirits, and tobacco. Yet with all this artificial demand, prices have not been forced up; and the revenue, with the aid of the income-tax, has barely made head against the innovations in the tariff, ventured by Sir Robert Peel. Without counteracting causes somewhere, this could not have been; and this counteraction is to be found in the deadening effect, which the bank-note limitation act has had upon all regular trade and ordinary dealings out of the sphere of the prevailing speculations. When these speculations find their end, then will the influence of that Bill be fully felt; unless, indeed, other events, in the meantime, put a sudden end to its enactments, as at present seems to be by no means impossible.

In the mean time, the partial revival of trade, brought about by the better harvests and the railway expenditure, by no means checked the agitation of the Anti-Corn-Law League, nor damped the energies of its leaders. The tone and language of the prime minister, ever at variance with his acts, had indeed given them fresh spirits; and their numbers and wealth went on rapidly increasing. Covent Garden theatre was thronged nightly, to hear the harangues of their orators; and the metropolis at last became pervaded with the spirit, which already animated all the classes of voters in the provincial towns and many of the counties. In short, the agitation seemed satisfactorily approaching its *denouement*, when it pleased an all-wise Providence to hasten the catastrophe, by one of those dispensations which change the destinies of nations. We have already seen how, for many years, the wretched root, the potato, which has long been the almost sole food of millions in Ireland, has, under the pressure occasioned by the debt and taxes, been becoming more and more the aliment of the once well-fed English labourer. We have seen, under the stimulus of the low diet, the population, formerly almost stationary, grow and increase; and thus, by morbidly swelling the numbers, increase the competition and lower the wages of the labourers. This we have seen and lamented; but the year 1845 was destined to set before our eyes a spectacle, than which nothing more appalling can be conceived by the gloomiest imaginings. In the year 1845, a mysterious disease made its appearance amongst the potato crops, not only in Europe but in America, and caused considerable destruction. In America this root is of no consequence. On the continent it is not a staple food; but in unhappy Ireland, and in some portions of Scotland, and even England, strong apprehensions of famine were excited. Against the alarm and panic caused by this circumstance, sedulously exaggerated by a large part of the periodical press, the now tottering corn-laws could not stand. A public letter by Lord John

Russell announced his conviction, that a total repeal of these laws was now inevitable. In this avowal, he was followed by Lord Morpeth and the greater part of the Whig party; and this, as a consequence, produced so violent a dissension in the Tory cabinet, that Sir Robert Peel, who agreed as to this point with his Whig opponents, at once resigned office. The die was now cast. After a vain attempt, on the part of Lord John Russell, to construct a cabinet upon the basis of an immediate repeal of all restrictive duties on the import of grain, Sir Robert Peel was again called to office; and by the aid of the "Liberals" and "free-traders," and of about one hundred and twelve of his own party, a total repeal of these laws, wonderful to say, was carried—a delay of three years only being interposed. The bill took date in January 1846. It enacted a short sliding scale of duties; ten shillings per quarter being the highest, and four shillings per quarter the lowest, until January 1849, when grain and many other sorts of provisions are to be imported freely into England. A very few days after this astounding event, Sir Robert, being in a minority on the Irish arms bill, again retired from office, to which the Whigs again succeeded, and which they still hold, amidst events the most extraordinary and by a tenure the most precarious. Thus, like the Catholic penal code, has the bulwark of the corn-laws at last been swept away by the very men who were put into power to protect both: and thus has the death-blow to aristocratic Tory domination been given at last by the hands of Sir Robert and the Duke of Wellington; a plain proof that events and not men now rule this country, and that the present system of government can only stand as long as events shall suffer it to stand. It is beyond all belief, that either Peel or Wellington, or Lord John Russell, were really moved by the influence of the arguments of the party styled "free-traders." These arguments had been for twenty years repeated *usque ad nauseam*, without the production of any such effect. Why then should they assume such potency in 1845-6? The truth is, that to overwhelming necessity we must attribute the whole. The prime minister had spoken against the injustice of repealing these protective laws, without a corresponding reduction of the taxation of the country, as strongly as man could do, in 1842, only three years before. He then said, in answer to the one-sided aphorisms of the men of free-trade—"The proposition of buying corn in the cheapest market, is certainly tempting in theory; but before you determine it is *just*, you must ascertain the amount of *burthens* to which land in other countries is subjected, and compare them with the burthens imposed on land in this country." In this one sentence, had he stuck to it, resides the whole *gist* of this matter. It is mere foolery to talk about the *exclusive* burthens on land. Sir Robert Peel must have known that all the taxes, *direct* and *indirect*, paid by those who live by tillage, and by those who supply necessaries to those who till the soil, are in reality paid out of the fruits of that tillage. In short, all these taxes come out of the land, and must be paid before either farmer or landlord can reap a shilling of rent or profit. How then is this land to stand the competition of countries where taxes are almost unknown? If land could be ploughed, as cotton is spun and woven, by machinery, it might bear this competition as cotton does, until foreigners equalled us in these machines. But without this, to talk of competition, is "to darken counsel by words without knowledge." How then came Sir Robert Peel, in 1845, to unsay that which he so clearly saw in 1842? The reply is, he did so, not from conviction, but necessity. He had convinced himself, that without some measure of this sort, there was left no chance of continued employment for the congregated masses of Lancashire and Yorkshire. This appalling risk he dared not face; and therefore preferred ruin for the aristocracy or the fundholder, one or the other, to rebellion amongst the starving millions of the North. It seems to me impossible to reply to this question in any other manner, or to apply any other solution to the enigma of the repeal of these laws by Wellington and Peel.

I now draw towards a conclusion; but, before finishing this letter, it is proper to observe the complete futility of all the schemes for bettering the condition of the country, that have been tried since the reform of 1832. This is apparent in the statistics of the kingdom, and cannot be gainsaid. The POOR-RATE, despite the cruelty of the amended poor-law, has again risen to the appalling annual cost of SEVEN MILLIONS, and yet the poor are worse off than before; are more harshly treated, and more ill-fed. This plain statement it is impossible to deny. Again, notwithstanding the spread of education and the building of places of worship of all sorts have gone on increasing since 1832, the COMMITMENTS of CRIMINALS have grown with them. This is shown by the following returns, which surely speak "trumpet-tongued" as to this matter.

Years.	Committals.	Years.	Committals.
1832	20,821	1839	24,451
1833	20,072	1840	27,187
1834	22,451	1841	27,670
1835	20,731	1842	31,309
1836	20,984	1843	29,591
1837	23,612	1844	26,542
1838	23,094		

The excess in 1842 probably arose from the extreme depth of distress that at that time pervaded trade and manufactures of every kind. The general result, however, speaks only one language. It tells us that all schemes, which do not go to lighten the enormous and crushing weight of the taxes, must be utterly vain. From that pressure arise the distress and the crimes; and by its alleviation alone can they be diminished.

The concluding letter of this series will contain a sort of general view, or "summing up" of the facts, and of the future consequences they are calculated to produce. In the mean time, it is proper to state, that in this, the thirty-second year of peace, the fixed or funded debt of the nation, or rather its government, is stated at the appalling sum of £727,835,934. If to this we add the value of the terminable annuities granted by government, the balances in the hands of the savings' bank commissioners, the amount of exchequer bills floating, the fixed debt of the government to the bank, and the various other claims upon the Exchequer, we cannot be above the truth in calling the whole in round numbers EIGHT HUNDRED MILLIONS OF POUNDS STERLING. Thus then, since 1815, no material diminution of this debt has been effected; and if we look at the following statement, we shall find as little hope for the future.

An Abstract of the Net Produce of the Revenue of Great Britain in the Years and Quarters ended the 5th of January, 1846 and 1847, showing the Increase or Decrease thereof.

	Quarters ended.				Year ended 5th Jan., 1846.	Quarters ended.				Year ended 5th Jan., 1847.	Year ended Jan. 5th, 1847.		Quarter ended Jan. 5th, 1847.	
	5th April, 1845.	5th July, 1845.	10th Oct., 1845.	5th Jan., 1846.		5th April, 1846.	5th July, 1846.	10th Oct., 1846.	5th Jan., 1847.		Increase.	Decrease.	Increase.	Decrease.
	£.	£.	£.	£.	£.	£.	£.	£.	£.	£.	£.	£.	£.	£.
Customs	4,402,506	4,499,548	4,848,363	4,354,789	18,105,206	3,961,918	4,523,391	5,310,835	4,514,721	18,310,865	205,659	..	159,932	..
Excise	1,917,485	2,965,684	3,955,106	3,838,837	12,177,112	1,626,458	3,104,711	4,181,926	3,608,155	12,521,250	344,138	..	269,318	..
Stamps	1,742,461	1,837,076	1,780,175	1,792,402	7,152,114	1,685,868	1,730,495	1,774,364	1,740,687	6,931,414	..	220,700	..	51,715
Taxes	145,945	2,000,567	201,279	1,876,051	4,223,842	146,142	2,006,427	209,940	1,909,899	4,272,408	48,566	..	33,848	..
Property-Tax	1,905,711	909,991	1,823,883	386,985	5,023,570	1,963,882	1,009,162	1,972,128	450,219	5,395,391	368,821	..	63,234	..
Post-office	178,000	155,000	209,000	189,000	731,000	215,000	181,000	217,000	263,000	816,000	85,000	..	14,000	..
Crown Lands	35,000	30,000	30,000	25,000	120,000	45,000	..	45,000	30,000	120,000	..	..	5,000	..
Miscellaneous (exclusive of China Money	22,951	13,652	15,102	68,612	120,317	91,522	18,001	177,910	29,657	317,090	196,773	..	..	38,955
Total Ordinary Revenue	10,350,059	12,411,518	12,862,908	12,031,676	47,656,161	9,735,790	12,573,187	13,889,103	12,486,338	48,684,418	1,248,957	220,700	545,332	90,670
China Money	392,065	..	450,000	300,859	1,142,924	..	440,000	227,644	..	667,644	..	475,280	..	300,859
Impressed and other Moneys	206,007	29,262	24,591	64,084	322,944	52,902	73,939	33,815	31,884	192,547	..	131,397	..	32,200
Repayments of Advances	418,545	182,354	473,881	404,179	1,478,959	456,473	111,607	199,882	302,449	1,070,411	..	408,548	..	101,730
Total Income	11,366,676	12,623,134	13,811,380	12,800,798	50,601,988	10,245,172	13,198,733	14,350,444	12,820,671	50,615,020	1,248,957	1,235,925	545,332	525,459
The Amount applied to Consolidated Fund, exclusive of Advances	7,273,077	8,255,562	8,869,973	7,859,997	32,258,609	5,468,353	8,476,134	7,617,435	8,615,898	30,177,822	1,235,925	Deduct decrease.	525,459	Deduct decrease.
The Amount applied as Advances	380,000	101,501	550,000	615,077	1,646,578	140,000	91,501	472,500	837,500	1,541,501				
The Amount applied as part of the Ways and Means of the Year	3,713,599	4,266,071	4,391,407	4,325,724	16,696,801	4,636,817	4,631,098	6,260,509	3,367,273	18,895,697	13,032	Increase on Year.	19,873	Increase on the Quarter.
Total	11,366,676	12,623,134	13,811,380	12,800,798	50,601,981	10,245,172	13,198,733	14,350,444	12,820,671	50,615,020				

The results of the above show, that it is only by means of the Income Tax, that the peace expenditure can be met; and that unless that impost can be greatly augmented, and with equally productive effects, there remain absolutely no resources on which to found a war expenditure.

LETTER XVI.

GENERAL STATE AND PROSPECTS OF THE COUNTRY.

HAVING now brought the historical portion of this work to a close, it only remains to fix the leading and most important facts of this strange narrative in the mind; and, from the view of the actual state and position of the country which we shall thus obtain, deduce the prospects and probabilities of the future. To arrive at this end, the best method (as it appears to me), is to construct a sort of condensed "summing-up"; which abstract, or summing-up, seems naturally to divide itself into *five* distinct general heads.

I. A brief outline of the position of the country, in A.D. 1688, when the revolution and its grand adjuncts, funds and paper money, were inflicted upon it.—II. Its position at this present time, when these inventions have developed a large part of their effects.—III. The perils resulting from the state of affairs at which we have already arrived.—IV. The certainty that some of these dangers must actually come to pass, in no long period of time.—V. The impossibility of now applying any palliative to this critical position of the country, and the general reflections that naturally rush into the mind, as to any catastrophe that may occur. Under these five heads, we shall obtain a clear and compendious view of the mortal maladies under which the country labours, and their assured end. To this compendium let us now apply ourselves.

I. If we look with the eyes of common sense at the state of England at the end of the reign of the much-maligned, but honest monarch, James II., we shall find that state to be very prosperous. The whole annual revenue required from his subjects by this king, amounted to only a couple of millions of pounds sterling; these pounds being in value equal to about thirty shillings of the money of this present moment. So well-off and easy in their circumstances were the mass of the people, that the poor-rates, which were in those days liberally distributed, only amounted to three hundred thousand pounds yearly. The population, being rich and well-fed, was moderate in numbers. No such thing as "surplus population" was even dreamed of. Every man had constant employment at good wages; bankruptcy was a thing scarcely known; and nothing, short of sheer and great misfortune or culpable and undeniable imprudence, could drive men into the Gazette bankrupt-list, or upon the parish books. In trade, profits were great and competition small. Six per cent was commonly given for money when it was really wanted. Prudent men, after being twenty years in business, generally retired with a comfortable competence: and thus competition was lessened, because men went out of business almost as fast as others went into it; and the eldest apprentice was frequently the active successor of his retired master, sometimes as the partner of the son, and sometimes as the husband of the daughter. In the intercourse of ordinary life a hospitality was kept up, at which modern times choose to mock at, because they are too poverty-sticken to imitate it. Servants had presents made to them by guests, under the title of "vails," which often enabled them to realise a comfortable sum for old age. The dress of the times was as rich, and as indicative of real wealth, as the modes of living. Gold and silver lace were commonly worn; and liveries were equally costly. With less pretence of taste and show, the dwellings were more substantially built; and the furniture was solid and serviceable, as well as ornamental: in short, all that it seemed to be.

The condition of the working classes was proportionately happy. Their wages were good, and their means far above want, where common prudence was joined to ordinary strength. In the towns, the dwellings were cramped, by most of the towns being walled; but in the country, the labourers were mostly the owners of their own cottages and gardens, which studded the edges of the common lands that were appended to every township. The working classes, as well as the richer people, kept all the Church-Festivals, Saints' Days, and Holidays. Good Friday, Easter and its week, Whitsuntide, Shrove Tuesday, Ascension Day, Christmas, etc., were all religiously observed. On every festival, good fare abounded from the palace to the cottage; and the poorest wore strong broad cloth and homespun linen, compared with which the flimsy fabrics of these times are mere worthless gossamers and cobwebs, whether strength or value be looked at. At this time, all the rural population brewed their own beer, which, except on fast-days, was the ordinary beverage of the working man. Flesh meat was commonly eaten by all classes. The potato was little cultivated; oatmeal was hardly used; even bread was neglected where wheat was not ordinarily grown, though wheaten bread (contrary to what is sometimes asserted) was generally consumed. In 1760, a later date, when George III. began to reign, it was computed that the whole people of England (alone) amounted to six millions. Of these, three millions, seven hundred and fifty thousand, were believed to eat wheaten bread; seven hundred and thirty-nine thousand were computed to use barley-bread; eight hundred and eighty-eight thousand, rye-bread; and six hundred and twenty-three thousand, oatmeal and oat-cakes. All, however, eat bacon or mutton, and drank beer and cider; tea and coffee being then principally consumed by the middle classes. The very diseases attending this full mode of living, were an evidence of the state of national comfort prevailing. Surfeit, apoplexy, scrofula, gout, piles and hepatitis; agues of all sorts, from the want of drainage; and malignant fevers in the walled towns, from want of ventilation, were the ordinary complaints. But consumption in all its forms, marasmus and atrophy, owing to the better living and clothing, was comparatively unfrequent; and the types of fever, which are caused by want, equally so.

Such were the physical state and condition of the people about this period. The national state was equally sound. There was nothing in the shape of Government debt, save some arrears of pay to persons in different services, and a sum of which the profligate Charles II. had robbed the Exchequer, being money deposited there by merchants for safe custody. These arrears King James II. had greatly reduced; and he had not only constructed a powerful and efficient navy, a service to which he was greatly attached and well understood, but had also organised a well-equipped and well-disciplined body of troops, the services of which were reaped by his Dutch successor. The results of all this prudence and excellent management were lost to him by one grand error. The people of England, thus happy in their external and internal affairs, living under a cheap government, now well administered, and for all ordinary purposes really administered by themselves, deprived of any real grievance, had made one for themselves. They suffered themselves to be tormented and distracted by religious feelings: and this soon led them into a bitter hate of the reigning monarch, who made no secret of his attachment to the old religion of the country; and into a jealousy of his prerogatives, which they feared he would use, and which he was no doubt too willing to use, to advance that form of religion which so many hated, and so many feared. The dangers which necessarily resulted from this state of affairs and this impolitic course, King James unhappily overlooked. He was, no doubt, sincerely attached to his religion, and willing to risk a good deal to obtain for it something like fair play in the country which he ruled. The king accordingly took at their word, those who stickled for what they were pleased to call "the right of private judgment in matters of religion"—and insisted, if every type, form, and description of faith was to be tolerated, that a form of religion, which had been universal in Europe for above a thousand years, should be tolerated too. The holders of the plunder of the old church now became alarmed. They plotted the overthrow of the government; and the result was the flight of the imprudent monarch, and the putting of the Dutch Stadtholder on the throne. Such was the state of England, prior to the commencement of the system of funds and paper money.

II. One of the grand outcries raised against the Stuarts, besides their attachment to the Roman Catholic religion, was their attachment also to the preservation of the royal prerogatives, and to the most extreme notions as to its nature and extent. They had been honest and open in this; and hence, every king of this family was, in some degree, antagonistic of parliament, and jealous of popular encroachment, and of the people's house, the Commons. For this honest adherence to their position, which was really a great safe-guard to popular freedom, they were most absurdly blamed. To blame them for this, was as truly foolish as it would be in a *jealous husband*, to blame a smart fellow for *declining* to be on very intimate and friendly terms with his wife. Such, however, was the case; and when, after James's abdication, the Dutchman was hoisted by the Whigs upon the vacant throne, this droll cause of complaint was cured. The Dutchman, before he was made a king, called himself "a republican"; and he soon showed that he had no objection to be on as *intimate* and *friendly* terms with the *Whig House of Commons*, as heart could wish! In short, this cunning huckster imitated the thief, who gives "the mastiff" a share, that he may get the remainder quietly for himself. He and his ministers set themselves, at once, to work to make plenty of (paper) money. They took care that the House of Commons should have *its* share of the good things going; and the "citizen king," and the stock-jobbers of the Whig parliaments, were speedily as *civil* to each other, as the greatest lover of "liberal government" could wish. The gradual results of this system of management we have seen. Let us get a look at the sum total.

Instead of two millions, we have to pay the taxes to make up an annual gross revenue that exceeds fifty millions sterling. We had lately to pay a poor-rate that nearly reached the heavy sum of eight millions sterling in a year; which, for a time, has been reduced to five millions by an atrocious law, which virtually amounts to a refusal of relief, and condemns the unfortunate poor to perish of actual starvation, or of the diseases consequent upon it. Bankruptcies and insolvencies are now counted by hundreds in a year; and hence become so common, that they have ceased to be regarded as a disgrace. By the mass of privations thus inflicted upon the body of the people, their increase has been so much stimulated, that the numbers now living in England are probably three times as great as the numbers in 1688. This increase has, at last, come to cause great alarm. In spite of all the extension in manufactures and trade, there is an increasing number of able-bodied men destitute of employment, and ready to turn against the government, which has been the means of putting them into this dreadful position. Another consequence of all these burdens and privations, is an alarming decrease in the profits of trade, and the creation of a competition which bids fair to destroy trade altogether. Nobody now can leave trade when once in it, because nothing is realised. Those who, by means of the funding system, get together huge capitals, are at a loss in what way to employ them, and will not go into trade. The consequences are, that all sorts of delusive schemes for the employment of capital are hatched; and men who possess nothing, unable to get subordinate stations, begin shops, etc., at a venture, on credit, until trade is choked up, and profits are at an end. In agriculture, the state of affairs is little better. The labourers have, by means of the new poor-law, and from being robbed of the common lands, been gradually reduced from their former state of comfort, to one of slow starvation and destitution. In plentiful years, when the corn-law is inoperative, even this does not enable the farmer to make his rent; and the consequence is, alternate periods of suffering on the part of the farmer and landlord, as well as of the labourer.

The great consequences of all this mass of misery have been:—first, the creation of a mass of half-employed paupers, so numerous that books have been openly published to teach the means to procure abortion, and to put infants to death without pain; next, a stimulus to crimes of all descriptions, and a vast increase of prisons, houses of correction, convict-hulks, and penal colonies. And, again, a total change in the manners of the whole people, as well as in their morals. This last is apparent, in a recklessness and want of good domestic habits and feelings, as well as knowledge, amongst the lower classes, and in extravagance and folly amongst the richer classes; in streets swarming with prostitutes, and covered with showy carriages; in bad domestic economy, dishonest servants, wasted incomes, and the love of show, contending with decreasing means; in taudry furniture and make-believe wealth; in cotton-velvet hangings, German-silver forks, and deal-tables, veneered over with thin slips of mahogany or rose-wood.

From this tissue of mischiefs, acting and re-acting upon each other, various other evils have sprung, amongst which must be noted a vast increase of bad and hasty legislation, a hardening of the criminal laws, and the gradual introduction, under pretence of improvements, of summary powers in the practice of magistrates and gaolers; a bad administration of the prevention of crime, by the disuse of the constable; and the introduction of a hired and drilled police, the constant employment of military power, and the paying and employing spies.

That which is called "the great modern increase in the business of the House of Commons," is merely the necessity to apply remedies to the various diseased symptoms and actions arising out of this generally diseased state; and the necessity for legislating for the various schemes for the employment of the plunder which constitutes "surplus capital," to which there is no end. Railway insurance, equitable loan, colonising, joint-stock building, banking, fishing, shipping, and other innumerable projects are constantly requiring acts of parliament; whilst new prisons, new tread-mills, police levies, powers for magistrates, bankrupt laws, vagrant acts, and all the apparatus legal and architectural for palliating a perennial growth of crime and mischief, are equally exigent upon the time of the two houses. A very little reflection is needed to show how the influx of misery and crime has worked these changes. The laws of our ancestors against crime were severe but open; because seldomer wanted. Murder and theft were comparatively rare; and therefore, murderers, robbers, and thieves were hanged or transported; and the example was not lost upon a population which was really moral. When crime, however, became with multitudes a matter of necessity, executions lost their effect, and the waste of life became as appalling as useless. Hence arose summary convictions; starvation in prisons; arbitrary powers to jailors; solitary cells; silent systems; and the adoption of a system of secret torture; whilst, in the "penal colonies," the inflictions now are so horrible, that the governor of one of them has openly declared "death, in any shape, *preferable*." That our jailors have gradually grown into governors, and our governors into jailors, is a melancholy fact, known generally to all observant and thinking men. For the details of the lamentable changes that have come over both the criminal law and its administration, the appeal can be only made to the lawyer by profession; nor has that appeal been made by me in vain. The following digest of the principal recent changes in our criminal code is furnished by a dear friend, who, to an accurate knowledge of the subject, adds the inclination not to gloss over or hide, for purposes of deception, that which he knows. No reader, who attentively peruses this minute dissection of modern legal tender-heartedness and philanthropy, can doubt whether or not I have asserted the truth, or be at any loss for the true meaning of the words "softening the criminal code."

Here are the details of the "softening," gentle reader! See; and as you see, admire!

DIGEST.

ABSTRACT.—"SOFTENING THE CRIMINAL CODE."

Of all prevailing delusions, there is, perhaps, no one so gross as that of our having a "*softened*" criminal code. Not only is it not softened, but it is in many respects most shockingly hardened. People have supposed that the law, in general, has become less rigorous, simply because the punishment of death has, in some cases, been abolished. They mistake, however, both as to the *motives* for such abolition, and the *actual doings* of the softeners. With a continual increase of crime, produced by our system of government, there has in fact been a continual action of the law-makers upon juries, and a resistance by juries against the law-makers. The makers of law have, for a long time back, kept the law more hard than juries could reconcile to their consciences to execute. This has produced, from time to time, and with various offences, a species of rebellion in the jury-box—a disposition to *acquit* instead of *convict.* The law-pressure was too high. Hence all those thousands of explosions of merciful feeling, in which we have witnessed verdicts of "not guilty" on the clearest evidence of guilt. In the state of things in which we live, it is difficult to determine how best to punish the offender. But our law-givers have had another difficulty, equally great to contend against—that of getting a jury of his country to allow the offender to be punished.

But if we look at this matter merely as one of suffering to the culprit, who will venture to say that the amount of that suffering is *less* now than formerly? There is still but the one extreme penalty, death, for the very highest offences, TREASON and MURDER. The next degree of punishment to that, is transportation for life. But that punishment has been *professedly* very much hardened of late, and, for the purpose of terror, rendered so intolerable, that prisoners have been told from the bench that they were "*going to something perhaps worse than death itself.*" What comfort, then, to the minds of those who recoil at the shedding of human blood, to be told that the victim of the law's vengeance is only condemned to what may be quite as bad, if not worse than an Austrian or Italian dungeon, or a mine in Siberia!

The crime of MANSLAUGHTER is punished with transportation for life. This is the extreme penalty now (3 Geo. IV. 38, § 1, 9. Geo. IV. c. 131, § 9). Formerly, with burning in the hand, and forfeiture of goods and chattels.

RAPE, until very recently, was capital. By 4 and 5 Victoria, c. 56, §§ 1, 4, transportation for life.

ROBBERY, by 7 and 8 Geo. IV. c. 29, § 6, and 4 Geo. IV. c. 48, was left a capital offence, but the judge had the power of merely ordering the judgment to be "recorded." But by the 1 Vict. c. 87, § 2, that discretion is taken away, if there be any stabbing, cutting, or wounding of the party aggrieved; and the sentence must be that of death.

ARSON of dwelling-houses or ships, exhibiting FALSE SIGNALS, and destroying SHIP-STORES, are capital, by the 7 Wm. IV. and 1 Vic.c. 89; and by the same act, several other species of ARSON are to be punished with transportation for life.

BURGLARY, before the 1 Vic. c. 86, was punishable as robbery above mentioned; but by this statute of Victoria, § 2, if the offence be accompanied by any beating, wounding, or striking of any person, the least punishment is death.

In all cases of a SUBSEQUENT FELONY, of whatever kind either of the felonies may be, the party twice convicted may be transported for life (7 and 8 Geo. IV. c. 28, §§ 9, 11).

The offence of RETURNING FROM TRANSPORTATION, transportation for life; and, before the transportation, the offender may be imprisoned four years with hard labour (5 Geo. IV. c. 84, § 22, and 4 & 5 Wm. IV. c. 67): and by 7 and 8 Geo. IV. c. 28, § 11, thrice publicly or privately whipped in addition.

SIMPLE LARCENY, or STEALING, is now punishable with various

terms for transportation; for life, 15, 10, or 7 years, or with imprisonment, hard labour, solitary confinement, and whipping. (The 15 and 10 years are terms for transportation, which have been introduced in some cases by the 7 Wm. IV. and 1 Vic. c. 90, in place of the 14 or 7 years enacted in the previous "Peel's Acts.")

RECEIVING STOLEN GOODS was at common law only a misdemeanor. By one of "Peel's Acts" (7 and 8 Geo. IV. c. 29, §§ 54, 55), it is made felony, and punishable with 14 or 7 years' transportation.

EMBEZZLEMENT, at common law, was not felony; but it has been rendered so by modern statutes; by the 39 and 40 Geo. III., c. 85, 7 and 8 Geo. IV. c. 29, and 4 and 5 Vic. c. 56. Under these and other statutes, a great number of embezzlements are punishable with transportation for various periods, for life, or for 14 or 7 years.

ESCAPING FROM MILL-BANK PENITENTIARY.—By the 59 Geo. III. c. 136, this was a capital offence. By 1 Vic. c. 91, the offender is to be transported for life. At common law, the offence of escape was but a disdemeanor, unless there were an actual breaking of the prison: but, by the late statutes, the mere escape is sufficient to create the felony.

Administering POISON, STABBING, CUTTING, or WOUNDING any person, with intent to murder, punished with death by 1 Vic. c 85, § 2. ATTEMPTING to commit like offences, with like intent, transportation for life by the same statute, § 3. (These provisions are nearly the same as those of 9 Geo. IV. c. 31, § 11, under which the judgment of death might be "recorded"; while under 1 Vic. c. 85, the capital cases leave no discretion, if there be caused "any bodily injury dangerous to life").

SHOOTING AT any person, or ATTEMPTING TO DISCHARGE FIRE ARMS, or STABBING, CUTTING or WOUNDING, with INTENT to MAIN, DISFIGURE, or *do grievous bodily harm*, or with intent to RESIST or PREVENT the lawful *apprehension* or *detainer of any person*, may be punished with transportation for life. Sending EXPLOSIVE SUBSTANCES, etc., throwing CORROSIVE FLUIDS, etc., with INTENT to *burn, main, disfigure*, etc., same punishment: 1 Vic. c. 85, § 4, 5. (These are nearly the same provisions as those of the 9 Geo. IV. c. 31, except that under the latter statute, judgment of death might have been "recorded").

FORGERY was, at common law, but a misdemeanor, punishable with fine, imprisonment, and such corporal infliction as the court might award. Pillory might have been added to the imprisonment but cannot be since the statute 56 Geo. III. c. 138, by which that latter mode of punishment was abolished, on account of its having given the "basest populace" opportunities to express favour towards political offenders.—Forgery is now, like all the preceding offences, a felony, and great numbers of forgeries have been created by statutes, from time to time. By 11 Geo. IV. and 1 Wm. IV. c. 66, forging Exchequer-bills, East India-bonds, bank-notes, wills, bills of exchange, promissory-notes, etc. etc., were still capital offences. By 2 and 3 Wm. IV. c. 123, all, except the forgeries of wills and powers of attorney to transfer stock, were made punishable with transportation for life only; while, by another statute of the *same session* (2 and 3 Wm. IV. c. 59) the forging of declarations, warrants, orders or instruments by the Commissioners for the Reduction of the National Debt, and of some other instruments, was again rendered capital.—The present forgery act (1 Vic. c. 84) enumerates a vast multitude of forgeries, abolishes the extreme penalty entirely, and awards transportation for life to the greater part of them.

Falsely Personating seamen and others, entitled to half-pay, pensions, prize-money, etc., etc., is punishable with transportation for life: 5 Geo. IV. c. 107, § 5; 11 Geo. IV. and 1 Wm. IV. c. 20, § 84.

Maliciously Injuring Property.—By "Peel's Act," 7 and 8 Geo. IV. c. 30, a great mass of offences of this class are created and consolidated, such as the injuring of trees, machinery, fish-ponds, goods, cattle, etc. etc. Punishment, transportation for life, and various other periods.

Cheating (obtaining money or goods by false pretences), a misdemeanor created by statute, and punishable with 7 years' transportation: 7 and 8 Geo. IV. c. 291, § 53.

Riot, and remaining assembled one hour after proclamation, or opposing the making of proclamation, was punishable with death by the famous Whig "Riot-Act" of 1715 (1 Geo. I. stat. 1, c. 5), after which were passed the 9 Geo. III. c. 29 and 56 Geo. III. c. 125, awarding the same punishment to rioters destroying or beginning to destroy buildings, etc. By "Peel's Act" (7 and 8 Geo. IV. c. 30, § 8) the "Riot-Act" was repealed, and new enactments added, by which rioters destroying or beginning to destroy any buildings, machinery, etc., etc., were still punishable with death.—

By one of the acts commonly called "Lord John Russell's Acts" (viz. the acts of Victoria above mentioned) the crimes created by the 1 Geo. I., are now punishable with transportation for life; and those created by the subsequent acts are punishable in the same way.

STOPPING OR SEIZING CORN, to PREVENT EXPORTATION; every second offence, transportation for seven years: 36 Geo. III. c. 9, §§ 1, 2. Pulling down granaries, or entering vessels and damaging corn, for the same purpose, the same punishment.

NIGHT POACHING.—After two previous convictions, the TAKING of game by night, or ENTERING LAND ARMED for that purpose, is an offence punishable with transportation for seven years: 9 Geo. IV. c. 69, § 1 (commonly called "Lord Lansdowne's Act"). THREE OR MORE entering land for same purpose, any ONE BEING ARMED, transportation for fourteen years: same statute, § 9. The "ARMING" must consist of an "offensive weapon"; but a bludgeon or a stick is within the meaning of the act, if the jury find that the defendant intended to use it as such; *The King* v. *Palmer*, Moody and Malkin's Reports, vol. ii. p. 70. The previous convictions may have been summarily before justices of the peace (that is, without jury) and the only *judge* a sporting squire! The Rev. Dr. Knox, in his essay "On the Animosities occasioned in the Country by the Game-laws," says, "the forest-laws established only one mighty hunter throughout the land; *the game-laws have raised a little Nimrod in every manor*," vol. iii. p. 3.

ASSAULTING, OR OFFERING any VIOLENCE to a *lord of the manor*, *owner of land*, *game-keeper*, or *servant* apprehending a poacher, the poacher having a stick or club, transportation for seven years: 9 Geo. IV. c. 69, § 2.

BEATING OR WOUNDING DEER-KEEPERS is felony; transportation for seven years: 7 and 8 Geo. IV. c. 29, § 29.

SMUGGLING. Three or more, being armed, assembled for the purpose of running uncustomed goods; felony, death: 3 and 4 William IV. c. 53, § 58. One being armed is sufficient, and a bludgeon or club is a sufficient weapon within the meaning of the act. See Archbold's *Criminal Pleading*, tit. "Smuggling." This punishment is altered by the 1 Vict. c. 91, § 12, to transportation for life. By these acts, and by 24 Geo. II. c. 40, § 28, and 6 Geo. IV. c. 80, § 143, there are other offences of smuggling made felony, and punishable with transportation, some for life, and some for seven years.

Administering, or Taking Oaths to *commit felony*, Endeavouring to Seduce any of the Army, etc. These offences were punishable with death, by the 37 Geo. III. c. 70, § 1, and 52 Geo. III. c. 104, § 1. By the 1 Vict. c. 91, § 1, they are to be punished with transportation for life. By the 37 Geo. III. c. 123, § 1, the administering or taking of any unlawful Oath, "*to obey the orders or commands of any committee, or body of men, not lawfully constituted*," was made punishable with seven years' transportation. (This was the statute under which the Dorchester labourers were transported; and this is still in force).

Training or Drilling to the use of Arms, or Attending a Meeting for that purpose, transportation for seven years; 60 Geo. III. and 1 Geo. IV. c. 1. This statute is still in force. It is one of the "Six Acts," passed in 1819, and which Mr. Denman, now (1843) Lord Chief Justice of England, described in the House of Commons as "Six Bills which went to overthrow all that was valuable in the Constitution."—*Hansard's Debates*, vol. xli. pp. 1072, 1501, A.D. 1819.

The foregoing specimens of punishment are quite enough to show that our criminal code has not been undergoing a "softening" process. Besides the general question of softening or hardening, there are certain cases in which our statute law exhibits a very gross partiality in the degree of protection it affords to one class of persons in comparison with another. For example, females in the higher ranks of life are but little exposed to the crime of rape. That crime, as above shown, is now punishable with transportation for life only. But it is also a felony, and punishable with transportation for life, to abduct an heiress, with intent to *marry* her (9 Geo. IV. c. 31, § 19). And night-poaching being transportable for fourteen years, it may be said, that a poor woman's person is now, in the eye of our "softened" statute-book, nothing very much more sacred than the carcase of a country gentleman's hare or pheasant! Again, an assault, with intent to commit rape, is punishable with imprisonment, with or without hard labour, not exceeding two years; but an assault on a revenue-officer, or on a game-keeper, may be punished with seven years' transportation!

Combinations among labourers, etc., were most cruelly punished by the older statutes of 1799 and 1800 (39 and 40 Geo. III. c. 106; 41 Geo. III. c. 38). The law, in this respect, has been modified; but that in a most insidious manner. For while it does not now, as it before did, prohibit any two poor men from agreeing together what their wages shall be, it punishes them the more heavily whenever any breach of the peace arises in disputes between them and their masters. All assaults, in pursuance of any conspiracy to raise wages, may be punished by two years' imprisonment, with hard labour (9 Geo. IV. c. 31, § 25).

Many other ASSAULTS, and other MISDEMEANORS, are also punishable by modern statutes, with hard labour, in addition to imprisonment. By the 3 Geo. IV. c. 114, hard labour is added in all cases of RIOT. Any assault, however trifling, on a policeman, puts the offender on the tread-wheel (9 Geo. IV. c. 31, § 25).

One serious feature in our modern state of things, is the necessity of providing punishment for the frauds of debtors. By 1 and 2 Vict. c. 110, § 99, the frauds of insolvent debtors are punishable summarily with three years' imprisonment and hard labour. By 6 Geo. IV. c. 16, § 112, the frauds of bankrupts may be punished with transportation for life. The mere non-surrender of goods, or non-delivery of books, is enough to warrant these penalties. The necessity for penalties like these arises directly out of our system of false credit. Take other instances again, where it has been deemed expedient to *encourage* credit; and there we shall find the law-maker actually promoting fraud by his own law, and *ipso facto* committing a double fraud, by entitling his handy-work "An Act for the *better Protection* of Property"! This is found to be the case in the little code of statutes relating to deposits, or pledges by factors and agents (4 Geo. IV. c. 83; 6 Geo. IV. c. 94; 7 Geo. IV. c. 7). In these, "in order to facilitate the advancing of money," we find an abrogation of the common law-rights of the owners of bills of lading, India-warrants, dock-warrants, etc. etc., to enable factors to pledge, and pledgees to hold; while, by the same wise statutes, the factor who may fraudulently take advantage of these new provisions, has a *new crime* invented for him, with the punishment of fourteen years' transportation!

But there is nothing in which the public have so much to *complain* of, as in those enormous and fast-increasing powers of summary conviction and punishment which are given to Justices of the Peace. In speaking of this species of jurisdiction, Lord Chief Justice Holt observes, that "all acts which subject men to new and other trials than those by which they ought to be tried by the common law, are contrary to the rights and liberties of Englishmen, as they were settled by Magna Charta" (*Rex.* v. *Chandler*, *Lord Raymond's Reports*, 581). Blackstone also makes some very strong remarks on the danger of this mode of administering the law, contending for "the necessity" (even at his day) "of not deviating any further from our ancient constitution, by ordaining new penalties to be inflicted upon summary conviction."—*Commentaries*, vol. iv. p. 279.

What, then, would these great constitutional lawyers have said, could they have foreseen the state of such matters in *our day!* At present, our very mixed body of magistracy have not merely such powers as that of licensing public-houses (which power even, as given in the reign of George II., is designated by Smollett, to be one enabling Justices of the Peace "to tyrannise over their fellow-subjects" (vol. iii. p. 346); but it is left to them to decide, whether we may use a room, or other place, for the purpose of delivering a lecture on the Corn-Laws, or talking politics with our neighbours, and if we so use it without their leave, we are punishable (36 Geo. III. c. 8; 39 Geo. III. c. 79). They now possess so wide a jurisdiction in case of Assaults, matters of Excise or Revenue-Law, Vagrant-Law, Poor-Law, Game-Law, in cases of Combination and Disputes about Wages, in Malicious Injuries to Property, and even in Larceny and Embezzlement (Felonies), as would require a whole volume to define. There is a small library of law-books upon this one subject; besides Burn's Justice, we have the works of Nares, Boscawen, Paley, Archbold, Woolrych, and Hulton, all relating exclusively to the one dread code of *Summary Conviction.*

By the 7 and 8 George IV. c. 29, STEALING DOGS, or other BEASTS, not the subject of larceny at common law, is punishable by one Justice of the Peace: the first offence, with the penalty of twenty pounds; the second offence, with imprisonment and hard labour for twelve months. Two Justices may order the offender to be twice whipped. By the same act, having the SKIN of a dog, or the PLUMAGE of a bird on your premises, with knowledge of the dog or bird having been stolen, similar punishment. By the same act, DAMAGING a tree, sapling, or shrub, second offence twelve months' imprisonment, and hard labour. By the same act, DAMAGING, with *intent to steal* any plant, root, fruit, or vegetable, six months and hard labour. By 7 and 8 Geo. IV. c. 30, MALICIOUSLY DAMAGING, with *intent to destroy*, any plant or vegetable production in a garden, the same punishment, or to pay such sum of money, not exceeding twenty pounds, as to the Justice may seem meet. Having EGGS of GAME, or wild-ducks, etc. in possession, knowing them to have been unlawfully taken, fine of five shillings for every egg; and in default of payment, six months' imprisonment (1 and 2 William IV. c. 32, § 24; the New Game Act). TAKING GAME by NIGHT, or ENTERING LAND for that purpose, imprisonment for three months, with hard labour, and to find two sureties in ten pounds each, at the expiration of the punishment, or to be again imprisoned for another six months, with hard labour. For a second offence, six months' imprisonment, with hard labour, and to find same sureties, or to be again imprisoned for a year, with hard labour (9 Geo. IV. c. 69, § 1).

Here are but a very few of the vast powers of punishment, in cases in which Justices of the Peace are the *sole judges of fact*, as well as of law.

In order, however, to have a true idea of the full operation of the law as it now is, we must narrowly watch its effects, and not be content with the bare words of the statute. To judge of the practical result of such refined distinctions, both as to *act* and *intent*, as we find, for instance, in the law of *stabbing*, *cutting*, *beating* or *wounding*, we must bear in mind circumstances like that of Cooke being hanged for striking Mr. Bingham Baring. Whether that punishment, in the particular instance, were right or wrong, is not the question. It is a question of softness or hardness; and that execution is undoubtedly hard, because it was awarded on the principle, long before then repudiated by our law (but now fully re-adopted), of *voluntas pro facto*, or punishing, not for the act done, but for something *intended*.—In the powers given to justices for the punishing of embezzlers of materials in manufactures, &c., they, the justices, are to be satisfied of the sufficiency of the account given by the party accused: if not so satisfied to convict him (17 Geo. III. c. 56, § 10). This statute, like others of the same kind, recites the necessity of rendering conviction "*more easy*" than it could be by the trial by jury! But there is no power in the law to determine *what* shall satisfy them; and who, then, can reconcile such a power of judgment to the spirit of our common law?—Again, after conviction we should see the treatment of the party *in jail* to know what he really has to undergo in the way of punishment. "Lord John Russell's Act" (1 Vic. c. 90, § 3) has magnified the torture of *solitary confinement* to one whole month at a time, and three months out of twelve. We should look at the "Reports of Inspectors of Prisons," and there learn the dreadful effects of this species of confinement and of hard labour, and the tread-mill, upon men, women, and children; and at the number of punishments inflicted by jailors without the intervention of a magistrate even! We should remember such cases as that of Charles Beale, who, having left his family in search of work (according to the spirit of the New Poor Law and the doctrine of "circulating labour") was sent to Northleach jail by the Gloucestershire justices as a vagrant, for neglecting his family, and there, according to the verdict of the coroner's jury, was killed by ill-treatment (*Times,* Nov 8, 1842, contains Sir James Graham's correspondence on this case). The *Cheltenham Chronicle* (quoted in the *Times* of Nov. 2, 1842) styles the discipline under which this man was put to death as one of "brutal atrocity." Look, again, at a more recent case, that of the jail at Knutsford, referred to in Sir James Graham's letter to the justices of Cheshire ("*Manchester Guardian,*" May 27, 1843), in which the Secretary of State blames those justices for being satisfied in condemning the conduct of the governor of the jail, which, he asserts, had been so cruel that they ought to have discharged him.

It frequently, if not generally, happens, that the greater part of the prisoners in a jail have been sentenced on summary conviction. For instance, the Report of Mr. G. H. Gibbs, Governor of Preston House of Correction, on the 27th June, 1843, mentions forty-seven prisoners that had been tried by jury, and 162 summarily convicted. The report of the chaplain of the same jail, Rev. J. Clay, presented to the visiting justices in October, 1842, states, that "no less than 502 indictments of males and 109 of females had been laid before the grand juries of the quarter sessions, within the year ending in the last preceding July; while, during the same period, the instances of *summary conviction* had amounted to 1,069 of males, and 174 of females; being, in the whole, 1,854 cases of offence, and, at the same time, an increase over the preceding year of 126 sessions cases, and 162 summary convictions."

The treatment of Lovett and Collins *before* they were tried, and the cropping of the two *unconvicted* persons in the Dover jail, charged with a common assault (*Times*, Nov. 8, 1842), show to what an extent the discipline of our jails is "brutally atrocious," even towards those who are by the law presumed to be innocent. What must it be with the majority of the convicted? The old duty of the sheriff, as the officer of the Crown, to take care of the party imprisoned, is abolished; and the prisoner, from the moment of accusation till the expiration of his sentence, is all in the hands of the justice of peace, who lays down the law, decides the fact, convicts, sentences, consigns to prison, and there goes to see execution done!

The New Poor-Law Commissioners' Continuance Act, 5 & 6 Vict. c. 57 (passed 30th July, 1842), enables guardians to set occasional poor a task of work, "to be done in return for the food and lodging afforded," the task to last for any time not exceeding four hours from the hour of breakfast in the morning succeeding the admission into the house. Refusing to perform such task, or injuring his own clothes, &c., by this act, renders the offender a rogue and vagabond, and subjects him to the summary punishment of the Vagrant Act (5 Geo. IV. c. 83, § 3), viz.: three months' imprisonment in jail, with hard labour.

What renders these summary convictions peculiarly unfair, is, that, while the great man who happens to be indicted for some misdemeanour, may, and very frequently does, remove the whole proceedings (as in the case of Lord Waldegrave, for beating a policeman), in order that both the law and the fact may be tried in the superior court of Queen's Bench, the poorer subjects are not only stripped of their right of being tried "by their peers" (a jury), but, by the express words of most of those acts which gave summary power, they are also stripped of the common-law right to a *certiorari* to remove the record of the conviction against them. For the legislature have taken care, in the far greater part of the acts which give the power, expressly to say, that no such removal shall be permitted; and in some cases, they have even enacted, that there shall be no appeal from the decision of the one justice, or two justices convicting, to their brother justices at the quarter sessions; or, when the appeal is allowed, it is only on the condition that the party appealing shall give security for costs—a security which, of course, a poor man can seldom find.

If the "conservators of the peace" were still, as originally, elected by the people, the people would have less reason to feel jealous of such enormous powers. But the "English Justinian," as he is called—the arbitrary Edward III.—deprived his subjects of this right; a right, to have which restored, the Welch Rebeccaites are now petitioning the Queen. (1 *Blackstone*, p. 350; *Lambard*, p. 20; *Hume*, vol. ii. pp. 319, 490, 491, 494; *Morning Herald*, Sept. 18, 1843).

The new discipline of close and solitary confinement said to have been adopted for Lord John Russell's "Model-Prison" at Pentonville, together with the professed horrors of the "Penal Settlements" of the transported; these things give us no idea of any "softening," no more than the Peel and Russell systems of town and rural police are signs of happiness or safety for the nation. The "Model-Prison" is, we are told, an imitation from the Americans, a people who have so far subjected themselves to corruption, as to want such things already, and to have actually become our teachers in the art of "softening" codes, by lending them new torments. At this moment, the Americans are blessed with "a good police-force," the honest citizen now having to run against a perambulating despot at every street corner. These torments are being increased at a time when reports, published on authority in both countries, are showing that they are beyond human endurance, and that the imprisoned are actually driven mad by them. Nevertheless, this most blessedly "improved age" would give almost as much for the discovery of a *new punishment*, as the tyrant of old would have given for that of a new pleasure. That there is the most abominable premium for accusing men *falsely* of crime, none who know the police-system will doubt; and the fact has recently been asserted, and offered to be proved, before the Marylebone vestry, by Sir Peter Laurie (a magistrate) and Mr. Soden. —*Morning Herald*, Sept. 18, 1843.

So far as the *wish* was concerned, it is evident, that our law-makers have never ceded the punishment of hanging but when driven to it; or in cases where the property or persons of the wealthy had little to fear from the crime; nor is it at all unfair to apply the principle of "the will for the deed" to those who, by their acts of parliament, punish men for "*intending* to commit a felony," when found in an out-house, or in a lane, *not* committing a felony (5 Geo. IV. c. 83).*

* This act (5 Geo. IV. c. 83) is one of the many acts relating to vagrants, etc., some passed previously, and others, since. By sections 3, 11, 12, every person wandering abroad, lodging in the open air, etc., not having any visible means of subsistence, and not giving a good account of himself, or herself; every person found in any house, or in any enclosed place, for *any unlawful purpose;* every *suspected person*, frequenting any river, warehouse, street, etc., etc., with *intent to commit felony*, shall be deemed a *rogue and vagabond*, and, on summary conviction by any justice of the peace (by the evidence of one credible witness), may be committed to the house of correction, with hard labour, for any time not exceeding three calendar months.—*D'Oyly and Williams's Burn's J.*, vol. 3, pp. 935, 936.

Mr. Serjeant Adams, Chairman of the Middlesex Sessions, in a "*Letter to Benjamin Hawes, Esq., M. P.*" (London: J. Hatchard & Son, 1838), gives the following specimens of *crimes and punishments*, among the extracts which he

FORGERY is a striking evidence of this. For forging bank-notes and bills, or passing them, the numbers of convictions returned were, in 1816, 104; in 1818, 227; in 1820, 352. From 1805 to 1818, the number of persons convicted of the crime of forgery was 501; of whom 207 died on the scaffold. In appears, again, from parliamentary returns, that, in the five years ending with 1820, there were ninety-four executions for the same offence. These malefactors, many of them to the amount of no more than 20*s*., used to be strung up in rows at a time (Sidney Taylor, *On the Punishment of Death*, vol. ii. p. 109). What a splendid "improvement" upon what existed even in the day of Sir Henry Spelman, who remarked, that, "while every thing else was risen in its nominal value, and become dearer, the life of man had continually grown cheaper" (!) *Glossary*, 350. The provisions of the statutes, taken in chronological order, show, that the enactors have given way only inch by inch, notwithstanding the horrors of jurors, and the failures of example from verdicts of acquittal. But, just as they have been forced to give up hanging in this and some other cases, they have most industriously, and insidiously, laboured to substitute other punishments as bad or worse, while, at the same time, they have never for one session ceased to create *new offences*, and to apply to them unduly heavy punishments.

Jurors, and the public in general, do not *know* what those transported have actually to suffer. They do not witness, nor have they fully described to them, the torments of "model-prisons," Northleach or Knutsford jail, states of solitary confinement, and the modern rack of the tread-wheel and jail-whipping. If they could see it, or hear of it all, know just what all these things are, to what increased numbers of persons they are applied, by what sort of *judges* they are very often applied, and, in thousands of cases, with what little pretence

makes from public returns of justice-operations in the County of Middlesex. The *criminals* here are boys of fifteen and sixteen years of age:—

"22nd March, 1837. Having in his possession two forks which had been stolen, *two months*.

"16th June, 1837. Rogue and vagabond, lodging in an out-house, *one month*.

"15th August, 1837. Possession of a loaf of bread, *one month*.

"25th September, 1837. Rogue and vagabond, and suspected, etc., *three months*."

"Against no one of whom (says the Sergeant, including these among a total of 383) had the *fact of theft*, or the *justice of suspicion*, been established by any previous verdict" (pp. 33, 34, 35).

of *justice*, many a mind that is now firmly convinced of our "criminal code" being vastly "softened," would regard it as having become harder and harder down to the last date on the statute-book.

The ignorance which has existed touching Mr. Fox's celebrated Libel-bill, strongly illustrates how easily people are duped with respect to the *actual* provisions and effect of the statute-law. That bill (32 Geo. III. c. 60) had been very generally supposed to make the jury judges of both law and fact in all cases of libel. It really gives them no such power. It is merely a declaratory act (that is, one deciding what the common law was previously, and, by inference, deciding that former decisions of the judges were wrong); and it simply declares, that "the jury, to try the issue, may give a *general verdict* of guilty or not guilty, upon the *whole* matter put in issue upon the indictment or information." The judges had held, that *they* were to determine the *libellous quality* or *tendency* of the words, and that the jury should only ascertain the fact of publication, etc. This act, then, just settles that they were wrong, and that the question of quality or tendency was one properly of *fact* (and not of *law*). The result of this famous act, therefore, as boasted forth to the public, was nothing more or less than a delusion, a grand, party, false pretence. As such it is exhibited by Mr. Starkie, in his *Law of Libel*. And Mr. William Scott, the barrister, a pupil of Mr. Horne Tooke, and who was engaged in some of the state prosecutions which gave rise to the statute, thus speaks of it in a letter which he addressed to the "*Sun*" newspaper four or five years ago:—"Mr. Tooke highly disapproved of this act. He knew it to be an act to gain false popularity; that, to constitute jurymen judges of law, proceeds upon a wrong principle, inasmuch as it presumes them to be—what they are not—a jury of lawyers." And yet this is what the act has had the credit of doing up to the present moment, in the opinion of hosts of Whig admirers.

PERORATION.—"Non minus principi turpia sunt multa supplicia, quam medico multa funera."—*Seneca de Clementiâ*, lib. i. vol. 10, p. 119.

Such is the naked truth, as to the merciful practices of our modern "softeners of the criminal-law." To it I deem it only necessary to add one more fact, relative to the punishments inflicted under the atrocious "amended" poor-law. It is simply this, that, under this law, the punishments inflicted, during the seven years ending with 1842, inclusive, amount to the appalling number of *nine thousand three hundred and fifteen;* the people punished in 1842 alone being *two thousand, two hundred and ninety-nine!*

III. The dangers and perils, internal and external, which necessarily sprung from the position of affairs herein-before described, must, for the most part, be palpable to the most careless reader. First, we perceive the certainty that, if the existing system of taxation can be continued to be worked for even a very few years longer, the country must at length sink under it; the government, like that of France in 1789, be brought to a stand-still; and national bankruptcy and confusion ensue. It is in vain to hope that an income-tax can redeem the system from its present difficulties; because it is evident, that this tax will either at last be saved from a person's own expenditure, or out of the wages of those he employs; and hence what the exchequer gains on one hand it will, for the most part, lose on the other. The farmer will employ fewer labourers, or pay them less, and the manufacturer the same; and, at the same time, as the general difficulty grows and increases, the means and incomes of the most opulent must be straitened and diminished. Hence this tax, like all other imposts, lately attempted to be wrung from a sinking people, must at length fail of its end, and ultimately deceive those who rely upon it.

In the recent repeal of the corn-law will, however, be found the most imminent peril to existing institutions and the system under which we live. We cannot apply machinery to the tillage of land as to the making of cloth. It must be done by the labour of man; and upon the land must fall all the taxes, direct and indirect, of all connected with it. With this load upon it, vain it is to expect the soil of England to stand against the competition of richer soils tilled by men who hardly know what a tax means. To stand against this, with wheat on the average at *four shillings*, or *four shillings and sixpence*, the bushel, is impossible, whilst taxes remain as they are. In 1790, when these taxes were *under twenty millions* per annum, rents could be paid with wheat at this price; but with taxes and rates amounting to *sixty millions* per annum this is not possible, except in a few cases of the finest lands near large towns. From this position of affairs, must at length arise that open war between the land and the funds, which has been so often threatened, and which the corn-laws alone postponed. These laws destroyed, the owners of the soil have only two ways left to avert almost total ruin. They must either repeal the taxes down to *five and twenty millions* at most; or they must alter the bill of 1819, and reduce the value of money to half its present value. But the grand difficulty will be, to effect either of these measures without a revolution. The minister who does either must have the great majority of the people of England to defend and support him. But this he cannot have, unless by admitting them within the pale of the suffrage, and that is itself equivalent to revolution. A return to inconvertible paper is the hope of many persons. The end of such a catastrophe would, however, probably be that of the French "assignats." Discredit and forgery would extinguish the whole.

A third peril is the external one: that is to say, the danger arising from the ambition of foreign countries at length forcing this country into a war, which it has not now the means to sustain, and the sure result of which would be universal panic and confusion, and a blowing up of the entire paper-system. This is another imminent peril. The reader will have already seen, in the course of these pages, evidence enough to prove, that other nations are wide awake to the crippled state of England, and silently engaged in taking advantage of that state. The American republicans have their eyes bent on Canada on one side, and on the West India Islands on the other. France has views on Egypt, and would gladly see Great Britain excluded from the Levant. Russia is clutching at Constantinople with one hand, whilst with the other she is silently undermining our sway in Hindostan.

Hitherto these powers, aggressive as their conduct has often been, have done nothing sufficiently *overt* to force upon us a necessity to appeal to arms: but how long may this caution last; and may it always be met by a similar caution on our part? Had not the recent war in Syria been as adroitly managed as it was audaciously begun, a war with France would probably have followed. As it was, hostilities were barely avoided: another experiment may be less fortunate.

The fourth and grand danger of all, is the continual risk that we now run of a domestic insurrection, arising out of the hourly increasing distresses of the people. Twice within the last ten years, we have been upon the very verge of popular explosion; and when it is considered, that the causes of national discontent are every week growing and increasing, both in England and in Ireland, this peril must be considered as imminent indeed.

IV. Such are the dangers that now hem the system of government in on all sides: and what is to avert them or turn them aside in any degree; or what reason is there for supposing that they are not permanent in their nature, and such as must go on until crowned by some catastrophe? A decay in national finances is a disease that experience has ever shewn to be cureless. When a nation has reached its maximum of exertion, then re-action takes place, as in the human frame; and a growing debility follows the reign of a strength, which has now seen its acme. This is naturally followed by desperate plunges in search of relief; and to one of these plunges we are already come, in the shape of an act of parliament to repeal the corn-laws. With a population increasing at the rate of a quarter of a million in one year, it was impossible that this plunge would have been longer delayed. Of its sure and certain consequences, I need not warn the reader of these Letters.

In the same state of tendency to a crisis, are our relations with foreign powers. The United States, despite the supposed settlement of the Oregon question, are still hostile in disposition and in tone, and evidently in search of some other hinge for a dispute. Russia is confessedly intriguing in central

Asia; and France is with difficulty reined in by her present ruler from headlong war against "*Perfide Albion*"! In the midst of all this, despair is fast increasing at home; and the fast-rising waters of desolation, which have long ago overwhelmed the cottage of the poor man, are now gaining height and altitude to ooze into the saloons and *boudoirs*, and gilded drawing-rooms, of the wealthy and the powerful: and this must go on.

V. Neither are there now left any palliatives or preventives of the certain fatal tendencies of our present position, which are practicable, or capable of being carried into effect, under the existing circumstances. The "trump-cards" of the system are played. The respite of the small-notes in 1823, was one. The Goderich joint-stock-banks were another. These cannot be repeated: nor has any man been found who could invent a third palliative, capable of being carried into effect and practice. There are, no doubt, two *conceivable* modes left; but they are impracticable. A return to "inconvertible paper" might be attempted; but it must be done, at once, by an order in Council; and what minister would dare so tremendous a responsibility; as the probable issue would be the total discredit of the paper, and consequent revolution? A "change in the standard" would be attended with equal difficulty; because it also must be preceded by an order in Council, arbitrarily prohibiting all suits at law for the recovery of debts, until after the act for lowering the standard (or, in other words, for making a golden half-sovereign pass for a pound sterling) was passed; if such a bill could ever pass the Houses, without producing irreparable confusion. That no minister, in times like the present, can be found to dare such responsibilities as these, is as certain as any thing in this world can be certain; and, therefore, we may safely conclude, that these two "conceivable modes" of palliation will never be attempted, much as they have been talked about by a certain class of political economists. The stoppage of the Bank by an immense import of grain, in consequence of a repeal of the duties on grain, has, indeed, been a subject of speculation, as if a return to inconvertible paper might be, in this way, managed. In a case like this, however, the alarm would be too great for the credit of the paper to stand up against it. A pretended "Bank Restriction," like that of 1797, would avail nothing: two prices would ensue, and the paper share the fate of the French assignats in the early years of the Revolution.

Thus, then, it seems evident, almost to demonstration, that ONE MEASURE ALONE can avert the violent destruction of the system; and that is the sweeping away of the debt, and the reduction of the taxes to about one-fifth of their present amount: but, under existing circumstances, what minister dares touch the debt at all? Lord Althorp's proposal of a tax on transfers of stock was instantaneously put down. What minister, then, shall dare to attempt even what is called "an equitable adjustment" of this debt; not to mention the extirpation of the whole corrupt and unnatural excrescence? It is clear, that, in our existing position, no man likely to possess power will dare to do this, notwithstanding the evident truth of the fact, that admitting the debt to be a valid debt, it might be justly reduced, to a very considerable extent, by deducting the amounts *overpaid* since the year 1816, in the shape of annual interest, together with the interest upon such overpayments. Neither need any "set-off" be made, in consideration of the depreciation of the money paid as interest upon such part of the debt as existed prior to 1797; because the holders of such part of that stock as may still be remaining unbought up, by the operation of the sinking-funds of Pitt and Addington, have, by the raised price of stocks, and the operation of the currency-bill of 1819, doubled their capital.

Upon a review, then, of all the foregoing considerations, it seems difficult to arrive at any other than one conclusion: and this is (to use the words of our greatest political writer), that "the entire system, debt, pensions, sinecures, dead-weight, and a thundering standing army, will be kept up to the latest possible moment, until, amidst the war of opinions, of projects, of interests, and passions, the whole paper-system shall go to pieces, like a ship upon the rocks!" At this prospect, no good man ought to grieve. Individual villains are often permitted to die in prosperity and unpunished; their retribution being reserved for another state of being: but corrupt national systems always meet their punishment *here.* God has never yet failed to give this lesson to the world, from Tyre and Babylon downwards; nor will this Government be an exception. The hand-writing is now evident upon the wall. If a choice be permitted us, every good mind would, of course, wish the suffering to be of a mitigated, and not of an aggravated kind. Be the price, however, what it may, of our deliverance, at that price it must be cheap. This is one consolation, under any circumstances; and this I state quite deliberately. If we consider the misery, the broken hearts, the starvation, the ruin, the pillage, of even ten years of this system, we shall easily see, upon the most moderate computation, that if its destruction cost one hundred thousand lives, and one hundred millions of property, it would still be cheaply purchased. Cost what it may, that its destruction is approaching fast, cannot be doubted. It may be retarded, or accelerated, by a few years. I may, or may not, live to witness it; but of its ultimate and speedy downfall, I have no more doubt, than if it were now passing before my eyes: and if this book shall be made to perform the office of a funeral sermon, it will have fulfilled my wishes.

LETTER XVII.

A FEW WORDS ON IMMEDIATE PROSPECTS.

It seems to be only consistent with propriety at the close of this strange, sad, and it is hoped, conviction-working narrative, to say a few words on the prospects immediately before us. A singular combination of circumstances, extraordinary in themselves, has made these both remarkable and important. In the first place, it is to be noted, that the national tendencies are plainly now, and by the pressure of events must continue to be, to prefer *direct* to *indirect* taxation. The proximate cause of this tendency towards direct taxation, in preference to the indirect mode, is sufficiently evident. We have now, and have for many years, had a population stimulated by toil, conjoined with a meagre or insufficient diet, to increase to a morbid excess, and in a *ratio* much beyond that of nations where food is plentiful and solid, and toil not extreme. This is admitted on all hands; and this being granted, it must, I think, be admitted likewise, that the excess of population, if it go on and continue, must and alone can be employed by an extension of manufactures. That it must go on I do not hesitate to assume; for it can only be stayed by some immense change for the better in the resources of the toiling classes; and that change can only follow other changes too important in their other consequences, to be hoped for at present. That this excessive population cannot be employed upon the land I also assume; because I shall afterwards show that the well-being of both landlord, tenant, and labourer, are already, and even now, in great jeopardy. For the employment then of this "surplus population" (which is the fashionable phrase), to manufactures we must come per force; but this admission includes many more. If manufactures are to be extended, so must the national powers of consumption; because the surplusage of goods so made, must either be consumed at home or abroad; and, if abroad, the commodities taken in return must be used at home, which comes to the same thing. Thus, for instance, if we are to send more cottons to China, we must be enabled to consume more tea, in order to support such a trade; for tea is the return-commodity from China To enable the people to do this, the high duty on tea must be lowered, and a direct tax on property or income substituted, to avoid shutting out some other article of consumption. This dilemma seems inevitable; yet, in this dilemma is latent a great difficulty; for then comes the question, on what property or income is the tax to fall? If on the land and its rental (and on these it must partly press), the difficulty at once rises into view, as we shall in due time perceive.

It was, from the first, apparent to all men who reflected calmly on the subject, that if the laws respecting the import of grain and other provisions were repealed or materially relaxed; and if immediately, or rather soon after such repeal or relaxation, any great scarcity were to arise in England, the consequences might be serious in the extreme. This supposed case has now become an actual one. It has pleased Providence, no doubt for wise purposes, to destroy, by a mysterious dispensation, that ill-omened root upon which so large a portion of the people of unhappy Ireland, and I fear also of England and Scotland, have for many years depended in great part, for subsistence. It now seems that no future dependence can be placed upon this wretched root. A great change in the habits and food of much of our people must follow: but, in the mean time, it seems evident, that a great and continuous importation of grain and all kinds of edibles into these kingdoms must be the consequence. This seems quite unavoidable, unless prevented by occurrences as singular as they must be important; and this being so, it seems also clear enough, that it is in vain to hope, that this sudden influx of provisions can be balanced by any manufactures that we are likely to send to the countries whence these provisions come. To establish a regular trade of this kind, a long series of years is required. It must gradually grow. But this influx of provisions is sudden; it has arisen out of a sudden dearth, accompanied by a repeal, as sudden, of all laws that used to restrict the import of grain or meat of any kind. It is the *surplus* of other nations which they are eagerly sending us; having found an unexpected market for produce which they used to grow on a sort of speculation. But it would surely be absurd to expect them, all at once, to take in exchange, manufactures which they really do not much want, and for which they have not acquired a taste. They will not, in fact, do so. Gold and silver will go in exchange for the grain and provisions, and not manufactures: and this, at once, leads to a state of things pregnant with peril to the existing system. If the year 1847 is to be as destructive to the potato as was 1846; or if even only a partial recovery take place from dearth, and consequent alarm and speculation, it seems to be a necessary consequence either that a continuous and long import of food must take place, or such import must be checked by something like main force! By 'main force' I mean such a forcible and violent revulsion in prices as shall suffice to stop it.

Thus then we have another dilemma. If the import be unchecked, and the precious metals continue, instead of goods, to be sent abroad to pay for the grain, and cattle, and meat brought in, the bank must, in time, be surely and totally stripped of her reserves. If, on the contrary, the importation be stopped, this check can only be by forcing the prices of grain to a level far below the present. In fact, to stop the influx of corn from the United States, and from Poland, the price of wheat must be reduced to about *four shillings and sixpence the bushel imperial.* It is well known to all who know the position of agriculture in Poland and in North America, that nothing above these rates will prevent wheat from these countries coming here in quantity. Even at thirty-six shillings per quarter, American and Polish wheat would be laid down here at some profit, though a moderate one; and therefore to check importation I hold that we must see wheat, on the average, at or under these rates. Now then, the questions, which press for an answer are, *first*, what would be the probable event, were the bank to be totally and completely drained of coin and bullion; and *second*, what would be the probable effects of wheat being at four shillings and sixpence the imperial bushel, on an average of years through many years together?

In the course of the foregoing narrative, we have seen, in detail, the mode and manner in which, in the year 1797, the measure of "bank-restriction," as it was cunningly styled, was at length brought about. It was accomplished without any discredit fatal to its ready circulation being thrown upon the inconvertible paper. But we have seen *how* this was done. The subject was new, and not really understood even by the ministers who had to carry through the audacious measure; and this ignorance, perhaps, helped them, by making them bolder and more confident than they would otherwise have been. At all events, they appeared to believe—and they succeeded in making the nation believe, that the "restriction" was only temporary—a mere state-manœuvre, and not a dire necessity. It was to last for seven weeks and a-half. Then for a few months; and, at last, only till peace came. In short, the ministry was always pledged, and by statute, to cash payments, when peace came; and we have beheld the consequences of this pledge. If, however, a bank-stoppage should again occur, no such delusions as these can be practised. If a stoppage again take place, it will be universally seen and believed to be *for ever;* or until the paper shall follow the French "assignats," to the "tomb of the Capulets." Hence, if a scarcity of food still continued, the price of bullion would at once rise so immensely, and the alarm be so great, that, in all human probability, two prices in the market for commodities—a paper price, and a gold and silver price—would quickly ensue; and the paper portion of the currency be at an open and heavy discount. There are the chances: and against such an ordeal, no paper-circulation has ever yet stood for any length of time. Everybody would recollect Sir Robert Peel's famous exclamation: "If we cannot pay in gold now, we never can!" All men would see, that, as the wants of the state caused more and more paper to be pushed out, it would depreciate to a ruinous extent. Hence, confidence would falter from the first; and when this is the case, an inconvertible paper-money is sure to fall.

Let us, on the other hand, suppose, that, by a violent, excessive, and continuous contraction of her issues, the Bank should stop importation, by reducing the prices of all goods, of all kinds, to about half, or two-thirds their present price, corn amongst the rest. Let us suppose, that, by a violent action on the currency to this extent, wheat were reduced to *four and six-*

pence the imperial bushel, and kept there for a length of time, then comes the question, What, in such case, will be the position of the landlords? What of the manufacturers? We have already seen, that, in spite of all the acknowledged improvements in the art of tillage, the expenses of tilling one hundred acres of average quality of land, are as much and a good deal more than were both rent and expenses of tillage in 1793! This is quite undeniable, I believe: nor will it be gainsaid by the best practical farmers that the North of England, or the South of Scotland, can produce. It will not, I believe, be denied even by farmers who mix grazing, in a considerable degree, with tillage; though this lessens the expense of the whole farm. If, then, wheat, on an average of years, is to remain as low, or lower than it was in 1793; and if stock is also to be sold at the prices of the same period, what must be the result? Must it not be that, excepting for the best lands, in the best localities, rents must cease to be paid, or the farmer be at once ruined? If there be any alternative, I should be glad to see it pointed out. There is no such alternative, however; and then comes the inevitable question: Will the whole agricultural body of this great country, submit quietly to be ruined? And if they will not, what must ensue? If we are to believe the unmistakeable hints given by their organs, it is evident they will *not* submit, but, rather, in their extremity, fly to a forcible repeal of taxes, and a reduction of the interest of the debt. Already has *Blackwood's Magazine*, a high Tory organ, and firm friend of the landlords, quoted the American adage: "Free trade means direct taxation, and direct taxation means repudiation of state-debts!" This language is surely plain enough. It plainly says, in case of necessity, that war between the land and the funds—so often predicted, so often threatened—shall commence in sad earnest; and that, if once the burthen of the debt be found too onerous for the landholders, they will appeal to the people, and throw it off.

Another query arises, and that is—Were it once to come to this, would the manufacturers seriously oppose it? Were grain to be brought down to the level of 1793 merely by the effect of foreign supplies, whilst cottons, and woollens, and silks, and hardware, kept their present prices, *they might.* But if, as is highly probable, grain be now to be *crushed down* to the 1793 level, purely by a desperate and continuous action on the currency, then must all other commodities fall together with grain; and what the effect of *that* must be upon manufacturers and dealers, I leave manufacturers and dealers to answer. All I wish to impress is, that this is the probable march of events. The chances run that way. It is, as the cards are, "the likely suit" just now, unless, indeed, the potatoes shall undergo a sudden recovery; and plenty undeniable succeed to scarcity and starvation undoubted, in the course of some three or four months.

Such seem, beyond all question or doubt, the realities of present prospects plainly stated. They are probabilities, not certainties; but contingencies as they are, they rest on *data* so indubitable, that it is impossible to contemplate them without an interest of the deepest kind. If to them we add the prospects of foreign relations, the whole presents a scene of complication hardly ever matched in this world, and surely never exceeded. In the conduct of foreign countries, both European and American, are to be discerned two plain symptoms of a feeling, not to be mistaken nor misunderstood. The one is a manifest impression, that all our recent or late commercial concessions and *liberalisations* (to coin a new noun), are merely the fruits of difficulty and dire necessity. The other is, that our pacific and coaxing policy, so altered from the former tone of the English nation, proceeds merely from a fear of war, arising out of the critical state of our currency and financial affairs. In fact, foreigners see, that all the mawkish sentimentality about the "wickedness and folly of war;" all the effusions of those sage bodies called "Societies for the Diffusion of Universal Peace;" and all the "lectures" on the blessings of friendly intercourse are really fashionable, because encouraged by the Government secretly; and that they are hypocritical, because they are *not* universally acted upon by those who, underhand, encourage and abet them. A war with France, or with Russia, or with the United States, is, they see, deprecated, because, as Mr. Gilbart has told us, such a war would produce Bank stoppage and universal confusion. A war with the Sikhs, or Chinese, or Borneans, is, however, they perceive, still "glorious," because these distant conflicts with semi-barbarous powers may produce pence, and do not produce alarm. Upon this impression, and with these views, foreign cabinets have now for some years acted; and the fact is now scarcely concealed. The Americans, in particular, make no secret of it. They send money to Ireland, and perhaps arms. They laugh at the very idea of resistance on our part. They take Texas into their territory, without adverting to its existing treaties with us as to the slave-trade. They openly set at defiance our claims on the Oregon territory, seize it, send an armed force, and compel us to submit. In the same spirit, they will conquer and annex Mexico. In the French Councils we see the same spirit of haughty disregard. Algiers is retained, in spite of stipulations to the contrary twice repeated. Our influence in Spain is a second time destroyed by main force, and the expenditure of French money. The Spanish marriages—though *not* any violation of the treaty of Utrecht, as has been hastily said—are in direct contradiction to our expressed wishes. Austria, Prussia, and Russia exhibit the same contempt of the British power. Cracow is openly seized in open violation of the treaty of Vienna: the intrigues of Russia in India are notorious; the Black Sea is a Russian lake; and Constantinople all but a Russian capital; and against this, British Parliaments and ministers only oppose feeble protests, and feebler complaints. The illustrious Earl Chatham once exclaimed, "not a gun should be fired in Europe, without England knowing the reason why!" Now England is seen not to dare to ask the reason why, whether the gun be in Europe, Asia, or America. In the same spirit, our commercial relaxations are viewed and met. They are put down to the account of fear and weakness, and the pressure of a surplus and half-starving population. Hence no reciprocal relaxations either do, or will take place; all the lectures of our political economists to the contrary, nevertheless, and notwithstanding.

Such are the immediate indications of the political horizon abroad, and of the political sky at home. They must appear necessary, inevitable, and quite in the natural course of things, to those who really understand the position of the country. To those who do not, they must seem perplexing and amazing in the highest degree. Every thing is giving way at home and abroad. The French alliance is dubious. The three powers who have at last annihilated the last fragment of Polish nationality, look at our remonstrances with scorn and contempt. The American congress resounds with speeches against the English government and system, whilst they are profiting by our submissions and concessions. At home, the phenomena are similar. There is a universal *palinodia* of statesmen. Protection is sent to the winds. The poor-law-commissioners are dismissed for doing that which it was intended they should do; and ere long perhaps we shall have Irish landlords unwilling to pay their debts, finding out that "repeal" is the *panacea* for Irish distresses; and *the Times* and Sir Robert Peel discovering that "sovereigns of gold" are an "incumbrance," and that a paper-money continually depreciating, or in other phrase "growing like grass under the cow's-mouth," is a Catholic remedy for that complication of maladies, under which the great historian Niebuhr described England as labouring.

To predict minutely, what is to be the course which these events shall take is impossible, save to that all-wise Providence that judges nations as well as individuals, and has decreed a sure retribution for national as well as individual crimes in this world and in the next. Let it suffice the readers of these Letters to be assured, that those general laws, which they have seen hitherto controlling events, will and must control them to the last. These laws are beyond the reach of ministers or parliaments. Policy cannot mitigate nor evade them. The dungeon and the bayonet cannot turn them aside. To time, then, we may confidently leave the solution of this problem; expecting much but wondering at nothing; certain that all will be ultimately decided in accordance with laws enacted by nature herself, and destined at last to conclude, in accordance with the dictates of stern and unswerving justice, a drama the most extraordinary that ever was enacted, for the instruction and warning of mankind.

Before concluding I must, however, record, that the gross sum of eight millions sterling is now being added to the already overwhelming weight of funded debt; that the exports of manufactured goods for the past year (1846), exhibit a decrease of two millions of pounds sterling in amount; and that the stocks of colonial, Baltic, and American produce are unusually low. These circumstances explain much, and predict and fore-shadow much. We now get a glimpse of the real motives which urged on Sir Robert Peel to the desperate step of a sweeping repeal of all restrictions on the trade in grain. It has become necessary to the continuance of our manufactures, and may impede for a time the progress of rivalship in machinery in the United States, and on the European continent. The low stocks of produce of various kinds add to the peril which is now looming round the position of the bank, and the whole of the paper-money establishments and system. With scarcity in France—famine in Ireland—and alarm and depression as to future prospects, as to food in England—the prices of grain must naturally rule high for many and many months to come ; nay, for years grain may not be cheap, unless made so by some violent action on the currency. To this necessity on the part of the bank, all circumstances seem to point. They absolutely appear to conspire to bring this crisis on, inevitably, and without chance of evasion. The event no man can predict; but it is quite within the verge of possibility that, as the scorpion, when surrounded by fire, is said to sting itself to death, so the banking act of Peel may, by force of circumstances, be made to bring down the very fabric it was intended to protect; a consummation of which the poetical would be not less conspicuous than the abstract and real justice.

INDEX.

J. Wertheimer and Co., Printers, Finsbury Circus.

Made in the USA
Monee, IL
04 November 2026

67391562R00243